Advance Praise

"Christine Hale's evocation of the bewildering complexities of life as a mother, daughter, wife (and ex-wife), and student of Buddhism is both a poem and a letter to those she has worked so long and hard to understand. On a journey that takes her through emotional and actual hurricanes, love and cruelty, urgent losses, and painful gains, she climbs to sometimes unnervingly high altitudes as she experiences "the joy and the sorrow of samsara." In beautiful, clear language, Hale explores the wounds life gives us, the wounds we give ourselves, and the long process of healing."

—Sarah Stone, author of *The True Sources of the Nile*

"Christine Hale's memoir *A Piece of Sky, A Grain of Rice* vividly and beautifully describes a chaotic life, and rather than the expected acceptance that accompanies a Buddhist memoir, this book finds several avenues out of pain, including tattoos, which come to represent the sometimes ragged fashion in which people are able to love. I couldn't stop thinking about this book after I read it: the many startling scenes and places brought so vividly to life, the rich detail, and the remarkable (if deeply flawed) people who populate its pages. A candid, deeply absorbing tale."

—Debra Spark, author of *Good for the Jews*

"When St. John of the Cross first penned *Dark Night of the Soul* in the 16th century, he clarified the halting and stumbling steps of a spiritual journey. Christine Hale's *A Piece of Sky, A Grain of Rice* takes this classic form and brings it into the 21st century, looking through the lens of loss, childhood trauma, Buddhism, and natural disasters, with tattoos and the author's love for her children front and center. Her narrative illuminates the experience of stepping through the chilly and often frightening darkness into a hoped-for new dawn in the company of a generous friend and trusty guide who's one step ahead."

> —Bernadette Murphy, author of *Harley & Me: Embracing Risk on the Road to a More Authentic Life*

"Christine Hale's *A Piece of Sky, A Grain of Rice* is an exquisite engagement with those tough human questions that must be asked even if they can never be answered. Hale writes toward acceptance, every page brimming with honesty, insight, and deep understanding. A truly beautiful meditation in lovely, lively prose."

> —Dinty W. Moore, author of *The Mindful Writer: Noble Truths of the Writing Life*

A Piece of Sky, A Grain of Rice

A Memoir in Four Meditations

*May all sentient beings under the sky
have peace, happiness, and the cause of peace and happiness.*

Acknowledgements

A Piece of Sky, A Grain of Rice is the story I have pieced together from memories of a life that's been called chaotic and that has certainly been broken, steep, circuitous, slow, difficult, instructive, full, rich, and ultimately very surprising: my path. Given the six decades spanned by the narrative and the dozen years it's taken me to write it, I find myself wanting to thank almost everyone who has touched my life. I must summarize. I wish to thank:

My children—my first spiritual teachers, who taught me the necessity of seeing beyond my own needs. My parents, who loved me, and did the best they could with the hand life dealt them. My sisters, who also love me, although they find me strange. My ex-husbands, from whom I learned much, often in hindsight. I wish them joy. My inexpressibly dear late-life love, Mc, who before we were married prophesied he would be the next opportunity for freedom in my life, and who has made good on that promise. Without his support and encouragement, at home and in my art, this book would not exist.

Two dedicated and talented clinical psychologists, Bryant Welch and Carolyn Reed, who at widely different times in my life sat with me for many hours over multiple years, and kept me from giving up. Women friends, dozens of you across the decades, who have listened, advised, foreseen, and kept tactful silence by wise turns. I salute you: some of you in my life still, some of you moved on or left behind, and some of you already passed away.

My root guru, the Tibetan Buddhist teacher whose name I keep secret out of respect for her fierce sense of privacy. Many years ago you suggested, Someday you write my story. I thought you meant a biography. Look what I have written instead: to the best of my ability, the truth you showed me. I never forget you.

Hun Lye, spiritual friend, without whom I would never have reached

Tibet. Sangha (spiritual community) members in Florida, New York, New Jersey, and North Carolina, for your distinctly individual examples of patience, generosity, and diligence.

I am grateful to the Virginia Center for the Creative Arts for writing residencies where the first pages of this memoir emerged unbidden and later pages were refined. I am grateful as well to the University of Tampa, Warren Wilson College, the Great Smokies Writing Program of the University of North Carolina at Asheville, and the low-residency MFA programs of Murray State University and Antioch University-Los Angeles for paychecks and the many supportive colleagues I found among faculty and students.

A big, happy shout-out to Raymond Wong, author of *I'm Not Chinese*, for bringing my book to the attention of Apprentice House Press. And much appreciation to the editors who have published excerpts from this book, and to the good people of the Carolina Mountains Literary Festival in Burnsville, NC, and the many, many readers and writing friends all over the country who have celebrated and boosted this work by talking about it, sharing it, blurbing it, and inviting me to read it and teach from it. You have made me understand the real value of memoir: to seek and claim one's own wisdom, and to offer the fruit of that effort in companionable aid to others.

We are already free, and were dismissed
where we thought we soon would be at home.
                    —Rainer Maria Rilke

Contents

Part One
What You Do Wrong

The couch, upholstered in textured velour, muted greens and gold, clashes with the view through the storefront window behind us: the buckling asphalt parking lot of a seedy Tampa strip mall and the words PIERCINGS * TATTOOS, blazoned on the glass in biker orange and gunbarrel-gray.

I am stuck.

Sunk to the hips in too-soft cushions, I will have difficulty—the middle-aged kind, knees and low back—when it's time to stand up. For now, I shove the cell phone hard against my ear for closer contact with my daughter. J is crying, stranded by a blizzard at an airport a thousand miles away. Beside me—the side opposite the phone—my son slouches, a six-foot, skinny, teenage mop-top. B's posture is defensive, his expression stricken.

We're in line to get our Christmas present—a together-tattoo, a rite planned for weeks—with only two-thirds of our three-person family on hand.

Garbled airline announcements reverberate from the phone in my palm; I picture J huddled in the cavernous terminal in Hartford amid hundreds of miserable holiday travelers. She flew north three days ago, her need non-negotiable, in a peak-traffic, weather-vulnerable season, to spend time with a boyfriend. Her problem, she says, is her brother B.

"It's more important to him to get *his* tattoo today than to wait for *me* to be there."

He can't hear her but he can read my face. He mumbles, "If we *have* to wait I will…" but we all three know perfectly well he will not. He and I are, after all, on this couch next in line for ink because he refused to wait. Tomorrow his winter holidays end and school will swallow him and, anyway, *today* is the day he's set to do this thing he will and must do.

She's twenty. He is sixteen. At this point in our story I have been between them, their single mom—one of me and two of them—for more than ten years. Flanked by their differences and failing to bridge them, I am trying hard today to enjoy as much Christmas present as I think I'm going to get.

My mother showered me with gifts at Christmas—at least until she stopped doing Christmas, in my mid-childhood, too sunk into depression to rise. Around age ten or eleven, I took on the holiday in her stead, decorating, purchasing, organizing and orchestrating with feverish passion. Once I left her home at seventeen, I "did" Christmas in my own household with the same solo fervor. But: in my early years, my mother was attentive and perceptive, or maybe just a good guesser. My Christmas-morning loot thrilled and satisfied me so fully, and so unexpectedly every time, that everything in the whole wide world seemed perfect—for the duration of that moment.

My two sisters' stockings hung at either end of the mantel. Mine dangled from its center. The gifts Santa brought me cascaded from the bulging felt sock to the chicken-wire lid my father had rigged to top the fireplace screen to the tiled hearth in front of it and out onto the ugly wool rug, dull pink and burgundy, covering the burn scar I'd once created—by accident, in terror—on the even uglier and scratchier carpet. I was given dolls, of course, and books and candy, and at just the right moment a tricycle or a bike and once a puppy, but mostly kits and projects: the props and instructions for a magic show, an electric cooker and bottles of multi-colored goop for producing plastic bugs, elaborate Rube Goldberg-type mechanisms that worked with gravity and marbles, pulleys or magnets—stuff that did stuff. Fascinating to figure out on Christmas Day, engrossing for some weeks if not months of the dull, dripping southern Appalachian winter.

In memory I lift my gaze from my own little island of radiant, satiated joy, and notice my mother, seated across the room, watching me closely, gauging her success by my pleasure. My older sister Betsy, cognitively disabled from birth, sits near me with head cocked, looking quizzically at her pile of gifts, smaller and less complex than mine. Her first exclamations of excitement have subsided; she requires explanation now about what exactly she's been given and what to do with it. My eldest sister Sara is not in this picture; she has left home, already and for good, for college, for graduate school, the first stages of her adult life. Furthest outside my circle sits my father, on the cheap, rigid living room couch where I'll one day be observed by him, stone-faced and thin-lipped, in the act of heavy petting with my high school boyfriend. My father on Christmas Day is inert, hunched, knees awkwardly higher than his hips on the low couch.

His face is impassive; he is not there, not really. My mother has made him come up from the basement or in from the yard for the unwrapping of the Christmas she has created. He is present but absent as he will always be at any family gathering where his role has been assigned by her.

The scar on the rug underneath my Christmas treasure was his fault in her eyes, because he was right there when it happened and *should have been watching.* He'd left the screen off the fire after tossing in a log even though she'd told him and told him *don't ever* do that. But the fault I could never forget nor forgive was mine: how I'd played with fire without knowing I did it even though I knew very well *never play with fire,* and just like that without ever meaning to I caused permanent damage to something she valued, that dull and ugly carpet.

I was very young the winter evening I touched the frayed end of a strand of kindling cord to the glowing embers of the fire he'd laid and lit and that toasted my face deliciously in that house always so cold in winter. I stared until my eyeballs dried out into the blue heart of every flare, feeling in my flesh the layered, flickering, concentric peaks of red, red-orange, yellow-orange and yellow that flamed above that center. I studied the glowing, pulsing hot-orange cubes into which the hardwood divided as it burned to coals because I saw a city inside those combusting bricks, a mesmerizing world they gated beyond the one I lived in—and I did not remember to remember that introducing fresh fuel to flame, that bit of temptingly raveled twine, would cause fire to race up the string toward my hand and when reflex made my fingers drop the flaming string, set the carpet on fire and smoke up the living room, I stared helpless and paralyzed while my father, present but absent, read a book on the couch.

Mama ran in screaming from the kitchen, incredulous, and enraged.

~

I listen to my children, but my eyes track the tattooist, Lefty. He is right-handed. He will reply to my eventual question about the provenance of his name with a laconic non-answer: his father's name was Lefty and they are Puerto Rican. He is a painter; his canvases—acrylics in shock-bright primary colors: skulls and swords, teardrops, gaping cuts, imploding crystals—tier the four white walls of his shop. Lefty concentrates with an artist's intensity on the canvas before him, the shirtless back of a client belly-down on a fully reclined chair, that man's attention, in turn, fastened on the portable DVD player he holds inches from his face.

In Lefty's right hand the tattoo gun buzzes like hedge shears. Car crashes, screams, explosions ebb and flow from the movie soundtrack. Nobody speaks except a twenty-something metal-head with a thick ring in his septum, a pointed stud like a displaced unicorn's horn protruding from his lower lip, and racks of barbells in his brows and ear cartilage. He lounges against the counter next to Lefty's workstation and talks to no one in particular about money and the sure-fire ways to find it. I hear "eBay," and "selling what's in my pocket, man," and "might as well, some guy's put up a box aliens gave him, and he's getting bids."

"It's me, isn't it?" I say to J, because now she's simply crying and one of us has to say something. "You're mad at me, aren't you, because I couldn't make your brother wait...."

Whatever's wrong among us, it has to be my fault because… because there has to be something I can do to please You, my loved one, because…because…otherwise, what will become of *me*?

"It's my way of being with you," J shouts through the phone pinched between my shoulder and my ear. "It's the only way I've got."

Oh. Is it not just me? She is herself, opened up and pouring out everything that's in her. Big crashing waves of pain, temper, disappointment, disempowerment.

She's always done this, and yet I never see it coming till it hits.

I glance at her brother, arms folded, face set. A peacemaker by nature, he's as passionate as she is, but the force of that comes out of him in stubborn attachments to his own will instead of emotional storms.

So. I apologize to her and sink deeper into the couch next to him, stuck with my familiar useless warring impulses to walk out, to side with one against the other, or to yell at them both to grow up and stop being…themselves. I never know how to handle our mess. I just know I can't quit trying to figure out who's wrong, who's right, and what I should have done to make everyone happy.

"It's *always* like this," J intones bitterly before she hangs up. "We never do *anything* together."

But we do. We hang on tight to each other and our views of each other.

When I shut the flip phone and it's just B and me, he says, "She's the one who left town."

"Yeah," I say, although I know better.

I can say You're to blame—*You,* the one I'm fixed on just now— but the trouble will still be mine.

I have a Buddhist teacher, and she describes herself this way: *I just old lady.* Next comes a chuckle that might or might not be tongue-in-cheek. She never reveals her exact age. My guess is she's somewhere between eighty and ninety years old.

She came of age, like the rest of the dwindling number of still-living Tibetan lamas exiled by the Chinese takeover in 1959, as an aristocrat in a feudal theocracy. Her form is stolid and lumpy, layered in many colors and textures of thrift-store sweat pant, skirt, undershirt, and sweater. Her breathing is often audibly labored. Her English is limited but her mind, her wit, and her tongue are razor sharp.

Most of her students fear her, but non-Buddhists who meet her in public places either dismiss her as a bag lady, or fawn on her with helpless, urgent affection. Her face is smooth-skinned, honey-colored, and square, the nose strong and the cheekbones prominent, a physiognomy more Native American than Asian—Tibetans and the Chinese who rule them are quite visibly racially distinct. Her eyes, so dark the pupil cannot be distinguished from the iris, are lively, youthful, and piercing. Her jet black hair, a matter of small vanity to her, hangs below her hips when she undoes it from the topknot into which it's usually twisted. The hands performing this operation are quick, small, and fine-boned, the fingers short and tapered almost to points.

My teacher's scent resembles the tang wafting from altar bowls of offered oranges just before their skin shows mold; it is, to me, as unforgettable and as enlivening as a lover's.

For the first years I tried to follow her, she did not acknowledge me. For some years after that, I had no name she claimed to remember. When asking others to fetch me, she referred to me, in a tone of mild derision, as *writer lady.*

When she did begin to address me directly, it was only to pound me each and every time with a single, horrifying question: *What you do wrong?*

My mother and I were, at least until I started school, alone together much of the time. My father stayed out of the house as much as possible, at his job, in the yard, or down in the basement. Both my sisters, ten and eight years my senior, had left by the time I was six for their respective levels of higher education. My mother stayed home. Although we lived in a small city in mountainous southwest Virginia, she worked like a farmwife. She cooked three meals from scratch every day, cleaned house on a rigorous weekly and seasonal rotation, laundered with a wringer washer, ironing every item after it line-dried, including my father's undershirts and boxers. She pickled, canned and froze the prodigious excess from his vegetable gardens; she tended an acre of perennial flowerbeds and, in two makeshift greenhouse rooms in our house, raised hundreds of orchids and African violets. Each weekday afternoon, religiously, she sat down to watch a single soap opera, *As the World Turns*. She spurned church, but sent my father and me to Methodist Sunday school. She did some drinking—a tumbler of grain alcohol or vodka stirred with a shot of limeade just before lunch or supper; my father, when he drank with her, termed this beverage a "rejuvenator"—and she controlled everyone in the immediate and extended family by means of irrational, vituperative, obsessive hatreds.

How regularly and over how many years my mother drank, I really don't know. The presence of a rejuvenator alongside her plate or at hand on the kitchen counter while she cooked was unremarkable to me until Sara, home for a visit during my mid-childhood, remarked on it, causing me to realize with a chilly shock that my mama's habitual drink constituted the kind of drinking I'd learned at church and at school good people were not supposed to do. Only with long hindsight can I speculate how much alcohol had to do with unleashing those rage-fits the family called "tears"—Watch out, Mama's on a tear—pronounced *t-air*, like the rending of cloth, which is what I heard and what I felt every time any one of us uttered the word: the indiscriminate fury of her scissor-tongue.

What is inarguable is how much I loved her. And how difficult it proved to do such a simple thing well. I was a late-life baby, a menopause surprise born when she was forty-five, in poor health, and very much alone with her fate, the permanent burdens of a bad marriage and a mentally impaired child. Again and again in those sequestered years, she told me: she prayed to God throughout her pregnancy and my birth that both of us would die.

The balance of the story, recounted in rage or despair, concerned what her doctor told her about me. He was my doctor, too; a figure of grave authority in my child psyche. A family doctor of the sort people had in the forties and fifties, he'd treated all her adult ills and delivered both my siblings and must have had some sense of what her marriage was like.

He insisted that I was a gift, and would bring You joy.

By the time my children and I calendared our Christmas tattoo, we all understood it was intended to ink us together in defiance of spreading separation. J lived out-of-state at that point for college. I'd leave Florida for a new job come spring, while B, having moved in with his dad at fifteen, would stay behind to finish high school. The Christmas in question was the last one we'd spend together in Tampa.

We scheduled the occasion the way busy families do things these days—in multi-point cyber dialogue: she cell-calling me, he IM-ing her, me emailing them both, he texting her (along with a couple dozen of his high school friends) to confirm the satisfyingly edgy plan. I found that edge pretty exciting myself. Three decades into holding up the conventions of the holiday no matter how bound up in despair, I felt oddly ready to eschew the tree, the shopping, the wrapping, even the gifts, and opt, instead, for a together-tattoo.

The question of who's responsible for our family penchant for tattoos is its own complex story. I wanted to believe J started it. The August she turned nineteen, in her last days home before heading back to college for her sophomore year, she spent a big chunk of that summer's wages (earned as a steakhouse hostess) in Lefty's shop, acquiring a glossy midnight-black tribal tattoo that transformed her entire shapely back into a graphic statement of her individuality.

I watched it blossom over three evenings, as she arrived home wearing first the outline, and then two stages of inking in: a sleek stylized caduceus-shaped scrollwork, its wings spanning her shoulders, its serpentine wand dropping nearly to her slender waist, a smaller, fibula variant of it seated in the hollow of her back just above the tailbone. On her petite and fine-boned frame that much ink loomed extra large. The uncompromising contrast of all that black pigment embedded permanently in her milky, vulnerable skin enthralled me as artist and repelled me as mother. The intricacy and restraint of the design—her own—pleased my eye. The audacity of her choices caused me sorrow—a little for her and a little for me. When she showed me the tattoo on paper, life-size, before she got it—not asking permission but definitely recruiting acquiescence—I told her my truth about it. Very beautiful. Very bold. Not likely to age well.

As if her forthrightness undid my objection, she told me: "Mom, me and my friends never think about getting old."

I was two and three and four when the two roots of my mother's story, her death wish and her doctor's prophecy that I'd be her joy, took hold in me. I spent all my daylight hours and many night-time ones in proximity to her flesh. The sweet, meaty scent of her clinging to the bathrobe, rose-pink chenille, she draped over me as a nap-time bribe brought exquisite sensual comfort. I napped on her bed, not mine, and in the wee dark hours, I often left my bed and came to my parents' and was taken in on her side of it, to doze against her body, my back flush against her chest. If I came to her room in full daylight and found her lying on the bed, face to the wall, her back a wall to my face, and climbed up behind her staring silence and held on, she might tell me the story all over again. She might say, "You are the only one who loves me."

You are the one. I hated hearing that. Hated knowing it. But I had to listen; the words anointed me. They made me responsible. They made me afraid. Not in my mind but in my child body I understood I *had* to do *something*.

We were just we two, after all, and if one of us died, the other would surely follow.

If You wanted us to die, I had better be ready.

I held on tight to my baby bottle right up to four years old. Black-and-white photos from the old Kodak Brownie attest to this: my lanky self lolling on the glossy-waxed linoleum of the kitchen floor, eyes glazed with bliss, head cradled on a favorite plaid-cased pillow, one knee cocked and the other balanced atop its fulcrum, free foot bouncing like Mitch Miller's sing-along ball.

My father liked milk, too. He drank more than his share according to my mother, and, worse, he raided the butterfat that topped the un-homogenized milk, using a spoon or even his finger to pop the cream coin from the bottle's mouth to his. I'd seen him do it, and imagined the greasy bite as repulsive, but what really gave the act its charge was my mother's response. Control of the milk, especially the cream, made a flashpoint in their mostly cold war.

Milk arrived at our house in heavy glass bottles, carried to a galvanized tin box on the concrete floor of our back porch by a milkman dressed head to toe in white. Two times a week he brought us two kinds of milk, homogenized and not homogenized. A paper hood with pleated sides covered the cardboard tab set deep inside the thick, worn lip of the bottles, rough from use and reuse. I liked to lift the box lid and look at tall bottles slick with condensation, but I knew very well *don't touch*. I loved milk but the bottles it came in spelled danger.

Early of a morning, just we two in the house, I might stumble from my bed to the kitchen in search of my mother and my morning milk, but stop short at the door, feeling danger like heat.

You stood at the sink. Ruddy-faced, sweating and swearing, ready to erupt. Working. In my body, bile ignited dread: the day not yet begun already a disaster. I should have fled and maybe tried but You sensed my nearness, it lit your fuse and let loose the awful tear. *I told him* never do that but he went right ahead *he defied me*.

You jerked me to the refrigerator and flung back the door: The only one who loved you would witness this evidence of wrongs done you. Underneath the pleated cover, replaced as if the glue between its folds had not been breached, beneath the tab set innocently back in place—the cream missing.

I don't know if I feared for my father. I know I feared for me. Exactly once I'd attempted to lift the sweating cool bottle from the misty-cold shelf all by myself. But the bottle lay shattered already at my feet, shards of thick glass awash in a pale spreading lake of ruined, wasted milk, my fault, my *fault*, blame beating like waves too big to jump that snatched me off my feet, ripped air from my lungs and dragged me mute across sharp shells to dump me raw on the sand, my mouth full of grit.

I remember my eardrums, my bones, the whole screaming world rattling with my mother's rage. In a heap on the kitchen linoleum, I cried oceans of hot, hysterical, self-abnegating tears.

There had to be some way I could cease displeasing You.
Some way to be as abject as You needed me to be.

My parents built their house, the only one our family ever lived
in, over a period of years beginning around the time my sister Sara
was born in 1945. A compact, one-story rectangle, asbestos-shingled,
devoid of any pretension to beauty, it faced busy, two-lane U.S. Route
11. The "Robert E. Lee Highway," so designated by the legislature in
the 1920s, ran the diagonal length of Virginia from Washington, D.C.
to Bristol, the little city where we lived, situated partly in Tennessee.
The state line, marked with bronze plaques sunk into the asphalt,
bisects the main street. Downtown, at what seemed to me as a child a
particularly unsightly location where the multiple rail lines responsible for the Bristol's bygone prosperity intersected State Street, a modest rectangular arch of steel scaffolding straddled the pavement to pro-
claim the city's slogan. Hundreds of incandescent light bulbs, always
a dozen or more of them dead, spelled out BRISTOL, VA.-TENN.
A GOOD PLACE TO LIVE. When the family car, a beetle-backed,
mouse-gray Chevy from the 40s, passed beneath the sign on the way
home from a trip to "the Tennessee side," the axles rattled across the
rusted rails with the same head-jarring violence set off by crossing a
cattle grate.

Our house, on the northeast edge of town, sat on two acres of
land; my parents raised flowers, vegetables, fruit, and at one point,
chickens. Indoors was much smaller than outdoors; the five-room
house had just two bedrooms. One was my parents', of course, and
the other Sara's. Betsy and I shared the attic.

My father had finished it out, walls, floor, and ceiling, in pine
panels, with a large window filling the peaked triangular wall on
one end, a walk-in storage closet occupying the opposite end, and in
between, running beneath the eaves, narrow storage tunnels accessible

by pull-out doors flush with the walls. The room was spacious and light-filled on one end on account of that single big window, but with no cross-ventilation and no source of heat except what rose up the enclosed stairwell, the temperature up there had seasonal extremes: meat-locker chill in winter and, in summer, sweaty airlessness. The attic smelled no matter the season of baked dust and Johnson's paste wax applied with a rag from a round yellow can and buffed, laboriously, on hands and knees. The scent was bristly, akin to the parched wood benches in a sauna. The only thing in the room not marked off into Mine versus Betsy's was the table between our two beds.

On my side of the stairwell that protruded into the room, dividing it less than evenly, I got the window, the majority of the floor space, the smaller bed, and room for a bigger mess. She got the door to the walk-in closet, which I would come to fear, and a dollhouse city I coveted.

I had my own dollhouses; built-in shelves on either side of the stairs held our separate neighborhoods. But her shelf was longer and had a second, lower level, supported on overturned cardboard cartons. Her neighborhood had a grocery store (fully stocked with tiny, bright-colored plastic food items, from canned soup to heads of lettuce); a one-room schoolhouse with an auditorium downstairs; a 60s split-level home of stamped aluminum wherein her city's high-end family lived amid two-dimensional representations of all the most desirable modernities of the era (matching pink kitchen appliances! a couch-sized console TV with rabbit ears! wall-to-wall *white* shag carpet!); and three much more modest family dwellings, one of them on the lower level beside the filling station (equipped with working garage doors and mechanic's lift) its occupants were scripted to operate.

My neighborhood consisted of a single "older" home, identical to Betsy's gas-station owners', of 40s vintage refurbished for me by Sara with furniture made from taped and painted cardboard, along with drapery, bedspreads, and cushions she'd sewn and stuffed with cotton, and a hospital, also constructed by Sara—industriously, ingeniously—from a warren of whitewashed shoeboxes accoutered in intricate detail. She'd tiled the floors with watercolor squares of chalk-white and institution-green, and furnished its many rooms with cardboard and aluminum foil examining tables, filing cabinets, and hospital beds, complete with scribbled charts dangling from the foot. Her effort and skill astounded me even then but I seldom played with this creation. I'd not asked for a hospital, and the precision with which it acknowledged the fact of sickness and death put me off it.

Betsy played with her dollhouse people only by dusting them and their dwellings with devotional regularity, gradually building up a thick veneer of Pledge textured with inadequately wiped-away dust. I played with a sprawling farm built from several bagged and boxed sets acquired as Christmas presents or bribes for grocery store good behavior: sheep, goats, chickens, ducks, dogs and cats, plastic ponds and hay bales and pitchforks, buckets and pumps and hard-lump sacks of grain, some full and some sagging, in a big plastic barn surrounded by miniature acres of plastic fenced field. She addressed her toys in a non-stop, incomprehensible sing-song patter, a self-language she still speaks until you ask her what she's talking about, while I silently narrated the troubles and triumphs of my animals and their keepers. I visited Betsy's dollhouse city only in her absence.

What I wanted, I think now, was access to the stories of the lives implied by the buildings, their objects, and the little figures inside them, frozen in a single pose and a single set of clothes. I ogled with fascinated revulsion the sterile perfection of the affluent family's furnishings, the molded plastic mother dressed perpetually in belted shirt-dress, pearls and pumps, one hand imperiously on her hip—no matter what she was doing—lying rigid on a bed or angled into the driver's seat of a car. I could not stop marveling at the disjunctions in scale of the schoolhouse, another of Sara's cardboard and paint creations, in which the hand bell, the apple, and the teacher—a giant with jointed legs of aqua plastic, a literal bluestocking—dwarfed her desk and her students, some of them in swimsuits and bathing caps, others in grease-monkey coveralls or suits and ties the same color as their pasty faces. I plucked the teacher from the schoolroom to her home—she lived alone, of course, an old maid with no pets, in an apartment behind the grocery store. With the aid of her jointed legs I seated her on her pink plastic couch before the blank pink plastic screen of the television she could not see since her un-jointed waist and neck directed her gaze at her non-existent ceiling.

When Betsy left home in early adolescence for the series of institutions where she would learn life skills and be abused or neglected in proportions she knows and I can only guiltily guess at, I spent hours and hours of after-school time alone in that attic. On a record player, a blue-and-white suitcase-style 50s thing, I spun 78s and sang along: Ol' Dan Tucker and his supper; Buffalo Bill woncha come out tonight; the home-on-the-range where the antelope played. I fenced my own plain, worn amber and smooth from many miles of sock-foot tread, and populated it with a herd of several dozen china and plastic horse figurines, while costumed dolls posed on chairs and shelves, actors in fairytale dramas I wrote in my head, silently delivered their lines.

Downstairs was my mother's realm, a militarized zone. The staircase separating us descended nearly as steeply as a ladder, with tall risers and shallow treads glossily varnished, a slick chute I fell down several times, once flaying the skin from the whole length of my spine. My mother attempted the stairs only when circumstances forced it, and then angrily, because of the arthritis in her knees. If she wanted me, she shouted my name up to fetch me. Clutching the rail, sick-anxious about the tear that might lie waiting below, I took my time descending.

When my father was in the house, whiffs of their communication—her stock phrases, his noncommittal grunts—might drift up the stairwell. I cocked an ear like a wary animal, guessing whether and how much trouble was about to break. Mostly, though, nothing emanated from downstairs but the pervading fixed fact of Mother—working and fuming, or inert with despair, curled fetal on her bed or laid out exhausted in the recliner in the den.

I can imagine, now, how my mother agonized between the rock and the hard place of choosing to exile her child versus struggling alone with Betsy's infinite un-meetable needs—her "throws" and her "spells," we called them: recurrent bouts of unexplained vomiting and emotional hysterics—given the school system's and my father's complete inability to help her. When Betsy left home, she was simply gone, mainly to my selfish relief. Except for the trips to visit her, retrieve her, investigate new places, and leave her—disturbing endpoints to interminable car trips, taut with my father's silence and my mother's angry outbursts at him, at her, at me—I thought very little about my sister's fate.

No one talked to me about You, Betsy; I was just a child.

As soon as J brought home her enormous, intricate, jet-black tattoo, B—fourteen at that point—initiated a tiresome nag. When could *he* get *his* ink? Sometimes I ignored him, sometimes I said no, and other times "when you're eighteen, you may do as you like." One Sunday afternoon the autumn before our tattoo Christmas, B and I strolled out of a movie house in Tampa's sleazy-chic Ybor City, passing a tattoo parlor on our way to the car.

I joked, slowing down, "Wanna go in?"

He said, planting his feet, "Mom, I want a tattoo just like yours, eye of Ra, blue, left shoulder."

I didn't say no, because I couldn't speak. I had mostly forgotten, because after ten years out of sight *is* out of mind, that I had a tattoo—the mark of my fortieth birthday and the savage divorce—a third eye that watched my back.

My boy had not forgotten.

"Does it wash off?" he asked back then, his innocent face perplexed, processing yet another event he hadn't ever imagined could happen. When I came home wearing that tattoo, he was six years old, in big trouble at school for the first time in his life—for punching other kids with the violence of his own blind pain—but familiar with tattoos only in their innocuous stick-on form.

"I want your mark," he said, the autumn afternoon he was newly sixteen. "Because you're leaving."

So. There You stand, my son, taller than I am, reminding me *I* started it, the tattoos *and* the separations. You—my second baby, the point at which I gave up trying to be a perfect mother—You clung to me in shrieking panic every time anyone else reached for You. But now You permit me to leave simply because I've said I need to, asking me only to allow You, please, to be scarred like me.

I looked B in the eye. I felt fear. I said, "You'll have to get your father to agree."

~

At four, I first left my mother's orbit a few hours a week, for nursery school at the Methodist church. I had to give up my bottle in order to go, so I must have believed I'd enjoy myself there, but I remember very little beyond the disturbing experience of being seen and directed by grown-ups other than my mother. Things she took for granted, my aversion to galoshes, for instance, and a habit of carrying my hands limp-wristed in front of me like bunny paws, appeared eccentric and in need of correction in the eyes of adults I encountered at nursery school.

At five, I entered kindergarten—in those days neither public nor universal—at a different Methodist church across town, populated by children of a higher socio-economic order because of the not-negligible tuition. It was a venerable kindergarten, chosen by my mother to provide a culturally and academically enriching experience; both my sisters had gone there before me. Amid the happy business of cookie snacks and field trips and games and songs and performances—every year this kindergarten put on a three-ring circus, in which children took the parts of animals, ringmasters, and trapeze artists—trouble reared up: the loving cup.

My mother wanted me to have it. She expected me to win it.

For what I recall as months on end she let me know in what she said and didn't say over meals and during drives to and from the points in our day: to not win the loving cup meant a lazy, worthless, no-account shirking of what I was capable, at the very minimum, of doing. With the least degree of proper effort, I would win this Best-in-Class award. I was smarter, prettier, and had better manners than any other child in the entire Anderson Street Methodist Church kindergarten.

This message puzzled me. I got wrong or didn't understand an alarming number of things. She often told me I was ugly; she said my mouth turned down. When on a tear, she berated me for having no decent manners at all. Who and what I really was, I did not know, but I understood, at five, that if my public performance didn't support her publicly professed truths about me, I was off my form, and could have done better if I'd actually tried, and *would* have done better if I really loved her.

I didn't care about winning. Maybe I already hated competing. But if You needed that cup, Mama, I needed it worse. Your joy = my responsibility, a matter of life and death.

I can't remember a single thing about the competition itself except an oral questioning, by the head teacher, Miss Maude, of the children deemed to be in the running for the cup. The questions, I imagine now, tested our knowledge of facts kindergartners should know, the names of the seasons, maybe, or of the president. During the test I felt some self-righteous contempt for how ridiculously obvious and easy the answers were.

I came to kindergarten knowing how to read without understanding that I did; my mother and Sara had read to me for as long as I could remember and I'd memorized any number of Little Golden Books. My disappointment was keen the day we received our longed-for first books, which turned out to be mimeographed pages bearing line drawings labeled with two or three baby words. It surprised me how far beneath my expectations the challenge of kindergarten fell. I seemed to have always known things other children learned with difficulty. I quickly learned the price for too often having the right answer and especially for too often volunteering it—alienation from my peers. But I liked having right answers: I yearned for the affirmation that praise and checkmarks conferred.

I don't remember if there were other categories of competition for this kindergarten Best-in-Show award. I vaguely recollect my fluttering terror-excitement on the big day during the hours that preceded the examination. But I recall with clarity what I would carry with me like a cup of gall into high school and beyond: an exchange between me and some other child's mother in the anteroom just after my questioning.

Maybe I was looking smug. Maybe my reputation as smart kid and teacher's pet preceded me already at that age. Maybe I seemed like a target because I was alone; for some reason, my mother was not with me as other children's mothers were. Or maybe the woman meant only to make friendly conversation with a kid who looked lonely.

She asked me if I'd studied. She might have said she bet I had. I had not. Until she mentioned it, I had no idea that people *could* prepare for questions. A strange feeling rushed over me. I didn't know what it was but it had to do with the size and force of my mother's certainty that I could and should win the prize. I swooned with sudden fear that I wouldn't, because I hadn't studied. And squirmed, at the same time, with deep shame at knowing I probably would win, without studying, because the questions were too easy.

The confusing, charged complexity of my emotions swept me

away from myself. I told that other mother a lie. I said, "My mother kept me up all night studying."

She was shocked. I was shocked. I had no idea such a thing was on its way out of my mouth; never in my life had I told such a whopping lie. I felt certain I'd be found out, with terrible, Old Testament punishment to follow.

From that moment until the loving cup was placed in my hands, I oozed the cold sweat of fear. Misery so overshadowed winning, I barely remember the award ceremony—some end-of-year event for which I was overdressed and desperately self-conscious.

My mother, my very first You, center of my world and the only light I see by at five, You have set me a single task. Please You, or die.

Years will pass before I notice other people called the object I won for You a trophy. "Loving cup" must have been your term for the prize. Nowadays I wonder if You meant to suggest the award was a cup of love, conferred on the winner by admiring teachers. But at the time I understood I was to love and desire the cup itself. The "why" I did not question; your desire was all the motivation I needed. Maybe I felt way down beneath all surface forms of five-year-old knowing that if I had the cup, I'd have loving I could hold in my hands.

Once I possessed the cup, I put it in your hands, pleasing You no end, of course. You put it on display in our house and showed it to everyone—relatives, friends, neighbors—any chance you got. If I heard You, I writhed.

The cup itself, I hated. When it came to live in my bedroom, I avoided its malevolent eye.

In my earliest response to the tired question that plagues small children—what will you be when you grow up?— I asserted with confidence that I planned to become a galloping white horse with an Indian on my back. I was old enough by the time I said this to know that people did not ever become horses, and that horse plus rider equals two beings, not one, but those were details I freely disregarded.

I couldn't overlook the laughter my career goal provoked in others. It became an oft-visited family joke. My next ambition I kept very private: I aspired to be a bird in flight. Playing alone in the attic, I projected myself beyond the glass squares of the big window into the empty space above the house next door.

When I grew up, I would fly free.

The sky, my Buddhist teacher says.

Those two words, no more. Her shoulders and the up-thrust of her chin provide the verb, her gaze the preposition. The pain she lives with and never mentions—a hip damaged decades ago in a breakneck horseback escape from a Chinese prison—supplies caught-breath emphasis.

Her English vocabulary is slender and specialized. *Compassion. More compassion. Visualize properly. Concentrate.* Exacting nouns, commanding verbs, and the very few qualifiers necessary to convey the essence of ancient Tibetan Buddhist teachings to eager and ignorant Western students.

My eyes follow hers to the cloudless dome above us—a moment of comprehending with the body the truth of What Is. The calm and empty sky always there, no matter the fog, the cumulus/stratus/cirrus clouds, the glare, the rain, or the darkness that occludes it.

My mother was an abuser who'd been terribly abused. A vicious, sensitive woman who never failed to feed and clothe me, support my education, inspire me to love the natural world and the arts. She never abandoned our family home and she never stopped loving me, albeit on her terms. She passed away at age eighty-nine. The following year, in the last stages of emptying the house she'd ruled and rotted in for six decades, I discovered the loving cup, furred with dust, awaiting me on a high shelf. I lifted it down reluctantly, marveling at a simple object's enduring ability to make me feel unworthy.

Why had I told that kindergarten lie? Even at five, I had a compulsion toward truth-telling, yet that day I lied easily and urgently, betraying my values. Betraying my mother, by calling her methods into question.

My values were her values, of course. *She* despised lies, *she* expected my success, but most of all she required—in order to stay alive—my absolute loyalty.

For years afterward, winning awards and A's while losing myself in early marriage, drugs and depression, I replayed the shame of the kindergarten debacle—the social faux pas, my moral transgression—and used it to beat myself down.

As a young adult I courted death by incremental self-neglect and wallowed in self-pity (never noticing how this behavior exactly replicated my mother's), but some essence of me that was quick-witted and lively found a way to survive by gaming the shame: I'll do it to myself before You, my loved one, can do it to me. If I played my game really well, I'd never have to be blindsided by disaster or rejection, never be caught out trusting anyone or anything that might betray me.

I racked up worldly success—often in school, sometimes at work or in love. Every time that happened, I'd catch myself compulsively dissembling to make it look harder so I could be both more special (look how hard I worked!) and more like everybody else (look how hard I *had* to work!). I compulsively disassembled, too—pointing out to myself and everybody else all the ways whatever I'd accomplished had not been difficult enough, not really, to count as real success.

All this, without ever comprehending why I lived the way I did, suffered the way I did, and wanted—so often, just like You, Mama— to turn my face to the wall and die.

~

One night during my decade as single mom, I dream I lose my purse while searching for V.T., the man I cannot have but long for like the Grail.

In the dream, though, it's the purse that's missing. The one material item I have most dread of losing and have, in fact, never in my waking life lost.

Flipping through racks of high-end suits, shirts, ties, I'm killing time. You're somewhere in here, V.T., near to hand; I can feel your imminence humming beneath a generic salesperson's detached supervision. The carpet in this swanky shop is very nice, a muted green, plush and thick. The hangers and shelving, glossy walnut, real fancy. Where *are* You? I grow impatient. Then, like a blow, I sense the absence of the purse strap from its always-place on my left shoulder.

Frantic searching. Silent panic. The salesperson staring coldly. Everything lost, disaster upon me, no purse, no ID, no money: ruin.

I find the purse. A modest-sized leather pouch, untouched. Resting on the cushions of a round settee—upholstered in sage velvet welted deep with covered buttons—right in the center of the store. I must have set it down without noticing and walked away, distracted, obsessing over You. I wrench the bag open and rummage. My wallet, still in there. Nothing, not a thing, missing.

I wake up shocked to sickness by the afterburn of the dream-punched adrenalin that's just surged through me.

I thought I lost my purse.

I *dreamed* I thought I lost my purse while looking for You, but didn't.

What does that mean?

~

For a couple of months after B brings up his tattoo—and

mine—on the Ybor City street corner, I hear nothing more about ink. But between him and J the wee-hours IM-ing and during-class texting and talking-while-driving cell phone scheming must have been under-way—in a rare cooperative effort. J, I suspect, took the lead once he let her know I'd caved. He would have needed her to lead because she's older, bolder, and, well, she'd not have followed. She thrives on connection but needs to head the pack; when those conditions mesh, she leads with grace, often to beneficent result. Whatever the mechanics of their collusion, it culminates one afternoon in November when she phones me from college to announce the plan they've devised, and not ten minutes later B calls, acting casual, admitting no complicity but clearly salivating to hear me confirm what she has—no doubt—texted him in the interim to report.

We shall, together, get three distinct and completely original tattoos, each incorporating a portion of the other two—both of theirs including an eye of Ra, mine made entirely from parts of theirs. Each person's marking will be witnessed by the other two. My children will do the drawings, together, when she comes home for winter break. Lefty, his skills a given, will do the ink. And I'll pay.

Okay, Mom?

"Okay," I say, first to my daughter and then to my son.

Okay, my kids: tattoos, together, let's do it.

I don't want another tattoo. I don't like encouraging them toward tattoos, either, but I know myself honored. Feel myself affirmed. My children's enthusiasm and initiative prove we've survived the divorce. I haven't ruined their lives. We *are* a functioning family, still.

Yet, to each of my children I voice a caution: "Don't tell your dad we're doing this."

You, my husband, offered me terms: "Bitch, how much do I have to pay you to get out?"

The takeover, at its origin, had not been hostile. You wanted badly to acquire me and I wanted—so bad—to be wanted. You pressed your case, bargained hard, closed the deal. From there to our dissolution the path ran sixteen years, mostly uphill.

Your opening bid marked me beautiful, desirable, intelligent: a credit to your powers to have and to hold. An opportunity within your driving necessity to trade up. You told me, more than once, about the loved one who came before: soft-bodied, like I wasn't; so sexy, such long straight black hair. Too little education, no ambition. You said she liked you too much. You said she never said no.

You did not like no, said or unsaid.

You made me an offer I was too diffident to refuse. I couldn't say yes. I never said no. Our wedding happened, testament to your will to succeed and my choking need to never be let go.

What stayed unsaid between us never did stop talking: my ambivalence and your determination to resolve it: a face-off on the fault-line we built on.

Sometimes in the we-two years with my mother, the doorbell rang and through the screen door she held wide I saw the uniformed deliveryman from King's Department Store downtown. In his arms, a rectangular dress box of thin, dull purple cardboard. Big—perhaps two feet by three—and distended by the contents overstuffing it. My heart lifted, twisted, plunged. Desire coupled to dread shuddered through me like a drug, and I slipped away to my room, awaiting a word or a sign from her that the box was for me, and that I should open it.

Sometimes, instead, the box sat waiting for me on my bed when I got in from school. Occasionally she pulled one down from a top shelf of her closet, and put it in my arms as a surprise.

But always, the same response in me. The addict's tremor. A sharp shivering certainty that lifting the lid would bring pain. And, complete clarity that no way would I not open it.

These Pandora's boxes closed with fat tabs like two-lobed clover leaves, purple on the outside, cardboard grey on the inside. Usually tape had been added to augment the latch. Cutting the tape, disengaging the tabs from their slots, raising the hinged lid, I beheld a pile of treasure selected for me by Mrs. Gallion, an elderly iron-haired saleslady in the girls' department who'd known my mother since, it seemed to me, the dawn of time. When my mother and I went inside King's Department Store (the better of the two in Bristol at that time) and rode the elevator up, operated in those days by a genial, uniformed black man on a stool, I dreaded seeing Mrs. Gallion because she wore black lace-up old lady shoes and fussy old lady dresses and smelled fusty the way maiden aunts did in those days.

She also had, at least in my memory, a prominent mustache. But she had excellent taste in pre-adolescent fashion. The boxes of just-arrived merchandise she sent out to our house on standing instructions from my mother to choose from whatever was new were full of the latest mainstream fads, everything the most popular girls at school were wearing, in just my size. I could try all of it on, and keep as much as my mother decided I could. But first I had to say what I wanted.

What *did* I want? How much should I ask for? That was the rub. I lusted for the most impractical and romantic things, velveteen or silk dresses and appliquéd coats suitable for the kind of occasions we never attended; I'd wear them once or never before I outgrew them. I chose by color and texture rather than taste or function. If I asked to keep too many pieces, I'd pay for the error: the clothes overfilling my closet would substantiate my mother's accusation, flung at me in a vulnerable moment, about my selfishness, how much I cost, how much she gave, how little I appreciated it. I tried to steer a perfect, pleasing middle path. Ask for less than I desired but enough to give me some affirmation—the tangible fruit of love—I craved.

The boxes tended to arrive not long after Mama unleashed on me one of her terrifying tears. *I'll wring your neck. I'll jerk a kink in you.*

You can just miss that party, that school trip; you can just stay home and HELP ME for a change; that girl's parents never pay back, they're in it for what they can get; she's not your friend, she envies your brains, your looks; she's trash, her people are trash, she doesn't like you, she's using you to get attention for herself. She fussed and shouted and kept at it for hours; I dissolved into hysterical, hiccupping sobs.

By the time I was ten I understood I was being bought off with dress boxes in place of apology or repair.

Well before I was ten, a dress box provoked not pleasure but entitlement yoked to resentment. Opening the gift box, I signed off on violence, made silent acquiescence that no matter how You treated me, I'd never, ever, go away.

The terms of our engagement are, first, that You must not be disturbed. And, second, that nothing's wrong with our marriage but my inability to get this right.

A chair whistles by my face, strikes the wall, and I refuse to forget it. I cry and want You to change. You've never hit me, You remind me, a point of pride. A matter of degree to me. But You earn the money. I've accepted diamonds. And dresses. When You shove me to the floor, I hiccup and sob, get up and acquiesce: my *fault*. I provoked You, I deserve it.

I believe this resent it reject it don't say so. Jigger reality as needed to line up your view with mine. Pound down the shame hammer, raise up the shame shield, wield the shame blade on the parts that hurt most: I'll do it to myself before You do it to me.

I have children, You change jobs, we move, and—trading up— move again. You don't do housework but You pay for maid service. It's okay if I write when You're out of the house. The house has a pool, the pool has a spa. I lack ambition, I'm frigid, make too many lists, cry so many tears. We barely hold on and on one thing we agree: the fault-line is my fault. All I want is what You are not: affirming and easy to please.

You up the ante. A boat and a horse if I'll continue to play. We try date night, more diamonds, champagne toasts in the spa. My resistant submission, your relentless insistence, it's soul-killing, hate-making. One Friday at my feet beneath your foot the champagne flute lies shattered. A burst truth of blond bubbles and razor-edged truth shards: Please me, or be crushed.

In the morning, the bell rings. It's a deliveryman. I open Pandora's box and find tulips, lavender and out of season. Expensive. Implicit in them, the terms of our marriage. You can say what You want and do what You want, as long as afterwards You show me the money.

One Sunday soon after I agree to our Christmas tattoo, B stops by to rehash the plan. We toast our triumvirate bravado with big bowls of ice cream and chocolate syrup at my kitchen table, and he voices, just incidentally, his reason for his investment in the scheme—a feeling darker than any he's ever admitted in my hearing before.

"We've been through hell together."

"Yes." I gulp surprise.

He says no more and I know I can't either. My son, after all, lives with his father and, ten years out from the divorce, an uneasy truce in the war he made on me for leaving barely holds.

Always, some kind of not-saying.

Always, the necessity to step lightly over trip wires to landmines that might or might not blow.

A foursome family's bitter end began like this: Halloween impending, the children's Gameboy in his hands, a quartet of pumpkins on the kitchen table, waiting to be carved. He drove toward his goal, hour after hour, level by level, succeeding. No way to save the victories. She knew that, she'd been told; each win mandated the next game. The children grew impatient. For their sake she transgressed. She disturbed. Spoke quietly, her lips near his ear, and just that way, nothing more, she made him lose the battle and the war. Everything he'd worked for, strived toward, invested in, all that holding in and holding on and holding out: he exploded.

The house tilted. Their world convulsed. *Her fault* their fault-line failed. He flung down the game, slammed out the door, peeled out the driveway. Tearless with fear, she summoned the children. Three at three sides of the table cut grins into orange gourd flesh beneath warm yellow light. On layers of wet newspaper, stinking piles of pumpkin guts. The big knife in her hand, little spoons in theirs. Her glassy shocked silence.

The boy says now he remembers nothing about this. The girl says it seemed normal at the time. Surely everyone's dad stormed out raging, sometimes?

He came home. No one said a word about it. She cried herself through the night. He slept. The sun rose, he went to work and the children to school, and she crept about the world, barely breathing, eyes down, apologizing to strangers at the grocery and the gas station for the small space in their path she took up. Then: the writing, the one thing wholly hers in this family's life was missing from its place on the hard drive they shared. Frantic searching. A novel lost. Ruin. But she found it. She found it hidden, not deleted. What did that mean?

His point of pride: I only moved it. Her matter of degree, the terms that went unstated: better behave, bitch, because I know how to hurt you, real bad, next time.

Dazed in mild mid-morning light, she sat alone on their king-sized bed. The empty house around her, her place inside it: nothing changed, but every last thing finally broken.

After that, she backed up her files every day and hid the disc.

After that, she held her tongue. Held her breath, too. Developed asthma. By the time she moved out—saying only, I can't breathe; I need air—she could barely speak for the choking cough.

~

Some stories I cannot tell because they are armed and dangerous, still. I project their pale shadows to this screen and watch them flicker from the forced, unsafe distance of *he* and *she* and *they*.

~

Exactly once as a small child I watched, on the sly, an episode of "The Twilight Zone," a television series prohibited by my mother as too scary for a second-grader. Simple curiosity caused me to break her rule; I'd heard kids at school talk it up. A single image from the single show lodged in my mind and never left: the bald, inert, pop-eyed face of a man kept alive inside a glass case, conscious but paralyzed, able to move only his eyes, his flicking pupils registering his spiking emotions, tracked by the jerking needle of an EEG monitor—and his wife, blowing smoke from her cigarette through the air vent of his transparent casket, smirking as his suffering torqued.

The man's helpless, interminable, glassed-in vulnerability triggered existential terror I could neither name nor cope with. Compulsively I fed my fear, rehearsing again and again the man's naked head, his bulging eyes, the suffocating smoke wreathing through his case, the wife's smug pleasure in causing him pain he could not escape. I must have confessed my horror to my sister Betsy because one night, as we lay in our respective beds in the darkened attic bedroom, eight years and eighteen inches apart, she told me that the man and his transparent casket were now housed inside the walk-in closet three feet from where we lay.

I was old enough to know this could not be true, but my cognitively impaired sister's imagination (to this day unrestrainedly bloody-minded) inspired her to state the preposterous with such confidence as to overturn my good sense. I still wonder if she intended to create torment, like any normal sibling might, but no matter, the terror she seeded in me took hold like a virus.

Some nights I lay awake for hours in a cold sweat. Some days I could not bear to play alone upstairs. The morbid tension I already felt about the distortions and impossibilities of her dollhouse-people's lives ratcheted into active fear each time I considered their world's proximity to the blank dark rectangle of the walk-in closet door. Its black iron knob—hollow, archaic, loose on the stem, the only one of its kind in the whole house—seemed by virtue of its singularity and its ugliness to attest to the presence of the profoundly unnatural.

Who knew when the knob would turn and the dark door swing wide? Anytime I found it slightly ajar, I slammed it hard. Behind that flimsy, hollow-core barrier lay the terrible possibility that malevolent force might keep a life captive, forever.

When You dictate the terms of our dissolution, I am crying. A hiccupping hyperventilating heap on the kitchen floor at your feet. I sob rivers and wail oceans, pleading on my knees: Something has to change. I cannot bear this marriage the way things are.

There has to be a way to stop displeasing You.

Is there no way to be as abject as You need me to be?

Your answer: Get Out.

I'll never know what he couldn't bear to say. What hurts he held so dear that no one and nothing mattered like they did. I can't ask; the breach is permanent. I speculate on this screen, instead.

Inside that rage at my failings, ferocious clinging to what he needed me to be.

Inside his right to be shed of me, implacable determination to never, ever lose.

Inside our complex disaster, a single, simple fact: I wouldn't say yes but I couldn't say no.

I refused to turn You loose. I made You cut me off.
I was the one You fixed on and the dead-wrong choice.
I never made You happy. I never brought You joy.

But, one more thing left too long unsaid: You loved me. And I loved You.

~

The grass surrounding the retreat house stands waist-high, an entire spring's lush growth left uncut through the thirty days of Saga Dawa, the holy month of the Buddha's enlightenment. To kill or even to disturb the hordes of sentient beings living on and inside and beneath the tangle would be inauspicious in this season.

Five days out of the seven I stay here, alone in one of my teacher's several properties, a derelict mom-and-pop motel in rural north-central Florida, rain falls. It arrives in slanting sheets, straight-down soakings, horizontal mizzles, and cathartic thunderstorms; a tropical depression has stalled off the coast. In the mornings thick mist makes a whiteout in the meadow behind the cinderblock strip of ten dank rooms, and the eaves overhanging the cement walkway to the one with a functioning kitchenette drip constantly, the building's flat roof draining old rain or new. I cannot walk into the meadow grass without becoming soaked, if not snakebit, and I have no way to dry my clothes, constantly damp anyway from the humidity pouring in through louvered windows cranked wide day and night to catch a breeze, so I stay put. I sit on my cushion in the shrine room, I lie on my sleeping bag atop a mildewed mattress to read, or I sit in the shelter of the eave above the kitchen door—a dry spot exactly as big as my chair—and watch it rain.

I have come here to fulfill a Buddhist practitioner's obligation: during Saga Dawa if at no other time, renounce the world entirely for three days, or better yet, seven, and best of all, fifteen. Seven days is what I can do this year, 2003, putting writing, friend and family responsibilities, money job, and housekeeping on hold. Each day I chant four sessions of prayers lasting at least two hours. In-between, observing the classical instruction for retreat, I rest, recovering energy and, as often as I remember (*drenpa*: remembrance), watching my mind (*shey-zhin*: mindfulness). During those hours I read books on the Dharma, and sometimes, indulging my writer self, novels and essays. I journal a few pages every evening about my physical and mental experiences. I cook simple meals and wash dishes and myself after shooing bugs, gently, from the kitchen counter and the rusty, leaking shower stall. But mostly the effort expended in chanting prayers and the body pain from long hours of sitting upright on a meditation cushion means I have to rest. When I leave the shrine room—dim, silent, low-ceilinged; the floor layered in antique, slightly moldy carpets of rich colors and intricate patterns; the walls thick with banners and the gilt-framed Tibetan religious paintings called *thangkas*—I relish the respite from discipline and exhaustion. I inhabit my relief deeply, guiltlessly—to an extent not possible had I been in the world, enmeshed in its duties and its din.

From my molded-resin chair I observe hawks, jets in the stratosphere, towering thunderheads, and the stubbornly veiled sun move across the sky in their requisite arcs. I watch leaves bend beneath the weight of individual raindrops and bounce back as each drop becomes a drip. The extent of the universe visible to me is a narrow swath of that impenetrable savanna grass, studded with an eclectic selection of planted or volunteering small trees, loquat, banana, avocado, crape myrtle (blooming hot pink), and ancient, gray-berried arbor vitae, bordered by tall pines dividing the property from fifteen miles of two-lane blacktop linking the nearly equidistant crossroads at Archer to the hamlet of Newberry.

The only living beings in this wet world are jays, cardinals, sparrows, crows, and grackles; innumerable representatives of a half dozen species of spider; a pair of half-wild black kittens (which I feed, as instructed by the usual occupant of the property, who has disappeared for reasons of his own); and the young but very self-confident raccoon who attempts to raid the cats' food bowl in broad daylight with me sitting right beside it. When I raise an eyebrow and address him, "Excuse me?" he lumbers off, no doubt to return in my absence. I hear, however, thousands or millions of the beings surrounding me: evening birds I cannot identify by their eerie calls; the rustle, beneath my window in the night, of four-footed animals larger or more clumsy than the freeloading raccoon; whining hoards of mosquitoes assaulting the barely-intact window screens; and the collective hum of all the insects that live in grass and warm up their lungs as the sun rises and sets.

I am by this time in my divorced, solitary state long-accustomed to living alone—my children are teens with lives of their own—but my complete isolation here, a woman by herself in what appears from the road to be an abandoned building, with no functioning locks and ample evidence that drifters have overnighted here in the past, this makes me jumpy, especially after dark. One night I panic that something large and angry is rifling the cupboards in the room where I sleep (the thumps and scratching suggest wrestling rats) but when I make myself get up and turn on the lights to investigate, fleeing cockroaches (the deep-South, four-inch, palmetto-bug kind) appear to be the culprits. Deep sleep stops visiting me, so that both body and mind run slow all day. Lassitude makes it easier to track my mind's flux—less going on up there. I turn soft and suggestible: more childlike, less defended.

Each successive day I spend less of my rest time lying down or reading and more hours parked in the resin chair, eager for the company of the two black cats. Kittens just old enough to be independent, they are clearly feral: narrow-bodied and spider-limbed;

extraordinarily long-tailed; slinky like tiny jaguars instead of sausage-shaped and plush like domestic cats. I never know their names, if they have any, so I think of them as Boy and Girl, gender being the sole distinction I can make at first. Soon the shapes of their individual faces, like their separate personalities, assert themselves. He has a solemn, low-browed face but a goofball's need to find fun in everything, even his slumbering companion's utterly motionless tail. She is petite with a heart-shaped, feminine face and a persistently avid expression about everything: meals, privacy or the jay that taunts her. Boy is full of bluster, Girl is tense about intruders. She'd go head-to-head, five pounds to his fifteen, with that young raccoon, given provocation.

My many repetitions of *sadhana,* a chanting and visualization ritual, are meant to deepen and stabilize my ability to concentrate. In the shrine room, new vistas of interiority do open themselves to me, and I enter them: the practice of releasing my clinging to notions about the boundaries of self. What I need. Who I am. I never know where "I" am going when a sense perception beckons. I try to neither wonder mentally nor resist by stiffening physically. There amid multiple altars piled with religious objects and time-dulled photos of sacred places and personages; dozens of tall, glassed candles suffusing the humid air with their heat and the buttery scent of melting wax; every fabric and each of my breaths saturated by incense brand new and decades old; that perfume almost-but-not-quite covering the acid-sweet odor of fruit offerings beginning to turn—I see, I hear, I smell and taste, I sense with my skin and my muscles and organs beneath it. I remind myself to relax, to allow the arriving and the departing of each sensation along with the emotions and mentations that form its wake.

When I leave the cushion, my heightened ability to focus fixes on the cats. Undistractedly I observe them sleep, eat, play at hunting, play with each other, and ignore me. The rain and wet grass keep them in sight—that single dry spot beneath the kitchen eave places their food and my chair in tight proximity—but they are too wild to be petted. They have no use at all for human contact; my presence neither interests them nor deters their interest in each other.

Because they are litter mates and still sexually immature, their play is really play, all exploration and rough-housed delight. His hind foot plops carelessly between her eyes, and she leaves it there, nonchalant at first, then licking it with motherly vigor, then shutting her teeth around it, a predatory gleam in her eye, stopping barely short of piercing flesh, to await his reaction: a no-claws swat. Next, a fury of wrestling. Legs wrapping and flailing, torsos twisting like pinned snakes, then her head nests beneath his chin. Girl licks Boy's chest while his tongue towels her ear. Half a moment later his fangs frame her jugular, her body slack, awaiting release. When it comes, she bounds into the grass and he gallops behind.

They incite each other. Completely enmeshed, they sustain each other. How long can it last, such un-cat-like loving kindness, this un-human equanimity about who did what to whom and what, if anything, it all means?

My life outside retreat feels like breaking rocks. I work hard to do everything right but I have no juice left in me. The novel I've labored over for ten years appears impossible to sell; I have a money job I can hardly bear; my passionate yearning for the answer I imagine the ever-silent, always-absent V.T. to be seems bottomless and permanent. My mother is dead but my demented father, slowly dying, calls me with urgent demands I can barely decipher, much less fulfill, and my two teenagers are worn out with me, distancing themselves from my world-weariness. Neither I nor anyone connected to me seems happy. Enmeshed, I can't stop struggling to do something to about that. *There has to be something I can do.* I think and think this at home and at work, my mind spinning like a bicycle wheel. But watching the cats from inside the confinement of retreat makes me stop thinking and stop trying to do anything.

Watching the cats, I relax—seduced by the joy of their agenda-less play.

Watching the cats, I forget myself.

Watching cats, I am free.

I even stop dreading nightfall. When the seven days are up, I hate leaving them, those kittens who have no use for me beyond the filling of their bowls. Packing my car, I hold back tears. I vacate with a sense of relief the decrepit room I've slept in; I padlock the shrine room like a jewel box I might someday reopen; but the resin chair, solitary in a wide sea of wet grass, Girl and Boy play-fighting beneath it, cracks my heart. Driving down the blacktop toward my mounded-up in-box and the puzzled or irritated family members, friends and colleagues impatient for me to resume my productive or supportive role in their lives, I feel bereaved about kittens. What if the property's caretaker doesn't return to feed them, won't it be my fault, somehow, for not making sure he did?

I am not all the way home, a two-hour drive, before it dawns on me that in the midst of retreat—a focused effort to cut attachment—I made a new attachment. To a pair of cats. That error, and especially the fact I didn't see it happening (where was my *drenpa?* my *shey-zhin!*), makes me writhe. Clutching the wheel, I label myself a bad Buddhist. That I've carried out my teacher's retreat instructions diligently but head home without fresh insight seems to prove it.

A year or so later, I'll discern what the cat incident taught me about myself: I have to have something to hold onto. That's my nature.

Unpacked, my insight reads like this: the cats' presence plus my habit of grasping incited my attachment. Then the two enmeshed things, cats and my habit, sustained each other. The attachment formed spontaneously—something *had* to arise to fill my habitual need to hold on—but I fed it. Indulging my attachment felt good, so I did it again. And again. Every day, and more hours each day. I became governed by my attachment—"conditioned" is the term for that. First I watched the cats because I had so little else to do, and soon I watched because I needed to, arranging my circumscribed life, the time of my meal, the angle of my chair, to keep the objects of my desire constantly in sight and my essential aloneness at bay.

Still more years will pass before I begin to give up my habits of guilty self-judgment and of seeking outside myself answers to my pain. I will wrestle with and be bested by one enormous, crashing longing after another. My needy father will pass away, leaving our frustrated connection forever unresolved. I will quit the distasteful job and find another, and then another, with different shortcomings. My children become adults moving further into their own lives but sometimes in their own time coming very near again. My novel finds a publisher, conferring upon me a baffling ambivalence about the necessity of self-promotion. And V.T., attainable after all, survives mortal illness and a vicious divorce to marry me—a man with feral mind and booby-trapped body, with whom I begin love again late in mid-life, not knowing what I have found and when I will lose it because—in the words of my teacher's teacher, passed mouth to ear down two generations to me:

You do not know what may happen.

Almost ten years after my retreat in the rain, another insight seeded then ripens in me. The benefit of mindfully experiencing attachment is the opportunity to taste fully its juice, bitter and sweet, and then—softly, lovingly, like a litter mate's jaws relaxing—release.

Inside a dream, an old one from the hard years of lonesome

longing, I step my way from yearning toward…what?

In this dream I think not *where am I going?* but *where I am*: sore-footed and astonished, wire-walking a razor-thin ridge line at strato-spheric height. The firmament I'm thrust into is black. To my left and to my right, near-vertical slick-rock slopes. Before me, a chain of peaks, bleak and barren. Atop some distant summits, three tall Tibetan syllables—Om and Ah and Hung—white, red, and blue, respectively, glowing like light timbers:

I am keenly alone. Dense silence weights my eardrums.

In a narrow valley vertiginous miles below me, luminaria nested in brown paper bags illuminate a labyrinthine path—

to You.

How is it I descended from the desolate high place?

Inside the dream I never wonder because faster than filings flee to a magnet, I am embraced by You.

We're waltzing, although we neither know how. We tried before and we failed but this time, like Fred and Ginger, we glide and we sway.

Your arms close a circuit that has been always broken. I light up. I am light, my feet float, blue eyes that are your eyes see me we dance me.

I found You, You fix me.

How easy!

Feels just-right.

But it's only a dream.

I wake up, and go on breaking rocks.

Part Two
Sky

When our together-tattooing actually begins, B is, by his choice, first up in Lefty's chair. Seeing him there causes me to reflect on how fundamentally grotesque it is to choose self-mutilation as a gift—and to have it inflicted by a stranger in a public setting while a family member watches.

The atmosphere in the tattoo parlor is a cross between the chilly sterility of a dentist's office—the antiseptic wipes, the latex gloves, the tipped-back, incapacitating chair—and a grunge hair salon in some trendy downtown location—the exposed ductwork, the uninhibited displays of narcissism. In either setting people pay for the privilege of undergoing a tedious, uncomfortable process while outsiders view the body and the procedures altering it dispassionately, and any emotions provoked by the body's vulnerability invite humiliation.

B, at sixteen, much concerned with being a man, finds himself in this awkward position in front of his mother.

I have no idea how to do this right.

Who is it You need me to be?

I last saw my mother alive late in the afternoon on New Year's Day, 2000. She lay propped up in a lounge chair alongside her hospital bed. She'd just undergone surgery for a broken leg, a pin now inserted into the crumbling bone above her knee. She had congestive heart failure, high blood pressure, osteoporosis, arthritis, gout and more. She was wan and vague. She'd been rambling on about her father and my father; she called each of them "Daddy" interchangeably. The gist seemed to be that both of them mystified her. Both of them she'd tried "no end"—her word—to please. Both of them had bullied her and, I believe, abused her, and at the end of her life she didn't know why.

My question to her had been, "What do you remember best?" I'd wanted her sweetest memories, and I got one. A pair of shoes, green suede and high-heeled, with a wide strap and a large button, that her mother had given her the money to buy, so she could be special, stand out, at some event, some ordinary school or church social. "She always had a little bit of money," my mother said of her mother, "and she gave it to me so I could get some of the things I wanted."

My mother had done that for me, all my life, even after I slammed out of her house and stayed gone from her life for years. The clarity with which I recollected this was piercing.

I lay my head on her chest, partly the penitent child returning and partly in humble respect for her old, exhausted heart. For the first time in decades, what she said provoked my tears, and she didn't want them. In a flash of her old, bitter strength, she commanded me, "Don't cry." Violating her chosen terms at the very end of her days seemed inconceivable; our relationship had, after all, always been her way or no way. I sat up and took her hands and held them. She changed the subject. Later I held her hands again, cutting her nails and filing them smooth.

"That feels so good," she told me. "They'd gotten awful long, and nobody sees."

I had dinner plans with my childhood friend Margaret, who would drive me to the airport. My job, my children, my writing, my diligent life awaited me in Tampa. When the hospital's automatic doors parted to let me out into a cold, flat dusk, the dregs of a day on which the millennium had turned, what surprised me was what I didn't feel. The frozen ground was dry, the sky empty.

In my mind's eye now, that moment is framed as I was. In a doorway. Me walking away from You.

What could I, what should I have done to stop your hurting?

B lies shirtless on his stomach in the fully-flattened adjustable chair. He is goose-fleshed. Gray-fleshed. Concentration gels his expression as Lefty gets started. Swabbing the skin clean, applying by transfer the drawing of the tattoo. Pulling on new gloves, loading the gun with fresh needles and ink. The buzzing commences. When he outlines, Lefty explains, he needles deep to make a dark, clean edge, the sensation, he warns, like a fingernail drawn firmly across a bad sunburn. After that, when he fills in, the strokes will be shallower, quicker, less stinging.

I try to do what I think I'm supposed to do: offer B support but avoid embarrassing him. I attempt chitchat, sometimes with Lefty, sometimes with B, alternating a tone of nonchalance with one of calm concern I developed while jollying my pre-schoolers through immunizations and dental procedures.

"Are you cold?" I ask my son. He shakes his head tersely. "You want a soda?" Yeah, he does. I pop the tab and place the can in his hand.

At ninety-six, my father landed in the same hospital where my mother died almost four years earlier, but death wouldn't take him. The doctor assigned his case—having pronounced the patient had seventy-two hours to live, and having acquiesced to my sister Sara's and my instruction to withdraw all but palliative care—reneged on his promise. He ordered an IV inserted to rehydrate a man taking too long to die because he was a tough old bird expiring of natural causes only. His immune system was failing, as well as all his organs, and he had a bladder infection from the catheter he'd worn for the last year or so, as an enlarged prostate slowly shut off his plumbing. The doctor put him on antibiotics, which he could not swallow.

He was miserable. He was disoriented. "Sometimes I don't know who I am," he told me, stating a simple fact.

When he was lucid, as he often was during the months preceding that hospital stay—me calling him dutifully every Sunday from Florida, sick myself with dread for the dead-end hopelessness of it, and him calling me anytime I came up in his squirrelly mind at a moment he could find my phone number and get his fingers to cooperate in punching the right buttons, no matter the hour of day or night—he asked again and again in a way that seemed not the least bit rhetorical, "How do I do it?" He meant, How do I die? He was ready to go. Worn out with suffering and loneliness but still a man of prodigious will, he could not figure out why it was so damn hard to get across the threshold from alive to dead.

That day I visited him in the hospital he was not lucid. But he was calm. And in this mysteriously blessed interval of not-suffering from the thrashing and the psychosis the rehydration set off in his body and brain, he cheerfully stepped from admitting confusion about his own identity to a child-like attempt to guess mine.

"Are you my sister?"

"No."

"Sara is my mother?" he ventured, his tone so guileless it felt playful.

It seems pointless and unkind to explain to You your mistakes. I sit with You, Daddy, instead, inside the uneasy peace of your not-knowing who You are and my not-trying to fix that.

Here is the thin shadow cast by another story I cannot tell.

At a convention in a faraway city a woman cornered the elusive man and said what she needed to say. She spit nails. He let them pierce him. Having said he must go, he stayed. Spilled secrets, hemorrhaged pain. Cradling his skull, noting how the bowl of it so exactly fit her palm, she wanted only to hurt what hurt her. But inside her own skull she heard her teacher's voice: *What you do wrong?* and *See own mistake.* She allowed his wet face to rest on her chest. His hands, chaste as ever, lay in his lap.

When he left, he closed again the door between them. A depression remained, in the armchair where he'd sat. Good silk damask, modest stripes of quiet teal and quieter gold-bronze, old elegance now well on its way to shabby. A dressing-room chair, a lady chair, built to accommodate short legs and full bustles, the seat wide in front, tapered at its short back, legs concealed by a straight, severe skirt.

She photographed that chair, an act of naked clinging that shamed her.

~

Later, much later, she walks into a tattoo parlor, bearing feelings that can't be fixed. Put a picture on me, Lefty, she says. Or should have said, if she'd known what she was doing, getting ink. Carve it into me, please: the colors, the coils, the pointillist scar that makes my hurting right.

~

She composed the embarrassing photograph with abject artistry. The depth of field shallow, the lens dialed wide to capture all the pale light slanting in through the drab room's one window, casting into plangent shadow the concavity at the center of the cushion: a portrait, she thought, of loss.

What will draw and hold the eye when the picture is printed, she failed to see through her lens: a square silk pillow, the magenta-pink of a Victorian valentine, edged in silk fringe of metal-bright gold, propped upright against the back of the chair.

This shot lies atop the stack when she picks up the prints. All the rest are primal dripping Northwest rainforest and jagged primal Olympic coastline. But first up, a coincidence: that chair, with its blazing incongruous impossibly transformative center.

My father named me, then renamed me. First he christened me Lucy, for his baby sister dead from typhoid fever at age three, one of several siblings or half-siblings of his who did not live past childhood. According to his one living sister, little Lucy was a great favorite of his. I threw that name away in first grade because classmates taunted me for the only association they could draw—Lucille Ball's redheaded ditz in television's *I Love Lucy*.

I altered my public identity at age six without telling my parents. I assumed my middle name. Chris. Short for the more prim and ladylike Christine. At home, my mother insisted for years on shouting *Lu-CY* or *Lou!* up the attic stairs to fetch me, but my father tried another tack. Somewhere in my mid-childhood he dubbed me Christopher and addressed me that way sometimes until he died.

I never acknowledged the shift, but I never said no to it, either.

B's self-designed signature tattoo fits snugly between his shoulder blades. Two red arcs, upright and mirroring each other's curve, strongly suggesting but not banally replicating a heart, nest within an intricate bramble of jet-black tribal branches and points borrowed from barbwire. An eye of Ra exactly replicating mine except in unblinking black is tucked artfully, asymmetrically, within the whole. The image is less than six inches square, but with two colors and a complicated pattern of narrow lines, the work takes time. B says little. His eyes fix on the DVD player a foot from his face. A post-modern, noir-ish Christmas story flickers on the small screen; I think none of us is actually watching.

"Give me a minute," B says abruptly. "I gotta have something with more action."

Lefty sits up, the gun ceases its burr, B flips rapidly through the clear plastic sleeves of a zippered album, then we are watching but not watching bloodthirsty dinosaurs in collision with human stupidity. Plenty of action, lots of carnage. I notice—taking care not to let that notice show—that the white-knuckled force with which B grips the chair preceded the switch in movie subject matter.

~

In a courtship letter to my mother, from the days just before their marriage in 1936, my father described plans to butcher a hog on the family farm. "I guess I'll have to shoot the pig," he says. "It was always my job to shoot the pig." He shot my dog after I outgrew her and she hung around her pen getting fat. He shot a pet rabbit when I got lazy about cleaning its cage. He shot the crows and pigeons that raided the seed he put out for songbirds. He once suggested in angry exasperation that shooting my cognitively impaired sister Betsy should have been an option. He was college-educated but he was country, too, and when some living thing seemed useless or troublesome or better off dead, to shoot it seemed to him a responsible response. As purposeful and straightforward as clearing up a mess.

He kept several firearms, all long guns—rifles, shotguns and a pump-action pellet gun—around the house, in different places at different times in his life. Cleaning out the house for sale when my mother was dead and he was too sick to help, I found his guns, one here, one there, under beds, in the closets, on shelves. I remember a different homecoming, some reluctant brief return in my young adulthood, when one of his favorite guns, a .22 with a scope, leaned up in a corner in the den, like a broom or a useful and portable piece of furniture. He'd left it there to facilitate firing out the open window at jays; they were stealing the sunflower seeds he meant the cardinals and the sparrows to eat.

My parents were elderly when my mother told me he had threatened more than once to shoot her. And himself. This was during their last years in that house they built together and lived in all their married life, when she could no longer walk and he had lost the strength he needed to plow and mow and plant. When they had no more work with which to buffer themselves from each other. When he jerked her arm and twisted it, breaking her wrist, an event she disguised as "accident" even from me, for a long time after it happened.

He did not shoot either himself or her. Was that a mercy? I used to wonder, watching them anguishing in their ailments and their hateful mirroring of each other. If it *was* mercy, in his eyes, did he grant it to himself or her? Or did he think himself a coward for having finally refused to shoot the pig?

When my daughter J was a toddler, she asked questions I couldn't answer. I remember the tenor, not the content, of the questions but the response I coined has never left me—partly distraction, partly a kind of existential punch line I still pull on her sometimes to set us both laughing ruefully. She wanted, in essence, to know *why* the inexplicable was the way it was. Maybe she asked why the doves in the shaded lane behind our house ran like chickens instead of taking flight when a car bore down upon them. Maybe she wondered why some neighbors were friendly, inviting us in for cookies, and others sour, complaining when we stepped on their lawns.

The point is, she wanted rules to apply.

Some do, some don't. That was my answer.

I remember your small fists balled against your thighs. I remember your moue of distaste and suspicion. You were perhaps three, and it was so not-okay that your mother had no better explanation than that.

My children loved my father because of his guns. And the bonfires, they were crazy for those, too. Twice a year, pre- and post-divorce, the three of us flew in from New York, from Bermuda, from
Florida—wherever their father's job had situated us—to the tiny
TriCities regional airport tucked in a river valley skirting the most
rugged ranges of the southern Appalachians. My father met us at the
gate, always wearing the bill cap and denim work jacket my mother
despised. Every time he was visibly glad to see us. We hugged, but
never found much to say. He loaded the suitcases, car seats, and
stroller into a Chevy Malibu station wagon my sisters and I would
give away at his death with only 20,000 miles on its twenty-year-old
chassis. Then, very slowly, on back roads to avoid the interstate highway where other people's need for speed made him nervous, he drove
us home—to dust and stasis and bad memories for me, and for my
children, fire, mud, and freedom, a frontier dream-come-true.

No matter the season, he helped them heap scrap lumber, cardboard boxes, wind-fallen branches and dead tomato vines, paper trash
from the cans in the house, whatever was available and flammable,
as high as they could pile it on a bare patch of garden. They lit it
themselves, a conflagration twice their height. Once he built them an
inhabitable-size teepee from dried cornstalks. Best of all, he set up
makeshift targets at the far end of my mother's abandoned flower garden, braced the pump-action pellet gun on bean bags atop the rotting
picnic table, and, municipal laws be damned, let them shoot.

They were five and nine—the year of the divorce—when this fun
began. My father was eighty-seven years old and had been sick for a
while, recuperating from colon cancer and prostate surgery. He was
more taciturn than ever, and short-tempered. It took three pumps
to give the pellet enough impulsion to fire, but he'd lost so much

strength in his arms he couldn't do but two. He handed me the gun and, struggling mightily, making sure to point the muzzle skyward, I bear-hugged the stock in both arms to eke out the third. I set the gun first in my daughter's hands and then in my son's. They were city kids, little Montessori-schooled liberals; the weight and terrible noise of a real firearm, and the bullet-pierced crayoned Xs they carried home to show-and-tell were transgressive experiences they relished way more than I realized at the time.

When it was my turn, I sighted through the scope that made a bull's eye at that distance easy, squeezed the trigger, and hit the mark. I felt good about myself. When my father praised my aim, I did not say abjectly, "It was easy, it shouldn't count."

We shot one after another, round after round, no one saying anything except Wait your turn, and Good one.

~

The first time I undertake a Buddhist retreat, I travel with no idea of what awaits me to a property my teacher and her family own, a rural setting in the Catskills a hundred miles north of New York City, known as Harris after the nearest unincorporated hamlet. When I set out, I'm not even entirely sure where I'll end up; I fly from Florida to Newark airport where others among the teacher's widespread and disparate following meet the flight. One of them drives me upstate.

This retreat property has been in my teacher's family thirty years, since their exile from Tibet in the seventies, but the half-dozen wood frame cottages—un-insulated, unheated, minimally electrified, and collapsing—originally comprised one of the numerous summer camps built by Hasidic Jews to escape the heat in Brooklyn and lower Manhattan. Many camps have gone derelict or been sold off by 2002, when I arrive, but directly across Big Woods Road a still vibrant one faces my teacher's property.

From May into June, for thirty days, I live in the least derelict of the cottages, often but not always alone. By day, the humid heat is enervating. At dark, the air turns surprisingly cold. In-between I discover, by accident of nothing-much-and-no-one to attend to, a fact of the natural world I've never noticed before: gloaming.

At day's end I consume my simple supper, wash out my bowl, and lie down, in sunlight still full, richly golden, and slanted. The view from my cot shows me only trees, a window-framed square of them, limbs and leaves so tightly latticing the sky I can see nothing beyond their translucent screen but the slowly dimming light. I begin this practice in happenstance and lethargy but very quickly my attention to gradual, complete extinguishment of each day's light becomes a sensory reward: a giving-in to the pure pleasure of stillness.

Mornings it's difficult to leave the warm sleeping bag. The hems of my pants and my shoes turn sodden on the short, misty walk through wet grass along a radius of the cabins' circle to the central one housing the shrine room. On my cushion, walled in with sagging shelves of holy books and salvage-yard tables heaped with candles, thangkas, and bowls of offered fruit, I chant long sessions of sadhana, the atmosphere within and without me shifting on the weather and the light: chilly gray before midday, airless and soporific on sunny afternoons, spooky if I remain there after sundown, the black windows speckled orange with reflected candle flame.

On Friday afternoons the Hasidic men come up from the City to join their wives and children for the weekend, and after supper, before sundown, before I go inside for the ritual end to my day, those families stroll pre-Sabbath constitutionals up and down the shoulder-less pavement of Big Woods Road. The men in full beards, prayer locks, calf-length black frock coats and broad-brimmed hats lead the way; the wigged wives in long skirts follow one step behind; several children trail each couple. All of them stare openly at the lone weird Buddhist in sweat pants watching them from her side of the road, long strings of kite-colored prayer flags flying in the trees behind her.

In the backyard of my parents' house where I lived from birth until I married at seventeen and left, two playhouses stood side by side. Wood frame cottages measuring six feet by eight, built by my father, silvered many times over with his favorite aluminum paint, they aligned perfectly with my mother's line of sight from the window above the kitchen sink. Neither playhouse was mine.

The better one belonged to my eldest sister Sara. By the time I was old enough to notice a playhouse, she was a teenager and almost always gone. The second playhouse had been built to accommodate our middle sister, Betsy. When I came along, Betsy's was designated as the one to be shared with me; I inherited full title when Betsy first left home for a residential facility at around age fourteen, when I was six.

No one—not Betsy, not me, not the neighborhood kids nor the cousins who occasionally visited—was allowed to play in Sara's playhouse. My mother, originator and enforcer of all family codes, forbade us even to open the door.

That door had a window, and each wall a double casement window with nine panes and cut glass knobs, but the once-starched, now-cobwebbed organza curtains blurred my view of the interior even when I mashed my nose against the glass. I seldom got that close. My habit of nervous compliance with the smallest of my mother's discernible wishes gave the entire little building a negative charge. Sara's playhouse had no locks—wooden blocks rotated ninety degrees on a screw to impede or allow the doors' and windows' opening—but I seem to have believed without quite knowing I did that my mother would know if I cheated.

Betsy's playhouse door sported a small metal knocker but had no window; its face was blank. Each wall had a glazed window, but one was a slider, one a casement, and one had to be lowered, two hands supporting the heavy glass, from hinges at its base. This effort and the disunity of effect I found aesthetically displeasing despite my inability at that age to think in those terms. A truly lovely small dogwood grew by the front door, and a flowerbed with a river-rock border graced the side with the awkward window, but it is only now that I can see this was so.

There came the day, of course, when I did open the forbidden door and cautiously enter Sara's playhouse. In my memory I transgress alone, but it's possible the rudest of the neighbor girls dared me to do it. A perfect vision of dust-furred elegance greeted me: built-in corner shelves stacked with miniature Delft china dishes and candelabra dangling plastic prisms atop lace doilies. A broad, wall-mounted counter-table at just the right height for a child-housewife, a range with an oven that according to the attached and batter-spotted directions heated up to bake muffins, and a sink that ran water via a hand-pumped reservoir. A down-sized ironing board, an iron with a cord and, at the juncture of wall and floor, a functioning electrical receptacle. Cookbooks and household diaries on book shelves with book ends. A silk parasol hung from a coat hook by the door, and beneath it, a tiny baby-grand piano with plastic keys that disappointingly only plinked when struck. But the plaster bust of Brahms on the miniature broad plain of its lid left me speechless with envy and awe.

In Betsy's playhouse, nothing was built-in. None of the kitchen appliances worked nor had ever been meant to, and anyone inclined to play-cook had to kneel or sit on the mud-tracked floor. Dishes and pots abounded, but in metal or plastic—mismatched, dented, or warped. Betsy's playhouse had no lace, fine china, or silk, and no instruments of art. Plenty of beat-up furniture—a couch, table, baby bed, rocker, and high chair of assorted scales, plus a full-size baby carriage in which I'd once been perambulated—and plenty of babies, a dozen at least in varying degrees of manglement. A little blue steamer trunk bulged with doll clothes, some of them elaborately embroidered and well constructed, but all of them decades out of date and almost none of them fitting the naked babies stacked willy-nilly in the crib.

Once I experienced the inside of Sara's playhouse, the shock of the distinction between her house and Betsy's never left me. I went to school with children who lived in our town's government-subsidized housing project; I'd even gone there after school with a classmate, once, before my mother put a stop to it, clarifying for me what the word trash meant when used to describe people. I don't remember a time when Betsy's playhouse had for me a meaning beyond her compromised status in the world and in the family. Because her playhouse was the one I got to share, I resented what that implied about my status. Perhaps in protest, and definitely in preference, I set us up with an alternate dwelling, pulling a few dolls and some dishes out to the bare damp dirt behind the playhouses, in a kind of cave beneath an overhang of quince I furnished with rock tables and stools, and flower-blossom foods.

I doubt it ever occurred to me that parental pragmatism—Betsy did tend to break, lose, and chew on toys—might have accounted for part of the difference in intricacy between the two houses. I know I never imagined that the mess in Betsy's house might have been partly of her own choosing.

I thought of her playhouse as mine to manage and evaluate because Betsy was my responsibility—and my social liability—when we played outside together, despite her being eight years my senior.

When the rude neighbor girl insisted more aggressively than I could withstand, I allowed Betsy to be exiled alone to the dirt flat behind her house, which I and my cohort then occupied, me skewered with shame and both of us smoldering with desire for what lay locked away behind lace curtains next door.

The wrong I did You then, Betsy, lives un-absolved inside me, still.

~

B calls several brief halts to his tattooing. Sips soda, shifts position.

Standing on concrete, my feet and legs and my head ache; his tattoo is taking a long time. I keep my eyes on B's face—it's resolute—and his hands—the tendons sprung. I don't like needles. And I don't want to see or even admit I know about the constant dabbing—the gauze square in Lefty's left hand lifting away blood beading like red dew in the needles' wake.

Each time B takes a break, Lefty sits up, strips off the gloves, rotates his stool away from his work to sip from a soda of his own. Taciturn, maybe thirty, stout, darkly handsome, he wears a close-clipped, clean-edged beard. What I take at first to be a mustache turns out to be a thick tattoo on his upper lip. In his answers to my small-talk questions, he's sardonic. In his actions and in the timing of his silences, he demonstrates exquisite tact about the emotional dynamic in front of him; his face and his body language remain blank as a curtain whenever B and I speak, and when we can't.

I imagine what Lefty must, in his work, witness. So many bodies, their most private as well as the public parts, in all their fat and bony, stretch-marked, spider-veined, hairy, odiferous imperfection. So many little human dramas too: ego and appetite, wastedness, grasping, grief, remorse, self-aggrandizement.

Later, when I begin to write about Lefty, I find myself describing him as "some kind of priest." He conducts the ritual that draws the blood that absolves penitents, and appeases furies.

Or so we believe, we who visit him.

~

Through all the years V.T. and I do not see each other and do not speak, a certain kind of dream recurs. Its narrative takes many forms but the theme is always the same. In the mornings when I jot down what I can remember in the journal that lives on my nightstand, I label these the Evil Twin dreams.

There You are, seated at a table, standing at a lectern, greeting me in an airport, and I *know* it's You, but your form is unfamiliar and your manner first confounds and then destroys me. Sly, duplicitous, charming, creatively cruel, You grind me beneath the heel of your supercilious speech, You shred me with a scimitar smile.

I wake up appalled and panting every time, reaching for the journal as if it is analgesic.

Which You is the real You?

Is the dream a revelation, or my confusion leering back at me?

In the first days of my month-long retreat at Harris, I try befriending the family of practitioners living on the property as caretakers, especially the mother, who has four children and a husband perpetually away at work. The three teens, whose job it is to mow and paint and tote trash, tolerate my attempts at conversation; I am a diversion amid endless manual labor, study, and prayers. The youngest child, a dreamy boy of nine, sometimes shows up at my shack with juggling pins or a clutch of kittens to show off. But the mother determinedly snubs me, resenting me, I decide, because my presence adds to her load. I have no car; she's been told to bring me groceries; she already has more to do than she can handle. I offer to mow, cook, or wash dishes but she ignores me. So I vow to minimize my requests to her, and give in to solitude. Once or twice I get word from my teacher to clear junk or sort books or plant flowers or weed, but more and more often as the days pass, I lapse into indolence between sessions of prayer, passing long hours on my back in the grass, gazing into blue or blank gray or cloud-puffed sky, experiencing—between jolts of guilt about my shiftlessness—pools of utter calm.

I have undertaken this retreat on my own initiative. My teacher has always told us—a regular dosing of her familiar pidgin English, syntactically incomplete, tonally identical: *do retreat sometime.* She's not pushed toward where or when. *Three days, one week, one month,* she says, often adding, *do retreat in own body, not necessary go here, go there.* I asked to come to Harris because I've heard it is the origin of her presence in this country, the first place her stepfather, a famous and learned lama of the old school, settled and retreated. I've chosen this particular year to come because the good fortune of "leisure and endowment," a necessary condition to sustained Buddhist practice, has befallen me: after years of freelance and adjunct work I've landed a temporary full-time teaching job that gives me my first-ever paid summer off.

But really I've come to retreat because I've reached the end of my rope of yearning. I can feel in my flesh that it is *time.* Time to give up writing a novel nobody wants, and past time to give up longing for my prince to come, because hating and fearing his silence and his fear does nothing to change our circumstance.

I intend, in a thirty-day retreat, to extinguish the notion that any-one or anything is so separate from me that not having it might extinguish *me.* I trust the teacher and the teaching to extinguish my desires.

But the teacher does not come. She ignores me. Each passing day I expect her more. I keep watch for the car that might bring her. After dark, I check anxiously for a light in her cabin, visible at a certain angle from mine. I have with me several books by masters in her lineage and daily I read from them; I stuff my head with information but no understanding comes. I do everything she's told me to do except one thing I'm not sure I really heard her say.

Had she actually whispered me permission to sleep sometimes in her learned stepfather's retreat house, the most decrepit of all the cab-ins, the only one that feels truly, palpably haunted? I peer through its dust-filmed windows at junk stacked to the ceiling in a web-sheathed jumble. I stand on its sagging porch, smelling rot and dreading its unlocked door. I touch its broken screen but cannot open it; I feel frightened and silly.

Finally, only because my timidity embarrasses me, I go inside. I clear a space on the filthy floor big enough for my sleeping bag and lie down, tense, fully dressed, ready to flee. Through that evening's long gloaming I read by flashlight and then chant prayers in the dark, as revved on adrenaline as if I were already running. Spiders the size of quarters rebuild the webs I've torn. Might they weave themselves into my hair if I sleep? Vermin rustle in the trash beneath the broken furniture that walls me in. I can't stop imagining slinking shapes sliding toward me.

All night I am on edge. Alert, and—oddly, at such a sharp place—quite clear about what's going on in my head. Aware that my mind is all that torments me, I sit with that fact. Uneasy, and awake.

All around the ample yard of the house I grew up in I found places to hide. What I hid *from*, I never named, but like a fugitive I moved often, favoring some refuges over others. I climbed trees and wiggled under shrubbery but avoided any manmade structure heaped with buckets or bricks where I might encounter snakes or insects. I tried and discarded a natural hollow at the center of a coil of still-living forsythia at the foot of the driveway. The cavity was roomy and pleasingly leafy but people passing in cars could see in. The dark square of bare dirt behind the playhouses where I'd exiled Betsy still drew me, screened from my mother's kitchen-window surveillance by the bulging trunk of a weeping willow and defended on the back side by a stand of thorn-bearing quince. I liked this hidey-hole especially in the seasons of rose-pink blossoms and blushing, dappled fruit, but after I caught the neighbor woman, Chub Creger, peering in at me on her way from her basement to her backyard clothesline to hang her wash, I abandoned it.

I'd been forbidden by my mother to ever step foot in the Cregers' yard, and not recognizing my mother as the true source of my dread, I feared Chub, a docile, hair-netted, ever-laboring housewife.

J took her first steps in the worn and grassless backyard of a secret safe house for battered women on a backstreet of a working-class hamlet in mid-state New York. I sat on the wooden stoop, a volunteer visiting for my weekly hour or two, flanked by women who'd come there to hide from men who, on bad days, wanted to kill them for failing to please. I'd begun this gig before I was a mother, soon after I quit my job in investment banking to stay home and write. I continued to visit while I grew bigger and bigger with pregnancy, and once J was born I carried her there with me, strapped in a front-pack until she got so heavy and wiggly I put her down and let her cruise. Without ever quite admitting to myself why I went to the shelter, I sought it out regularly, learning what I intuited I needed to know: how to run, what my rights were, and just how difficult and profoundly unsafe it would be to assert them.

This particular June day was warm and soft. All of us wore shorts. I glanced away from J and back again, and she'd done it: turned loose of my knee and set off down the gravelly path. At nine months she'd blacked an eye the first time she tried to walk with nothing to hold on to, but this time, at eleven months, she didn't fall.

Off You toddled in summer-gold light, unafraid—leaf shadow on your shoulders, and three bruised women behind You cheering your impulse to get on your feet, and go.

I took in my mother's rules and in my small-child years observed them religiously but ended up, again and again, on the wrong side of her law. I left the yard with permission, came home on time or early, found myself overdue on her clock by an hour. I was punished. I arranged to bring home a school friend to appease her worries I had no friends; afterwards the visit was an imposition my thoughtlessness cost her. Retribution followed. I could, for no reason I understood, walk into a room unsuspecting and her fury, as from divine right, ambushed me. No matter how I listened, I could not avoid mistakes. I heard her say yes; she shouted she'd said no. On the very worst of the very bad days, she sent me outside to the forsythia to cut her a long switch. Obeying her always, I brought it in. She stripped the leaves from the supple stem and whipped the bare backs of my legs. The slender switch sang. She cursed. I stood silent; never to cry when she punished me had become a point of pride. When she quit, blood oozed from a long ladder of red welts.

Afterwards, sitting on my swing in the yard, I contemplated those stripes. They told me she was wrong. I knew mothers should not make their children bleed.

But your view was my one view: please You or die.

You had to be right, so I had to be wrong.

I must be stupid, I must be bad; I'd better try harder to understand how pain was good. The older I got the more complicated the calculus became. I made myself badder. But I had to make the world bad, too. If I couldn't learn how not to be wrong, getting punished must be right. Whatever I did was wrong, by definition. And by simple, illogical extension, everything anyone did not like was my fault.

~

When B's ink is done, we send J—still stuck in Hartford—a photo, from his phone to hers, of him laid out in Lefty's chair, his new tattoo glistening beneath its protective coating of A&D Ointment. We each speak to her, briefly, everyone's tone cheerful, disappointments and differences masked. Afterwards, suddenly, B has an attack of shivering. Lefty's shop is chilly. I am chilly and exhausted and hungry, and we have my ink yet to go.

Stepping outside, where daylight is fading, I pull from the trunk of my car the only thing I have to offer either one of us for extra warmth—this is Florida even though it's also January, so neither B nor I thought to bring a jacket; we'd run the AC on the way to the shop. I take in my hands a scrap of the tough, brown, corded bedspread that covered the day bed in my first writing room twenty-five years before, five houses ago and a dozen states away, that has since addressed many away-from-home kid emergencies, from soccer-field blood-lettings to embarrassing motion sickness events.

The sun is down. It's not yet dark. The sky is the color of tired foil stripped from a tray of ball-field potluck. The darkening shapes of the last vehicles in the lot, the traffic rush along the four-lane, the habit with which I suppress my wish to be somewhere else, writing or at the very least aware of myself being a writer, these sensations and that tension are familiar, the nearly comforting discomforts of parenting.

In a Kodak Brownie snapshot dated June 1955, my mother's gaze fixes on me. She is forty-five. I am a three-month-old baby—fat, droopy-diapered, and ham-fisted, punching myself upright against her seated thighs, between her encircling hands. I am looking elsewhere, over my shoulder, anywhere but where I am. She looks at me with love and a brave small smile, but everything else about her is ravaged. She is gaunt. There's no other word for her hollowed cheeks and temples and her sunken eye sockets. The shape of her skull is barely disguised with flesh. Excess skin, from which fat and health have fled, hangs in wrinkled dewlaps from her jaw onto her neck. Her hair is thin and oily and caught back any-which-way with pins; it is receding from her already high forehead.

She looks like a concentration camp survivor. Like a refugee holding someone else's baby she hopes to save. I can see in the strain of the tendons in her forearms that she's barely got the strength to try.

By April 1959, the love has burned out of her eyes. In a photograph that might have been taken on Easter, she stands among her three daughters on the church steps. Sara, nearly fourteen, almost the same height as my mother, appears neat, poised, and carefully self-possessed. Betsy, twelve years old, her face expressing her condition in a characteristic squint of anxiety and impaired comprehension, fits under my mother's chin. Four years old, I stand to the side, clutching my tiny purse and looking elsewhere, wanting something else, my socks slipping into my shoes and my wispy hair crawling out of its barrettes. My mother stares straight at the camera, bone-thin, slump-shouldered. Her hair is neat this time, but cranked back painfully tight on either side of a razor-white center part. Her eyes are sunken so far in they appear as two black holes.

In the picture, she looks like hell. From where I stand now she looks insane.

It must have been my father who pointed the camera and pressed the shutter button. He was always the one who posed others for snapshots, which he always dated on the back.

I wonder what You saw when You framed that shot, peering through the Brownie lens at the four females fate dealt You: your responsibility and your puzzle.

Did You see, when You looked back, more than You expected to see?

Back inside Lefty's shop, I drape the strip of corded bedspread around B's naked narrow shoulders. He welcomes the gesture, and me, with a grin. Wearing the scrap like a royal's robe, he strides round the shop floor, shaking his hands, swinging his arms, loosening up. He is relieved. He rules. He's done this thing he had to do.

~

As a child, a teen, and a young adult, I have a recurring nightmare. The setting details vary but the situation is always the same. I make my way alone through woods, the path difficult, damp and slippery, all the leaves down, wind-fallen branches blocking it. I come upon a nest of snakes, short and thick, black with copper cross-hatch markings. Because the dream is familiar, I recognize from inside what's coming. The first sight of the tangled mass of reptiles ratchets my dull dread of empty woods into breathless, nauseated panic. I am barely able to command my body to go forward but I do, I must. I step right into the midst of the snakes because somewhere behind me is the man with the gun. He stalks me like a deer. I run, I cannot look where my feet land, the snakes may strike but I *must move.*

I already know, because the dream recurs and recurs, that I will never get away from the man; there will be nowhere to hide in this vast forest of naked trees. Always, eventually, he shoots me but weak-kneed, desperate, I run, every single time, until I can run no more. Then I drop. My back against a tree or a rock, cornered, cowering, I wait for the bullet to hit. There's no question but that it will; the exquisite horror of this nightmare is recognizing the dream—oh, *that* one—then knowing there's no way out but to endure each dilated second of the bitter dream right through to the end. I never see the man who stalks me. He's a shadow, but I can see, as if with binocular vision, his long rifle trained on me. And once I give up running I can see the bullet, too, deforming the air as it bears down on me, in excruciating slow-motion. When it strikes my chest, there's a hard thump of impact and a burst of shattered flesh and...I am awake, gasping, so relieved—oh, glory—it is only that dream, and it's over.

~

In my earliest memories of my father, he was a lap, gruff but welcoming and warm. I curled into the animal comfort of him, his arm wrapped round my middle as *Bonanza, Paladin, Rawhide, Branded, Maverick, The Virginian*, or *Gunsmoke* flickered black-and-white on the square screen of our ancient Motorola. If we spoke it was only the smallest response to what we watched: "Good shoot-'em-up, huh?"

I paid close attention to our shared focus: fifty years later I still remember the terse nicknames and scruffy faces of all those male heroes and anti-heroes, their horses' grace and prowess, the salutary carnage at the center of the men's lives, and, with the exception of affable Miss Kitty, the utter absence of women from their stories.

When my father had to be in the house, he was more likely to read than watch television. I loved to read, too. But we never talked about books, ever. Stacks of them, carried in from the public library, surrounded his chair: Zane Grey westerns, history, science. He enjoyed Rudyard Kipling's stories, and Sir Walter Scott's novels, and he particularly admired Shakespeare's history plays. Sometimes he spontaneously recited a passage, which caused me to stare as if he'd grown a second head. Every Sunday he read the funny papers, another pastime I loved, too, and occasionally he directed my way an avuncular remark on Prince Valiant's or Li'l Abner's adventures. Nothing he said to me ever developed into a discussion of story or character, or any discussion at all, that I can remember. I never knew how to talk to him. The way I remember it, he spoke rarely and in single sentences, each one registering on me as a small shock—criticism or non sequitur—that reminded me I did not know him, really.

~

So much of what I remember from thirty days of retreat at Harris is the texture of time I spent waiting for something memorable to happen: the blissful indolent stillness I relished but could not quite trust, and the inconsequential but brightly colored small events that decorated and complicated the emptiness of hours passing.

I never knew when lines would form for the leaking toilet and tepid shower in my cabin, the only functional ones on the property save at the unhappy caretaker's house. Visiting practitioners in need knocked or walked right in, sometimes before dawn. One of them stayed with me for a week, washing her beloved pet turtle in the kitchen sink, slinging, I felt sure, a slick of salmonella across the freshly washed dishes. A carpenter, a hard-living, ex-wife-done-me-wrong non-practitioner charged with shoring up the sagging cabins' frames, set up shop some days on my porch, the site of the only functioning outdoor electrical outlet. He plunked down his beer cooler, plugged in his power tools and boom box, then sang along—with equal, full-voiced enthusiasm—to the you-left-me yearnings of country singer Reba McIntyre and blind operatic tenor Andrea Bocelli.

I fell into love, privately, with each of these inconvenient visitors in turn because, I suppose, there was no one else to attach to; as with the kittens, my need to need had to fixate somewhere. But one day, a memory with a different feel: circumambulating the property briskly for exercise, from within a woodpile I'd been warned to avoid I heard right through the crunch of grass beneath my feet and the crickets' seamless humming a dry, dangerous ticking. Bone on bone. Chilling. Hair lifted on my neck, and I fled. I'd never heard a rattlesnake's warning but in my flipping stomach and racing pulse I got the message: death is usually unexpected, and often nearby.

~

When J was about three, my father took her fishing, at a trout-farm pond to make it easy. She shrieked with joy at what probably seemed like magic, her wished-for fish shimmering and twisting, plucked from water by a line on a pole her Granddaddy steadied in her hands. But when she found out that fishie had to die, whacked on the skull with a pair of pliers from the tackle box, she crossed her arms on her chest and cried bitterly to go home.

My father was exasperated. Next visit he bought her a purple tri-cycle with pink streamers on the handlebars and plastic flowers on its basket, but when she didn't ride it much, he gave it away; he couldn't bear the waste.

That made her, and me, hopping mad.

⁓

I am very young, not yet school-age, and the waxed-paper sleeve of saltines I clutch is supposed to be my snack. But the swarming fish lunging at the crumbs I sprinkle on deep green lake water are hungry, too. The deck I kneel on, slick with algae, dampens my pants and chills my knees as I scrunch down for a closer look at the small storm of churning gaping fish mouths. My father and my sisters and my father's best friend Charlie are on all on the other side of Charlie's houseboat in a cove on South Holston Lake; they can't see me because the house part of the houseboat is between us. I hear them talking as they try to catch fish with worms and hooks. All the fish are on *my* side of the boat.

I am cold and moist all over from the motorboat ride across lake, which sounded more exciting than it turned out to be because the boat, an aluminum fishing skiff, has only a small outboard motor and does not go fast, and I was bored almost to tears until somebody put these crackers in my hand. I shake the last crumbs from the wrapper into the water. The fish go crazy. I wonder what else I can drop in the water to feed them and then I'm upside down and under the water.

Cold encloses me and I am sinking; all I see is green and I don't know what to do; but my brain is working, a shocked, slow-motion calculation in which I comprehend that if I do not somehow push my head back into the air and keep it there, I will breathe water and die. Grown-ups have told me about drowning, and I'm not going to do it. I bicycle my legs with all my will, my head breaks the surface and at the same instant my father's hand shuts hard on my upper arm. He hauls me up that way, a big fish, dripping. He is not angry, and I am very glad to see him.

Chilled to the bone and very frightened by how bad that feels, I am ferried back across the lake to the dock, a miserably extended trip at the boat's modest top speed. The way I remember this ride, no one speaks. At Charlie's home near the lake I'm put into someone else's clothes, far too big for me. Mine tumble dry. I watch them at first through the window in the dryer door. At home we do not use a clothes dryer; my mother pins things to a wire in the backyard in summer and to wires in the basement in winter. I am glad Charlie's house has a dryer so I can get my clothes back fast. I do not like the strangeness of what I recall as a cashmere cardigan sweater, on me as long as a dress, skimming my naked skin. No one scolds me about the accident, an anomaly that really scares me. At home an accident always sets off one of my mother's tears. I sit on a wooden swing in the sun in a yard not mine, while Sara crouches nearby. She coaches me quietly and urgently that I must never, *ever* tell Mama.

Growing up I spent many hours of drizzly-gray winter hunkered down on the furnace floor register—a cast-iron waffle three feet square, the only source of heat in the house. It filled most of the floor space in the tiny hall bounded by two bedrooms and the single bath and was close enough to the basement door to be imperiled by its backswing. The blower pushing hot air from the furnace through the register cycled on and off with a click, each one triggering a lift and then a droop in my body temperature and my spirits. Inside the rough bliss of each hot updraft I roasted my backside and parched my sinuses, half-lidded, a lizard on a stone. Each time the blower shut off I waited, cold and vigilant, for heat to return. If a footfall sounded on the basement stairs, I tensed: a parent on the way in from the garden, the garage, the world beyond our property, whose face—the set of her lips, the cast of his eyes—made a clue I processed fast about how quickly and in what direction my day's terms might shift.

When the door swung open, basement scent flooded through, a primeval cave-dank made acrid by fumes from the coal bin. In hot, muggy weather, the poured-concrete basement, windowless, completely below ground, remained cool. In winter, its floor and walls stayed as frigid as the earth they held back while the furnace—big coarse slabs of pig iron seamed together with cement rough enough to tear skin—glowed dull orange and could burn a hand that brushed it.

Before daylight and again at dusk, the harsh scrape of metal thrust through coal reverberated up through the floor register—my father feeding the furnace. In my youngest years the coal he shoveled came in stone-sized lumps lifted directly into orange hellfire I could glimpse, from behind him, through the unlatched furnace door. But the coal I really remember was stoker coal—a slippy mountain of anthracite chips poured into the house by chute from the tipped bed of a blackened, dieseling truck.

Just once, inciting my mother's wrath, I carried some dolls and their dishes into the coal bin and tried to homestead there amid the heaps of black crystals stinking of oil and staining like ink. I don't know why I wanted to touch coal and play near it, but I did. The smell and the grease both drew me. In the aftermath of the whipping my adventure earned me, I avoided even glancing into the bin, as if the ghost of that particular rage of hers might snatch me. But sometimes when no one was home I lifted the hinged lid of the wooden box my father built to house the stoker screw and stared with tense fascination at the steel spiral forcing coal into the fire.

That I must never tell my mother about falling in the lake became a curse I could not bear. A nervous condition I was constitutionally unable to withstand. I comprehended in my body that I might have died. The understatement of the aftermath compared to what I'd been trained by my mother to expect—plus the shock that adults (I surely included Sara in that roster) might *dare* to conspire to pull wool over *her* eyes—unsettled me. I understood the necessity for secrecy, though. I did my best to hold the awful responsibility inside my small body but it grew bigger as days and maybe weeks or even months passed until finally, as with my lie about the loving cup, the truth busted out of me like an incubated monster.

My memory of this event is more feeling than fact but I see it in the mind's eye this way: the whole family is in the car headed some-where on some errand. Both inside and outside the car the world is black dark. At a stoplight from the backseat without provocation I speak the fatal phrases: "that time I fell in," and "I'm not supposed to tell."

A spreading silence swallows my words, a nothing-ness I instantly understand as bigger and more dangerous than the something I've uttered. I sense—as if I smell it—my mother's rage begin to boil, and I register—in the stiffening of my father's straight spine—a cold rift between him and me, immediate and widening. My sisters' held breath is a vacuum sucking up oxygen I need to stay alive.

In all my senses and every cell I feel how bad I have fucked up. I've betrayed my father, who saved me from drowning, and I've loosed on everyone involved, even Charlie and his family, a plague of my mother's vituperate and morphing hate. She will tell and re-tell this story for years as hard evidence that my father and his friends are no-account liars.

All this injustice is and forever will be *my fault*. I have brought exile upon myself; no one wants to be around me now.

In a corner of the front yard, bounded on one side by Lee Highway's hurried two-lane traffic and at right angles by quiet Meadow Drive, some ancient, very tall hemlocks had dropped a decades' deep pad of needles, twigs and cones, compressed but springy, soft to my feet despite the prickle of the newest dusting of needles, which stuck to my bare thighs in shorts season and sifted into my shoes when barefoot weather ended.

The trees' living boughs had long ago receded toward their crowns, making of their scaly black trunks the columns of a dark mansion. In the distant past quince bushes and forsythia had bloomed at the hemlocks' feet, but those bushes had been shaded to death by the time I played there. Inside the exoskeletons their slumped naked limbs suggested, I wiggled and then crouched, gradually enlarging the cavities into rough low-ceilinged rooms, digging shallow basins in the black dirt after peeling away the needle pad. With the dirt I removed I sculpted low mounds to serve as chairs, tables, and serving platters. I never had much use for dolls or the paraphernalia of clothes and crockery that always came with them; I preferred to dish up yellow-and-white blossoms from the flower garden as scrambled eggs, along with fresh sweet black raspberries, sun-warmed from the briar patch in the orchard, or the apples themselves, green, ripe, or desiccated depending on the time of year. I did not eat these things; I arranged them. Then I talked the story their placement told me—but silently, all sound and action sealed inside my head.

At night, to find my way to sleep, I built houses in my mind. Every night I furnished a different room of a many-roomed mansion, placing each carpet, each curtain, each piece of furniture or décor just so. Every room was a different color, every item in it entirely and solely that color. I saved the result in my head each evening as I finished and reopened the picture the next night. A soothing compulsion, always available, always only mine. I imagined no people in my mental house, ever.

Each spring when the wild onions came up, I built my imaginary houses outdoors. I gathered the longest and strongest leaves from each grass-like clump, tied them end-to-end to form juicy green threads many feet long, and strung them like police tape from limb tips or upright sticks thrust into the dirt to delineate rooms in buildings only I could see. I segmented entire sections of the lawn, angering my father, who had to tear them down to mow. My mother railed against the green stains on my hands and my pants' knees and the powerful garlicky scent that so permeated my skin no amount of soap and soaking removed it completely during the wild onions' long season, from late spring to early fall.

I ended up forbidden to handle them, but I did it anyway sometimes: I plucked a single, whip-thin leaf and inhaled a soothing whiff of its pungent juice—another guilty compulsion, another comfort, another story all *mine* no one could take from me.

Eventually it's my turn in the tattoo chair. I perch sidesaddle, my back to Lefty, shirttail rolled up and waistband rolled down. I will receive my Christmas tattoo in a spot midway between coccyx and waist that only weeks later will B slip up and refer to as my "tramp stamp," the idiom of his high school peers for what I will then discover—to the profound wounding of my cool—to be a ubiquitous peek-a-boo location for teen girl tattoos, exposed with every squat or bend that separates her too-short shirt from her low-riding jeans.

But my stamp will be the mark my children have made on me: the slenderest suggestion of wings, two inches in height, eight in width, hinged at a vertebra's bump, and profoundly asymmetrical—the left arc B's barbed wire branch and the right J's cursive curl.

Because this is my second tattoo, I think I know what the sensation will be, but because the old one sits in soft flesh beneath my shoulder, I learn something new when Lefty takes his gun to me. Each time the needles drill across the spine they set the nerves there to firing, the result not pain but strong neural static surging up the spinal cord to a brain that can't make it mean something but won't quit trying.

~

In my young adult years, my memory of the lake accident and its aftermath sufficed to explain to me and to therapists my non-relationship to my father. That day was the day it happened: after that betrayal, no more connection. He never forgave me, and anyway Mama put her foot down; she never again allowed him to take me with him anywhere. But I've come to see a more complicated truth, in which I'm even more helplessly culpable. Every year of the we-two years with my mother, she claimed me more fully. Her doctor made me her gift; she made me her ally and her pawn. Every year my eyes aligned more fully with her lens: I saw my father not as human being but as unfeeling brute, the object of her disgust.

Beside him on a back road in the company car—a cobalt-blue Ford with a six-foot whip antenna—I sat stiff on the bench seat in a silent rage she'd taught me. The two-way radio connecting him to his job as assistant manager of Bristol's utility crackled and yakked. A loaded .22 lay across his lap for taking pot-shots at crows. Rocky pastures and falling-down barns and shaggy cattle rolled past the cranked-down windows; I knew he might follow a power line for miles to investigate a new transformer or substation. If he came upon linemen working he might well stop to talk for half an hour or more. Worst of all, he might come to a dead stop right on the two-lane blacktop, draw a bead on a crow, and drop it. I could hardly bear my contempt for the way he flouted the law—my mother's and the state's—firing that gun out the window when I should have been already dropped off at ballet.

Once in my early teen years when I had become almost oblivious to his existence, he insisted I go with him to the shooting range he and friends built over a period of years in a wooded cove way back in the mountains. He was not patient and I had trouble using the scope because of my glasses but I hit the target, down in the corner, way outside the bull's-eye, firing a .222 varmint rifle with a kick that deep-bruised my shoulder. I did not tell him how much the blow surprised me, nor how much it hurt. I simply hated him for making me do something I did not want to do.

These are things I remembered only after my mother was gone, my children were adolescents, and I flew in alone to visit him, renting a car at the airport, picking him up at assisted living where he sat all day, deaf and bored in the wheelchair that was my mother's before him. Desperate to do something he would experience as nice, I took him out for a ride, a completely aimless expending of gas and time. I drove back roads I hadn't traveled in thirty years. We found very little to say, but he directed me sometimes by pointing or uttering a few words. We followed the power lines, I managed not to get lost, and when we parked for a little while at a substation he knew something about, he looked out the window, apparently pleased.

The minute Lefty begins his work on my back, B finds a stool and sits facing me, very near. He is solicitous, a surprise; he is, after all, sixteen and has chosen to live fulltime with his father. His attention taxes me a little, too. Occupied with bearing the stinging and the zinging, trapped in that chair when I am so eager to finish, to go home, to get supper, I don't want to make conversation. It dawns on me finally that he is uncomfortable watching me submit to something he finds painful—later he will say to J, his voice taut with anxiety, "Mom just *sat* there." My eyes on B's face while Lefty's needles rattle my spine, there must be something I should do or say to make this feel better for B.

Yet I can't think what that would be. He offers me soda, asks if I'm cold, adjusts the position of his stool to look more directly into my eyes. The tedium of getting a tattoo—time passing slowly, the necessity of being patient through one moment and the next and the next with a process that hurts but cannot be evaded—this makes me think about childbirth. B's was a homebirth, an un-medicated labor I found merciful and intimate compared to the over-engineered, frighteningly lonely hospital birth in which J was literally torn out of me. Finally B asks me straight out if I'm in pain, and without knowing I'm going to, I quip, "It's nothing like having babies."

My son's stubbly, blemished face turns stricken. There's a beat of silence while the needles go on pounding. Then another. Then he breathes out, "Thank you."

You are grateful I brought you into the world? After all that's gone wrong?

With my fingertips, I barely touch your bristly teen-man cheek.

A tattoo is a yearning—or its expiation—incised into the flesh.

B was born in the wee hours of September 11. When he turned twelve, that ordinary date that had been his special day became 9/11, no longer his and forever imbued with passions that don't come in birthday colors. It had been our plan, that day, after school, to buy him a stereo for his bedroom at my house. At supper, he cried and refused to shop. He said he couldn't stand to have a present when so many people were dead and dying. That evening, I made him go anyway; he *did* deserve his present. The three of us set out for the store, a forced march, uncertain whether it would be open, given everyone's uncertainty about whether we were or were not at war or under siege. It was a grim business, choosing that big, silver, multi-feature boom box. The salesman almost unable to sell, the birthday boy nearly in tears, and his mother, a hard-ass, insisting the day was still in some part his.

I told You: what went wrong is *not your fault*.
But I don't think You could hear me.

My son didn't want that gift I forced on him. It plagued him, sitting in his room, staring him down, reminding him of losses he could never make good.

My teacher did come to Harris, sometimes, during the month I stayed there. But only on a Saturday afternoon or a Sunday morning when everyone else came, too—the tiny shrine room abruptly packed with practitioners and too many children of all ages, and she on the phone with absent followers or leading hours-long sessions of prayers and admonitory teachings in a room stuffy and stale with collective body heat, anxiety, and exhaustion. Breaks were long lines for the single toilet and frantic effort among the women to cook up enough vegetables and rice in too little time and too few pots. I disliked the onslaught of people and work, resented the chaos, and longed for the teacher's attention, knowing I wouldn't—and shouldn't—get it just because I desired it.

One particularly hot and busy Sunday, several hours into an intricate ritual, the two dozen or so adults packed into the airless shrine room struggle to withstand the added stress of a small boy's extended tantrum and his father's suppressed but boiling shame and anger. Seated cross-legged on a cushion like the rest of us, chanting like the rest of us in stumbling weary tandem with the teacher, the man trembles visibly. His face is thunderous but he, like the rest of us, tries to persevere in attending to the teacher's fierce directive: *Concentrate.* She chants in rapid energetic Tibetan, gesturing with bell and *dorje*, striking a cymbal and clattering a small, two-sided drum. The desperate child kicks and screams and scrambles across shelves and furniture like a deranged squirrel, knocking objects, mundane and holy, to the floor. The room bulges with titanic emotion tides: angry, hungry, hurting, incredulous, outraged people trapped in close quarters.

My attention cuts in, cuts out. Fixates on brain buzz and muscle cramp. This suffering—unjust, pointless, crazy, infuriating—will it never end? I might just faint. I might jump up and strike someone, seize the child and fling him from the room. I may shriek at the teacher how much I hate all this. My own children swim in my turbulence: far away in Florida, busy with friends...or not...are they needing me, missing me, *blaming* me? *Why* have I come here? A grain of rice strikes my face, and I sit up. In a burst of *drenpa*—remembrance—my awareness—*shey-zhin*—sits up, too.

The teacher's eyes meet mine. Draw my gaze with hers to the boy's face: rapt now, and inches from hers. Entranced like a charmed snake. She sings prayers, rings instruments, commands the group and—at the same time, effortlessly, playfully—flicks rice at him from an offering bowl, one grain at a time. She mugs and she grins. Her features dance. He giggles and squirms, pinned with sheer delight and surprise. He shouts. He bounces up and down like a piston while she chants, flings rice, fuels him, snares him.

In the midst of a solemn ritual, they misbehave in tandem. In tandem with them, I catch on for half a second to what she's directed me to see: concentration *inside* chaos. Full engagement *amid* full awareness of what is. I light up, lose my misery, fill up with their joy.

The very second I notice it, the feeling is gone. In subsequent hours and days, I replay the circumstance in which that clarity arrived. Carefully at first, and then frantically, mind whirring, intellect straining, I try as hard as I can to hold on to something that was nothing tangible. Grasping at the breeze that billowed a curtain, I catch only limp cloth in my hand.

The doctor who jerked my father back from death's door against his wishes died just days later, struck and killed by a passing car while attempting to change a flat tire on the highway shoulder. The next physician assigned to my father, a very young woman, new to the practice of medicine, put up no fight to keep him hospitalized. She let him return to assisted living to get on with his business of dying by inches, his mind more ready to do that than his body. When he became too demented and physically incapacitated for the staff there to cope, the director summoned me to move him to a nursing home. I still had the temporary fulltime teaching job in those days, and flew up from Florida just before classes recommenced in January 2004.

My father seemed to know me but couldn't speak. As the aide seized the handles of his wheelchair to push him from his room into the hall, he grew agitated. He tried to stand up. He struggled to form words. The aide, middle-aged like me, plump and kind, someone born and raised in those mountains who had not fled them like I had, leaned down and spoke at his ear. She said firmly, "Mr. Hale, you're going with your daughter."

Her compassionate half-truth calmed him and upset me. I couldn't look at him as the automatic door swept open with majestic slowness and frigid winter poured through it. I felt angry and inadequate in the role I'd been dealt: ferrying my frightened, feeble father to a strange place where I'd leave him, alone, to die.

As a child my eldest sister Sara did her best to save the baby birds, nursling rabbits, and once a barely furred opossum orphaned by predators, careless drivers, or the blade of my father's plow. Wrapped in rags, tucked into shoe boxes, fed diluted milk and mashed bread from a medicine dropper, they all died anyway. Every one of them got a funeral. I can barely remember the time when both my sisters still lived at home but those burial rituals left a clear imprint: Sara at the head of our procession, preaching from the Methodist hymnal; Betsy, forever fated to hold the short straw, pulling the Radio Flyer hearse; and me tagging after, barely comprehending more than the solemnity of what we were doing.

Way at the back of my mother's ample and well-tended perennial garden, behind a river-stone birdbath flanked by thick stands of pampas grass and a pair of big hemlocks, little graves were dug and cardboard coffins covered over. When I was older and my sisters long gone from home, I tried out that spot as outdoor safe house. The hemlocks' shaggy branches screened it completely from all eyes. The birdbath made a compelling sink, offertory, or cauldron. Proximity to the stocked aisles of the flower garden grocery was a plus, but because the place had been the destination of those funerals I almost did not remember, the dim enclosure of that shaded spot felt creepy instead of cozy, and I moved on.

Revisiting that failed refuge as an adult brought to mind another picture tinged dark, at least in hindsight, with the pervasive presence of fear and loss. That red wagon the stagecoach in a game of cowboys and bandits. Sara, six-guns figuratively blazing, galloping her stick horse in ambush; Betsy, the conscripted dray horse, running pell-mell down the grape arbor bounding the flower garden, the Radio Flyer jolting behind; and toddler me the forced passenger, clinging to the rim in stiff-lipped terror at my role in someone else's play.

Each of us had a stick horse made by my father—broom handles topped with pressboard silhouette heads bearing painted-on features and real leather reins, but by the time I rode mine—called Silver, just like the Lone Ranger's steed—Sara's horse and Betsy's stood abandoned in the basement alongside the rakes and hoes. Almost all my memories of that yard are solitary and shadowy. In a bright photo that shocks me freshly each time I see it, my two blond children gallop through that same grape arbor on some early autumn visit, and everything in the picture is golden—the leaves, the grass, the light, their hair—except for his scarlet coat, her hot pink sweats, their matching red rubber galoshes.

My mother served our meals on a set of pastel Fiestaware, ownership established by color. The blue plate hers, the yellow plate my father's, the pink one, mine. I disliked pink but would eat from no other plate because I'd come to associate—that alignment of my view with my mother's—the hue of my father's plate with the viscous matter he sometimes deposited on it, food he removed from his mouth because his loose dentures couldn't chew it. Repellent too was the crumpled napkin alongside his plate filled with snot from his ever-leaking nose. I hated even to wash his plate; I never believed it sufficiently disinfected by mere dishwater. Whenever I could I doused the yellow plate with boiling water from the kettle on the stove. Occasional glimpses of my father's tongue as he chewed revolted me. When he gave up on the dentures and removed them to a soaking cup on the shelf above the sink, his tongue appeared a swollen mass inside his lipless slack cheeks. I shrank away from his rare attempts to kiss my cheek because I did not want that tongue, that mouth, that nose in proximity to mine.

On some school or Girl Scout field trip, I once purchased little souvenirs in a mountain gift shop for each member of my family, taking care to pick just the right emblematic thing for each person. For my father I confidently chose a silvered-plastic loving cup, two inches high, emblazoned "World's Best Liar." I don't remember that I had any direct evidence of my father telling lies but my mother told me so often what a liar he was that the gift seemed simply perfect. It was not until I presented it to him—and he turned on his heel, unmistakable pain and fury on his face—that I considered what the designation might mean to *him*. I was frankly stunned to realize he had *feelings*.

That betrayal of him on her terms made me loathe myself in that moment and any time I recalled it for years afterward. In each bout of regret I would try for a while to become more neutral toward him but it was too late; I had the habit of dismissing him, and he did not trust me. He did not like me, either. He told me as much at some point in his last years. How superior and stuck up I'd acted; how all I'd ever cared about was pleasing her; how as a result she gave me, at his expense, anything I wanted.

But my father did love me. He never injured me and he didn't fight with me. For most of my life he stayed out of my way and off my radar, living his life and bearing his troubles in complete silence, as far as I was concerned. When I came home to visit as a young adult, infrequently until I had children, his bear hugs at the moment of my arrival and my departure book-ended whatever chaotic emotional engagement I'd had with my mother. Each time my children and I boarded a return flight to New York or Bermuda or Florida, he stood by himself on the observation deck to watch the plane out of sight, before driving home alone to his recliner and TV in the basement, and my mother, inert and fuming, upstairs.

I felt for him then. My children had softened me, my miserable marriage had wised me up. His lonely, unrequited, old-man devotion made me burn with shame and pity I had no words for.

~

The morning after my tattoo and his, B heads into a new term at his high school, juiced by the possibility his fresh ink will draw reprisals from the authorities when classmates gather round to gawk. J has gotten in from Hartford in the wee hours after spending twenty-four straight sitting up in the terminal, and gone straight to bed. I leave the house at dawn to drive the sick cat to a biopsy, fighting rush-hour traffic on a classic mom mission.

Squinting into the sunrise, hurtling bumper-to-bumper at seventy on Tampa's overloaded freeways while attempting to tune out the animal's frightened yowling, I feel a leadenness in the muscles and even the bones of my lower back signaling, I think, the presence of lactic acid, biochemical afterburn from the surges of adrenalin that clenched those muscles involuntarily tight during the waiting, the watching, the empathizing, and the getting-mine-done in Lefty's tattoo parlor.

The feeling is familiar. I can't place it and then I do: the morning after six hours I spent in the emergency room of a third world hospital trying to prevent, solely by my stubborn presence, my then-husband from dying from anaphylactic shock and a medical staff uninterested in the woes of one more ignorant, unlucky tourist. He'd been struck by hundreds of Portuguese man-o'-war stingers and almost stopped breathing. I left J, then four years old, parked on the beach, uneasy in the company of my visiting childless childhood friend Margaret. I rode in the ambulance, seven-month-old B clamped on one hip because those were the days he wouldn't let me leave him anywhere with anyone. So intent was I on keeping the father alive that I never set down the child until the whole ordeal was over.

When I rolled out of bed the next morning to answer B's wake-up cry, still on my own inside a marriage that scripted me to be forever loyal and always strong, I fell to the floor, crippled with pain from locked muscles in my arm and hip. Only at that moment did I *feel* the whole truth of what transpired the day before.

You, my husband, wore new scars, and so did I, but nothing changed: we'd go on another five years as if that near-disaster hadn't shown either one of us a thing. Until its lesson finally caught up to us, and flung us both to hell.

Then I'd know again in my body that leadenness and toxic spasm— flattened by our divorce to a futon, laid out in front of a cheap television on the floor of an under-furnished and ratty rental house, one child curled wounded and fetal under each of my arms. Just short of destitute for the year it took to reach a settlement, harassed and threatened, too terrified to eat, sleep, or think straight, I'd done nothing to earn this except speak too much truth; my attorney confirmed this, when affirming You could not take my children from me. Cornered, I'd blurted what I knew I must never, ever tell. I admitted I wasn't coming home from the breathing place I'd fled to and in jealous rage You filled in a blank: if I didn't want You, then who? V.T. looked like a culprit—over-supportive, over-kind, but innocent; we were both so innocent in those days—and in your mind You fast-forwarded me and him through events that wouldn't transpire for a decade.

Prescient construction on your part; a karmic fault, gaping, on mine.

Charged for what I'm guilty only of wanting, someone who listens and cares, I end up stuck with the bill: I am at fault for everything each one of us suffers. I carry on breathing and earning in order to care for my children; for their sake I give up once and for all my naïve fantasies of suicide as escape but—paralyzed by shock and loss, rigid with determination—I have nothing to give them sometimes but the animal comfort of my nearness.

Through cold light on a clear mid-winter day, I drove my father twenty miles from assisted living to the best of the nursing homes that would accept his circumstances. Aides there put him to bed while I signed the necessary stack of documents. The director red-flagged the DNR order. I put my father's shoes and a few other items of street clothing I knew he'd never need again into the cupboard on his side of a tiled, sparsely-furnished room that appeared clean but stank in the urine/cleaning solvent/diseased flesh way every nursing home does. I sat on the bed he lay in, trying not to feel what I felt, the horror of having delivered him like a parcel to a holding pen for the dying.

He gave me his hand, work-battered, icy cold, already stiffening. I held it like a book between my palms and watched passersby in the hall through the open door, some of them glancing in before quickly glancing away. Some time passed. He asked me with sudden, sensible directness, "Where am I?"

I plucked one potent word from the nursing home's otherwise generic name. "This is Grace," I told him.

He had the right to a real answer to his question. And, word-worker that I am, I couldn't keep myself from claiming the available irony.

"Grace," I repeated. Near his ear, because his attention was waning, I added, "That's a good place to be now, isn't it?"

He nodded, half-smiled, seemed content.

I left him then. Went outside to the rented car, drove to the airport, flew home to my job and my children in Florida.

~

Another truth I can bear only with a long lens of distance.

Squinting, white-knuckling the wheel in a rented Taurus, an angry woman drove a desperate man straight into a blinding July sunrise. Mountains crowded the highway, a shrug of mist on their green shoulders. Frozen-faced, V.T. slipped and she slid with false brio over the glassy knot that gagged their speech.

At a café one town clear of any place eyes might recognize them, they ordered. A hefty cinnamon bun and a gaping bowl of soy latte for her. For him, a single slice of zucchini bread and coffee, black. Her stiff jaw torqued tighter. He was still as he'd always been: restrained. He steered them past the sagging comfortable couches to straight chairs. They sat down face to face, divided by a square table lamed in one leg. When the corner dipped, she compensated, pressing it up with her thigh.

Small talk ensued: jobs, books, the grown-up children. They did all right with that. Around them china clattered, cutlery rang, customers called greetings. The espresso machine hissed and fumed. Palms pressed firmly either side of the breakfast she couldn't eat after all, she stopped listening to V.T. Studied, instead, his deep-bitten nails—familiar—and the ring, also familiar, incised into the meat of his finger. Her gaze ricocheted off that, up, to the gray at his temples—abundant, and not familiar. The lightning bolts migraines had etched into his brow, deeper than she remembered. *Remember.* She checked her watch, the minute hand much farther advanced than she'd guessed, their single hour almost run out. This, a little blow. A tiny revelation. They would not, after all, change anything, fix anything, go anywhere with what had always been, face it: impossible. Out-breath. *Okay.* In-breath. *It is what it is.* Old awkward friends catching up, about to move on.

Next breath. Her gaze rose to his eyes. *Your eyes <u>your</u> eyes, so exactly.* Still blazing. That face. That *face.* The absurd, exasperating grin.

Out-breath. Like someone hit the pause button, that's what it felt like, her mind sitting up, taking notice of what it noticed: *How long has it been since we stopped talking and started staring?* A breeze touched her teeth. A sharper revelation jerked her upright.

I am grinning. Like a chimpanzee. Like a fool. At You, grinning back at me.

~

When my children were young, I carried my 35mm Canon everywhere, freeze-framing what I could not believe I was seeing, much less feeling.

In a glossy color print their soft faces bracket my mother's, a cheek-to-cheek trio. They adore her. J and B lean into her wasted body across her wheelchair's arms, their lips pursed with photogenic kisses. She, owl-eyed behind thick cataract glasses, looking more startled than pleased, stares through those lenses and the camera's at me. She hated those glasses, having once sworn she'd never wear them. It was I, not my father, who drove her to an out-of-town hospital for what was in the days before lasers a significant surgery. Newly sixteen, licensed just in time, I visited her daily after school, then coached her through learning, at sixty-one, to wear the rigid contacts that in those days replaced an excised clouded lens. When she couldn't take her contacts out and cried hysterically, I pulled them out for her with a tiny plastic plunger.

In the photograph, she holds her fingers splayed in front of her chin. Perhaps she's just eaten a jelly bean from the Easter basket my children have balanced in her lap. It's her right hand that's upraised, the one with the thickened wrist, broken in the "accident" that took place sometime in the half-dozen years I stayed completely away from her, never visiting and seldom phoning.

By the time J was born and I resumed visiting my mother, she was seventy-five, crippled, chronically ill from self-neglect, and self-isolated to the extent she'd not left the house for several years, even to step into the yard. She propelled herself from bedroom to kitchen to den and back again, seated in a wheelchair with the footrests removed, "paddling," my father termed it, with her house-slippered feet. She seldom bathed because of the logistical effort and no longer did housework; he opened cans, washed the dishes, and stacked up the attic, the spare bedroom, and the living room with the boxes of merchandise she ordered from catalogs, some of which would be still untouched when she died.

I don't know if my mother ever wanted grandchildren. When I announced my first pregnancy, at thirty, she raged at me for months for risking the birth of another mentally retarded child like my sister. But it would turn out that J and B, her only grandchildren, were gifts who brought her enormous, evident joy. For them, she ordered cartons of toys and games. For them, she bathed and got dressed and lurched down the back steps clinging to the rail, barely balancing on arthritic knees and gouty feet. She inched across the yard using the walker she otherwise spurned and dropped heavily into a lawn chair, as gleeful as my children about leaping flames, jumping sparks, long supple sticks of skewered marshmallows and the hotdogs she taught them to call wienies.

When I had to tell my children one day after school that she'd died, it flattened all three of us. We lay down on my bed to cry, one of them crooked in each of my arms. I couldn't understand why it hurt so bad to finally be free of her. J and B, then thirteen and nine, already five years into divorce hell, were plenty familiar with loss that would not heal but they refused to accept the complete, immutable erasure death brings. There simply had to be recompense. Within a month of her funeral, when the elderly diabetic cat we'd had since J was two had to be put down, they insisted on a replacement. A fresh being to adore. I agreed to a trip to the animal shelter even though I knew they'd soon outgrow this pet and I'd be stuck with it. J pulled from a cage a black and white female cat almost identical to the one who'd died, and said, "Her name is Karma."

For most of the next seven years, Karma—afflicted for half that span with the incurable running sores of "kitty leprosy"—was my closest and often my only companion.

When she dies in my lap, from the mercy of the vet's euthanizing injection, I will cry as if I'll never be consoled.

As my month-long retreat in Harris draws toward its close, time passing in much the same way it has from the beginning—prayers, indolence, heat and cold, light and dark, solitude, stillness, bright scraps of event—it dawns on me that even if I give up on my novel, I'll have to go on writing and trying to publish. I've become, for the time being, a writing teacher fully installed in academia, publish or perish part of the job description.

With respect to V.T., I simply give up. I cannot excise him from my heart or my head no matter how I try. I have no option but to persevere in forbearing his confounding behavior and my own stinging need.

In thirty days of retreat I've achieved no cure for my desires. I've come to terms with two of them, but that seems a pale conclusion to an effort I'd thought would make me stop hurting—and stop needing.

During my very last days on the property, the beleaguered mother in the caretaker family takes me along on a trip to a Super Walmart some twenty miles away. I asked early on for a chance to shop for dry socks and some toiletries. But by the time she offers me the chance to climb into her minivan, I don't want to go. My world in retreat appears beyond beautiful: the sky excruciatingly blue, the grass and pines incomprehensibly green, the flowers brilliant and perfect.

At Walmart people rush in and out the automatic doors looking doleful, harried, down-at-the-heel. Their heavy carts loaded with merchandise, a fraction of the plastic-and-cellophane-wrapped bounty bulging from the shelves inside, seem to make them—and their children—angry. The force of the shoppers' collective misery sends me cowering into my hoodie. Before I've quite made my way inside the store, a woman shouting at her whining toddler yanks him upright and out of the cart-seat by one arm. The child's reflexive accusing shriek sends pain slicing through me. The woman's face, bulbous with rage, stiffens mine.

I flee. The minivan in the parking lot is locked, so for the hour my hosts shop, I huddle on a hard bench in Walmart's foyer between the two sets of doors. I manage not to cry, but people stare; I know I look ill and crazy, so deep in that dirty hooded sweatshirt on a summer afternoon. I feel, in its flimsy shelter, as yolky and defenseless as a newborn. Re-entering what most people call the real world is too much. I have no skin, no shell, no separation of me from You to shield me from what is.

I feel everything everyone feels, and it's too much, I cannot bear it. I beat a retreat back inside myself like a rabbit down a hole.

Repeatedly as a small child I got up in the night, made my way to my parents' room and my mother's side of the bed. I wanted in. I wanted to sleep between them. "I had a nightmare," I told her, every time. Occasionally, that was true. Usually, it wasn't. Usually, my mother let me in and always she placed me on the outside, between her and the edge of the bed.

I had most of what I needed.

My father did not want me in their bed. I sensed tension, in him and between them, but I arrived often, compulsively, and my mother never said I had to stop. I gave it up on my own; I suppose I got older and stopped wanting that intimacy. Maybe, too, I got tired of balancing on their edge.

Later, when I was a teenager and my mother and I were most consistently estranged, she insisted one night on sleeping with me in my bed, on the flimsiest pretext. I had a cold, and she said, "I want to stay with you to make sure you're all right." I was outraged by this newest intrusion into my most private space. Nothing about me was mine alone; her eyes were always on me.

What did she think I could do, asleep in my bed, that she wouldn't like? Just to show her, I turned my back and masturbated while she lay beside me in the dark.

Not until many, many years later will it occur to me that You might have come to my bed seeking safety—fleeing a nightmare my father pressed on You.

The apple orchard, the part of the yard furthest from the house and entirely beyond my mother's line of sight, held my favorite refuge. Most of the dozen trees were several decades old by the time I played there, some with un-pruned branches spreading like hoopskirts, their tips skimming the ground. Crawling beneath those boughs in summer I entered a tent lit green with leaf-filtered light, pungent with rotting apples, and buzzing dangerously with the industry of honey bees, wasps, and yellow-jackets. A moment or two of that heady risk was enough; I knew too much about bee stings. Honey bees hurt bad but only briefly if I plucked the stinger from the welt and poured on camphor; yellow-jackets struck in silent droves and set me afire with their limitless stinging; wasps were the worst, their stings made me ill.

Honey bees land-mined the entire yard—I preferred bare feet to shoes, and most of our grass was clover—but in the orchard they ruled. Only my father never deferred to them. He placed their stand of hives at the center of the orchard, flush with the raspberry patch for pollination of the fruit and berry blossoms, and he took from them their honey at his will, wearing a beekeeper's veil but seldom bothering with the smoke pot. He brushed away their stings, which he said he did not feel. At breakfast, lunch, or dinner, he forked up dripping chunks of honeycomb from a forest-green Fiestaware bowl and gobbled it down, wax and all.

I gave the bee hives wide berth, and taking care not to place a naked foot on either a rotted apple or a bee sucking it, I seized the lowest horizontal branch of my favorite tree, swung my feet to its gently sloping bole, and scrambled up into its crown, disappearing from the world. Up there, I day-dreamed the perfect tree house. One long limb running parallel to the ground six feet below I designated as living room. Another, where I balanced a sandwich or a bread ball wadded from a crust-less slice of Sunbeam white bread, was the kitchen, and yet another, higher up, the bedroom. Stretched full length on my stomach on lichened gray bark, I silently narrated the picture-stories in my mind: a real tree house somehow sustaining actual rooms, as fantastic but more personalized than the ones I read about, over and over again, in *Adventures of the Swiss Family Robinson*. Years later, as a teen on a band trip, I would eagerly make the Family's tree house my first stop in Disney World, an embarrassingly un-cool choice, only to be gravely disappointed by the un-treelike concrete and I-beams from which that commercial fakery was constructed.

I longed for an actual tree house and must have asked for it out loud because at some point in my early adolescence, when I was too old to appreciate it—my interests tilting already toward boys, the Beatles, and acceptance by a peer group—my father built me one. *He* called it a tree house, but for both my mother and me it was an eyesore. At the edge of the orchard, facing the house, he erected four wooden telephone poles trimmed to ten feet in height. Atop them he mounted an industrial-sized wooden shipping crate, turned on its broad, four-by-four-foot side with its narrow lid removed, creating an open front, accessed by a long wooden ladder. The creosoted result was hideous. Even I thought so, but for my mother it was an embarrassment rising above the tree line of our property; the neighbors could not fail to notice and judge. For me, the salient failing was that it was *not* a tree house: no tree stood anywhere near it.

I recall the grating dissatisfaction every glance at the structure and every climb up its ladder exacerbated in me. My father had gone to so much trouble—I was old enough to get that—and still he had not got it right. Yet, I also remember the good use to which I and two neighbor girls, both older than I and neither one an appropriate friend in my mother's eyes, put it. T, a budding delinquent, required me as the price of her friendship to shoplift penny candy from the small grocery nearby. D, three years my senior, had a much more developed interest in boys and was the source of most of my earliest (and mostly erroneous) information on sex. The treeless stilt house gave us a place to hide contraband—Sugar Babies and Tootsie Pops so tainted with the terror of un-prosecuted larceny I could not eat them, and dog-eared issues of *Playboy* borrowed and later returned to the bottom of D's father's basement stash. I could never have imagined without those glossy visual aids that any woman anywhere could have such abundant flesh to display, much less find so much apparent bliss living inside its rosy, air-brushed perfection.

Hunched in the skyward crate, breathing creosote fumes, I turned the pages of soft porn slowly, well beyond my mother's gaze and, so I assumed, her imagination. I began to freshly intuit the vastness of space available to me inside the refuge of duplicity. Look like one kind of person and be, in secret, another. My private life began a darker turn then, from ether-worlds explored only inside my head toward corporeal adventures sought out in back seats, band buses, and basement rec rooms.

~

On the morning of the day I am to leave retreat, I wake to find the teacher's car parked in the grass before her cabin. She'd come in the night, at last, without warning. My heart swoons. I have to leave, but she has come in time.

I wait all morning to see her. My flight home will leave Newark, 110 miles away, in mid-afternoon. I get word I'll be riding down in the teacher's car; she intends to head that way once her business at Harris is done. This news thrills me—the teacher is taking me to the airport!—but it makes me nervous: the *teacher* is taking me to the airport. She arrives everywhere later than she's supposed to. She does not experience time according to Western convention. Airlines do not make accommodation for this different way of being, so she misses most of the flights booked for her.

An hour after I should have been on the road, given the drive time and post-9/11 security protocols, my teacher summons me. She has gifts for me. From India, a small folding prayer table and a three-by-five-foot carpet to place under it, beautiful items, astoundingly so, but a quandary to pack. I thank her humbly, and we walk together through tall grass studded with summer wildflowers. A slight *umpf* of effort punctuates each shift of her weight to her damaged hip. The pine tops sway in a light breeze. Prayer flags lift. She speaks the familiar terse admonitions in the familiar fractured syntax. Birds sing and soar. Across the road, at the Hasidim's camp, children shout boisterously from the playground. My mind and my feelings argue. This one-on-one stroll with the teacher, is it bliss, or expensive carelessness?

I'll miss my flight.

I can re-book.

That will cost some money.

I have some money.

Just before we climb into the car, my teacher pats the crown of my head with a folded silk banner emblazoned with Tibetan icons known as the Eight Lucky Signs. She places it in my hands, another gift. I thank her and feel my gaze rise in tandem with hers.

The sky.

Blue and blank.

Perfectly clear.

Always there.

I dream again and again during my divorced and man-less years of babies and children, not mine, for whom I am responsible. But in one particularly vivid and disturbing dream, I am pregnant. In my too-old-for-it middle-age, I walk about at that so-pregnant ninth month point that my navel has popped out, an obscene little mound extending even further into everyone's face this inappropriate fecundity.

All of You just stare. My ex-husband. My mother. Bosses, teachers, old friends and old enemies: tight lips and hard-faced disapproval. I am frightened and embarrassed but—having no choice; what is, *is*—I lift my chin and go about my business.

I offer no explanations for the belly, and no apologies for its back-story. I believe, in the dream, I am pregnant *with* V.T. rather than by him, but my truth does not matter. People will think what they think. They will say what they want to say.

My belly and I make our way through the world while onlookers ogle and flinch.

On the long tense drive to Newark, I sit up front in the teacher's big Lincoln Town Car, beside the fellow student tapped to drive. She is white-knuckled and lead-footed. There is traffic. Plenty of it. With luck, we'll reach the airport at just about the time my flight is scheduled to take off. My teacher rides in the backseat with another student. She chants prayers and speaks by cell phone to followers, and issues instructions to one or another of us, the kinds of things with which she is always, unendingly, busy. Somewhere still upstate, trees instead of asphalt surrounding us, I hear her say—I think I really do hear this very near my ear—*I like you.* As we near the airport, navigating knots of concrete viaduct and clots of taxis, she reaches over the seatback to press into my hand four dollars, crumpled singles folded together like a note, borrowed from the student beside her.

This good luck, she says.

Miraculously, I make my flight. It's been delayed. All my baggage goes aboard, too; the skycap at the curb eagerly produces a cardboard suit box and a role of tape, gratis, and expeditiously packages up the prayer table and carpet. He is, I think, Pakistani, and might have some inkling of their function. I have to pay extra, of course, to check my excess baggage. But I have some money. I do.

A few weeks after I delivered my father to Grace Healthcare and Rehabilitation Center, I returned to say good-bye. Under hospice care he was gliding through his last days on a slick of morphine. He greeted me with joy. Bliss softened his coarse unshaven face as he pulled me toward him for a kiss on the lips I couldn't quite evade.

"There you are! *There* you are, I knew you'd come," he cooed, and I knew—because I saw in his eyes and felt in his touch an ardent young man's greeting to his love—that he welcomed not me but some essential lost someone back into his embrace. Transformed by a drug haze, I became his one and only, the bringer of joy after all and at last. There's no telling whom he thought he saw in his opium dream, but at the time—perhaps because I know I look very much like my mother—I felt uncomfortably sure it was she he kissed.

The following weekend my two sisters and brother-in-law visited him. They told me afterwards he seemed to recognize them. They said he was calm. Betsy fed him a little applesauce. Sara read him a Psalm. A couple of days later, he was gone.

Once during the ten days I spent emptying my parents' house under the gun of a closing date, dust and too much déjà vu drove me outdoors. The air smelled mountain-sweet, flowers and bushes bloomed in profusion, the bees were busy: late May, high spring in the southern Appalachians. A lovely contrast to Florida, already steamy by that time of year. I sat down in damp ragged grass beneath the last sagging remnants of my mother's many clotheslines. The abandoned playhouses stood near at hand. The sandbox and swings, the wrecked, weed-choked gardens all in my view, the same line of sight that had been hers from the kitchen window above and behind me.

Beneath the buckeye, the sugar maple, and the enormous willow oak, where her hundreds of orchids once summered, the two dozen tables they crowded (my father's creation, built from the flat sides of the giant wooden spools on which industrial grade electrical wire was shipped to his employer) had slumped to the earth beneath heavy carpets of thick, vibrantly green moss studded with mushrooms. Twice a year throughout my childhood, I and sometimes my father provided unskilled labor for the seasonal migration of those orchids. In spring, we lugged them from her flower porch (an ordinary front porch, enclosed by my father) or its poor relative, the basement flower room (a cinderblock cube he'd wired with tiers of Gro-Lux fixtures). Until fall they basked in filtered light and proximity to a water spigot. Then we lugged them back inside.

The big awkward plants weighing two pounds or more in their thick clay pots had to be carried individually down six brick steps from the flower porch, and down another four concrete steps to cross the driveway, and up four brick steps to the tables. My father once tried to streamline the effort with his rubber-tired wheelbarrow, setting a half dozen pots in its bucket and bumping it down the stairs and up again, but she put a stop to that, once the first terra cotta pot cracked. All this took hours in the heat of late spring amid her grating anxiety about whether the last frost had indeed passed, and more hours again in the nip of mid-October while she worried aloud whether or not we would really finish before first frost. Red clay rubbed off the pots to stain my clothes, and the sharp green scent of the orchids' air roots clung to my hands; my short legs went rubbery with fatigue, sweat burned my eyes and hair straggled from my ponytail into my mouth.

In the spring once the plants were all outside, the trays and the over-turned pots that had pedestaled them beneath their winter lighting had to be carried out, scrubbed with hot water and bleach in the driveway, then dried in the sun to kill that year's crop of algae. At day's end, all of it got toted back indoors. The next day the curtains, stickered with dried leaves and dead bugs, their hems stained green from contact with the pots and the water-filled trays, came down for the laborious washing/starching/ironing process until, the years passing, cotton organza was finally replaced with permanent press polyester, and, gradually, because she had no help once I left, she stopped taking them down at all, and the curtains greened, and then grayed and

tattered, and ended up in the trash, the windows bare except for ugly
and effective insulation: the heavy-gauge plastic my father had stapled
to the frames outside.

My mother in the grave, I'd returned to undo the little of her that
was left so the house could be sold. Seated alone in the backyard I'd
played in and retreated to thirty-five and forty years before, I qui-
eted. The darting flights of song birds, the harsh comments of a crow,
the ratcheting of a freight train from behind the backdrop hills, the
drone of a small plane invisible in a ceilingless sky, converged slowly
with their ghosts from seasons past. Into this charged moment there
dropped a phantom figure of my mother. I was awake but I saw her
plainly, as if in a lucid dream: a thick figure stoop-shouldered, wearing the familiar, ridiculous conical straw hat she favored for gardening.

Her back was to me. The long grass bending around her knees
bore a heavy load of dew. She walked slowly, a metal bucket in one
hand, the opposite arm extended for balance. She had nothing to say
to me; she was working. A coolie in a flower-print duster, wading into
an un-mown field.

Her mess was my mess, that day—the sorting and sifting, the tossing out of detritus. My responsibility. But when I finished, I would
walk away. She could never do that. That place, her responsibilities,
her enduring, recombinant mistakes—her nature and her times did
not allow her to escape. She made a nest inside her misery, and burrowed down.

In my vision You make your way deeper into the field, Mother,
through tangled grass, lugging that bucket.

Inside the jet climbing skyward, lifting me out of Buddhist retreat
toward home and job and children, the real world of compromised
joys, painful constraints, and abundant disappointments, I felt lucky.

I felt kindly toward the people strapped into seats around me, preoccupied with reading or typing, listening to music, or parsing the contents of their heads. They wished to be happy, every one of them, just as I did. However stupidly we went about seeking it, and to whatever end, the same need impelled us.

I did not open a book, nor write in my journal. I looked out the window, at the sky. So many things I had done wrong, and could not undo. So much I did not like, and could not avoid. None of that left me but—the plane nosing through clouds so apparently solid, so utterly vaporous—a grain of insight struck me. I smiled at what I felt: wordless clarity, and peace. A breeze of release billowed the curtain of my mind, interrupting for one instant my lifelong struggle to separate myself from my troubles.

Stilling, for a moment, my always-effort to cut myself free from You, and what You mean to me.

Inside a dream, I wake up. Something dangerous lies near me. Very near. So close that fear dead-stops my muscles, almost halts my breath. The reflex of cornered prey: freeze. Don't run, don't flinch, too late now, just wait to find out if what holds you in its sights will strike, or move on.

I view myself from the outside even as I writhe in the grip of this dream. From this angle I can see clearly what threatens me. Millimeters from the crown of my head is the head of an enormous snake. Black, or so dark in the dark as to appear so. Obscenely thick, and long. Muscle in reptile form as big around as my leg and far longer than I am tall.

Paralyzed, cowering, I wait for the strike. I wait to die.

The dark snake's mouth is so near its breath stirs my hair. This cold-blooded beast's out-breath is...warm. So warm my scalp heats, and the heat spreads. My body quickens.

How odd, asserts a small clear voice from the outside-of-me mind observing with calm compassion my fright-frozen body.

Instantly this grain of insight enlarges into pressing, inarguable intuition: if I can allow this terrible, inevitable thing to happen, it will save me.

Part 3
Lucky

When B and I return to the shop a few days after receiving our tattoos, J's already in Lefty's chair. Sitting up, tipped back slightly, her legs extended—her portion of our together tattoo will reside on her lower leg, just above the bump of her ankle. Lefty's working, concentration keen, needles whirring. J watches us walk through the door; she looks displeased.

Today is the last possible date our schedules could be jiggered, inconveniently in each case, to allow all three of us to be in the shop at once. It's the day before she returns to college and the hour immediately post-school-day for B. I arranged my day to pick him up so we could get there together and on time, but we are late anyway, held up first by B's drama practice running long, then further delayed by the heavy traffic of Tampa's afternoon rush. J's chilly affect—just sitting there, expressionless, getting ink—tightens the tension I already feel: once again I've proven inept at getting things right.

"Does it hurt?"

The question is voiced by a young Latina, slight as a reed and visibly trembling, who's entered the shop right behind me and B, sheltered beneath the arm of a beefy boyfriend. J's fists and her jaw clench the way they did when she was a toddler and yet another non-negotiable truth about the world had once again made her spitting mad. She answers, "It's not bad."

Weeks later, someone with personal experience will tell me that "ankles *really* hurt, much more than anything on the back." Ignorant of that for now, I watch J's new tattoo take shape: a single cursive curl lifted from the twining wings of them on her back, reshaped at her ankle into a perfect circle opened in one quadrant by the eye of Ra that replicates mine. Brutal blue-black on her pale skin, yet barely three-inches in diameter. The work goes quickly, so fast B and I could have missed it entirely had we arrived only minutes later.

My eyes keep slipping off J's immobile face, drawn by the beading blood, the dabbing of Lefty's hand. B stands nearby, distracted, I know, by his cell phone vibrating vigorously, again and again, inside the latched pocket of his cargos, but he does the right thing; he foregoes pulling it out to look. Emotionally, I'm skidding. Nowhere to stand. Here at this culminating stage of our long-planned, much desired triumvirate-tattoo, no togetherness, just a doing-it-cause-we-said-we-would rush.

Then it's over. She's called no breaks. I hand Lefty the folded stack of twenties, and the shaky girl and her guy step up to the chair while Lefty stretches his back, swigs soda, and begins again his expiatory presence to his clients' need to hurt just right.

My tattooed kids and tattooed me, out we go, into a winter twilight. Purple, yellow-green, and gray, the color of a fading bruise.

In the midst of an angry, bitter fight during her mid-teen years, J shouted at me: "You made a mistake."

We had been discussing what I needed and expected from her and why, in her view, what I got was what I deserved. By "mistake" she meant, that time, my marriage to her father and especially my inability, thereafter, to get it right, to stay in my place, to forego blowing up a life she and her brother felt they knew how to live.

My answer: "You're right."

The simple awful truth I spoke drilled a hole in my chest—and got us nowhere, except bloodied—because...what can I do to undo in You the damage I've already done?

Immediately post-tattoo, I guilt B and J into dining out with me because that was what we'd agreed in the original plan we'd do.

"Christmas dinner after Christmas tattoo!" I hear myself chirp. They roll their eyes.

At my favorite Indian restaurant, seated two-facing-one in a particularly uncomfortable vinyl booth, the seat too hard and the back too straight, I'm the only one eating. My children piddle and stir in their entrees; they confess one after the other (in what seems to me callous disregard for my feelings) to having eaten (in what seemed to them famished necessity) immediately before the tattoo.

The minute I've paid the check, J heads straight back to Lefty's to meet a guy friend who's become a tattoo addict, she explains, after witnessing the inking of her back—his third tattoo scheduled tonight. B is visibly impatient to get to the privacy of his room and answer all those missed calls and text messages, and maybe make a pass at his homework.

Driving home alone after dropping B off at his dad's, I can't fail to notice how J is right, again: we never do anything *together*.

And I keep on making mistakes I cannot fix.

The dinners boxed into three disposable containers lined up on the back seat signify the reality of every eat-out meal we ever had as a live-together threesome—one or both of my children always preferring, and needing, something other than I was capable of giving.

~

During the dozen years I am divorced, I dream repeatedly of toilets I must clean. Crap-stained, sock-stuffed, filled-to-the-brim-and-overflowing with piss and blood, pus and sputum and diarrhea slopping over the sides, the stench exceeding my worst gas-station restroom experiences: it's up to me to put my hands in the mess and start wiping up. I long for rubber gloves and never have them. Sometimes what's before me is just any old filthy toilet. Other times, it belongs to someone I know. Resistant, amazed, I get to work. I can't say why I know there's no escape from this wretched task; I just know.

When I wake up, the repugnant images come with me. This goes on for years, the repetition and variation of this dream. When I begin writing this book, I say to V.T., by this point my late-life last-chance You, "There's so much shit in my story!"

You answer: "You should write about that."

In some other fight at some other point in J's stormy teen years, I slapped her face and she slapped me right back, shattering the pledge I'd made for all of us when she was a toddler: no hitting. My capacity to abuse—the involuntary, volcanic urge to shake her, to strike her, to shut her up—boiled in me more than once when she was a baby and so I shut it down. I ruled it out. Took a vow. No spanking. No corporeal correction of any kind.

We made it that far, to perhaps age fifteen, and whatever she said to provoke me hurt bad, but the detonation of *my* fear, *my* frustration, *my* desperation into rage I needed to inflict on *her,* it felt like primal sin reasserting.

My *fault.*

Was it the day of the slap that B, eleven years old and never in his life struck by a parent, burst into wracking sobs? Was it that day he began to need to leave me—to put the safety of some distance between us?

In my mid-twenties, I told a psychiatrist in New York City about the recurrent snake-and-gun nightmare from my childhood. That stalking hunter and his inevitable bullet had started to revisit me in the tiny midtown apartment I shared with the man who would father my children. We'd been married just a few months, and already I feared his temper. I was working very hard, first in retailing and then in investment banking, making more money than I'd ever imagined possible. I was depressed and anxious. Prone to crying jags. On occasional clothes-buying sprees at Bloomingdale's or Lord & Taylor, I spent more money than we could afford, but nothing, and I mean *nothing,* made me happy. Except lighting up a jay and losing myself inside a dopey stupor.

This doctor was abrasive, unkind, and unreliable about keeping our appointments. I wonder now if she had her own problems, with drinking or drugs. She said not much in response to my report of the recurring dream—she said not-much in response to anything—but that day she made a statement that astounded me: "You were abused."

Absolutely not, I told her. Your view of my relationship with my mother is preposterous. Mama is sick, and sad, and so many things have worked out horribly for her, but she loves me very much. And I love her back. I have to, I'm the only one she's got.

That psychiatrist didn't know what she was talking about, I felt sure, but still her words triggered an explosion of deep-buried shame that threatened to blow my head off. Child abuse was *trashy,* exactly the kind of thing my mother most contemptuously hated. I could not allow that term to be associated with her, or me.

The therapist insisted. Oh, yes, you were. You were *abused.*

I was not.

The doctor recited back to me what I'd told her over the course of our sessions about my childhood. She was cold and mean and constructed her case with exquisite logic.

I walked out of her office terrified. I'd heard this dreadful thing intimated once before, by my first therapist, a calm, warm-hearted man who for several years stood between me and suicide, but I'd pushed the treasonous notion from my mind. This time, I was able for just a moment to see my life the way the psychiatrist viewed it. I had trouble walking home, as if the sidewalk tilted. Manhattan's sky-scrapers leaned in above me, their heavy shoulders almost touching.

If I change my view of You, everything I believe about myself and everyone else will change, too.

Already, even as I re-buried the shock, change took root.

If everything that's wrong in my life—and yours—is *not* my fault—if I'm not what You said I am and must be—then I'll have to do something to assert myself.

I might have to see what I look like, distinct from your view of me.

Well within my mother's view from the kitchen window stood a building we called the summer house—a place I never played. I avoided it because it emanated misery I could feel but never quite fathom.

Gracefully constructed of crisscrossed slats painted white, the walls more suggested than solid, with a door and four large windows cut out, roofed but dirt-floored, a brick grill and chimney centered at the back wall, the summer house had been designed and built by my parents for casual entertaining al fresco. My sister Sara remembers when they did regularly host friends out there: the benches built in beneath the windows sported striped cushions custom-made by my mother, and a picnic table and chairs filled the center space. It never looked that way in my lifetime.

Sometimes as a child I stepped inside the summer house, trying to understand what felt so wrong in there. Silty dust from the perma-nently desiccated floor puffed up between my bare toes. Spider webs stuck to my shins, and a sharp flake of peeling paint might wedge accidentally, painfully, beneath a fingernail. A smell odd and old and sad veiled me despite the open air just on the other side of the thick and woody grape vines and wisteria that once trellised the walls decoratively but now threatened to pull them right down. Most of the floor space was hogged by the ancient and enormous rotor tiller my father fired up only in spring to bust up the winter-hardened garden soil; that dormant beast smelled slightly of gasoline, and shreds of dead weeds hung like dried flesh from the tiers of dull steel talons visible behind its tin mud flap. A lawn mower or two lived in there—he never threw them away but like some people with several cars in their yard, kept at least one running by pulling parts from one to another—along with rakes, shovels, rags and other forms of handyman detritus, and the little tiller he used to turn up flower beds, and the hand-powered, one-blade harrow he wheeled along to lay open the furrows for seeds I'd be conscripted to plant.

I could wedge myself in among the tangle of blades and handles, but I never stayed long, ceding it to the spiders and wasps so at home inside the dry solitude.

But in the late summer of 1971, a season I was sixteen and about to begin my third and final year of high school, I spent many sweaty hours scraping away the scaling layers of aluminum paint with which my father had preserved the wood, then applying coat after coat of new white paint. The project took a very long time; who knew that much open space could have so much paint-able surface—six faces to every slat, narrow but long or small but rough and thirsty. It took *forever*, especially in teen time, and I hated every minute of it. I persevered, however. My mother had made the job one of the conditions I must meet in order to be allowed to marry the following June, at seventeen, and everything—my whole *life*—depended on that wedding.

I was in love. I had found my one and only, a You who would make all wrongs right.

Just like in the movies, Juliet and her Romeo, if I could not be with the one I loved, I was gonna die.

A less romantic truth was operative, too—one I overlooked given how hard I worked that year to keep my mother, my boyfriend, and myself on task for the big event. I needed, in order to stay alive, to get out of my mother's house. Out of her orbit, out of her sight, and away from the crushing dark force of her unhappiness.

~

The spring before J left for college she gave me, for my birthday, a Mr. Potato Head toy. Overtop the words "Potato Head" on the box, she pasted stickers inscribed "Right."

Mr. Right. A standing bitter joke in our two-girl household at that point (B having shifted, by then, to his dad's). Mr. Potato Head-Right, my wise daughter pointed out, was completely available to me and came with no baggage of any kind. I could even rearrange his features at will, swap his mouth for his nose just for cathartic spite.

She dated. She put on fishnet stockings and thigh-high boots and went out to parties and clubs. I did not. I sat at home chanting mantra, and writing and rewriting my novel. She knew I was lonely; she felt bad for me. We both felt certain my romantic situation was hopeless. I was an uptight, middle-aged loser bleeding by the drop to death for lack of my elusive one and only.

~

My mother wanted her children to play the piano. She had a strong connection to classical music; she'd trained to sing *lieder* in college. My sister Sara took to piano eagerly and well, but I don't remember ever expressing interest or willingness. The church organist, Miss Henley, taught children in her home weekdays after school. She was kindly—open-faced and un-critical—but clueless, I now think, about how to deal with me.

Once a week I dragged my feet from Thomas Jefferson Elementary School to the little house she shared with her widowed mother, a modest frame house squeezed in by its similar neighbors on an old residential street close to Bristol's never-thriving downtown. I arrived hungry and dirty. I was required to wash my hands before sitting down at the venerable upright piano in the living room. Before I put my freshly-scrubbed fingers on her real ivory keys, Miss Henley wiped each key with a tissue dipped in rubbing alcohol—surely a necessary precaution between child students whose noses and fingernails were rife with germs. I didn't like the smell of the alcohol; it reminded me of the doctor's office. I didn't like the old-people scent of her house, either. Miss Henley, likely in her forties then, seemed plenty old to me, and her mother positively ancient. They greeted me with acceptance and warmth I found suspect, given the expectations I was actively defeating every time I crossed their doorstep.

During my lessons I believe I was truculent, inattentive, and unpromising. Miss Henley kept trying, of course, as all decent teachers do. I tolerated her. I lied to her, too, about the time I spent practicing. She required students to keep a log, and awarded a prize for the biggest grind. I remember the look on her face when I handed in a soiled sheet of notebook paper detailing my fantastic efforts, several hours a day, and I recall even more clearly the squirming shame with which I accepted the prize—a plastic bust of Listz, a composer I did not know nor comprehend, and an object obviously inferior to the three busts made of plaster my sister had won during her stint as Miss Henley's pupil. My music teacher surely knew I didn't deserve the prize but couldn't figure out how to say so.

I wonder if my mother knew I lied. I assume she did but it's not impossible that she was simply too depressed to pay attention to the relationship between the half-hour or so I actually sat on her spinet's hard bench clunking through the exercises, and the figures, inflated by a factor of two or three, I recorded on the paper she signed.

I got my comeuppance for lying. Twice a year Miss Henley required all her students to participate in recitals. The music had to be memorized, and once I was seated before an audience—usually in the church basement and consisting only of parents and other students—I could remember very little beyond the need to not fail.

For these recitals I did practice—and practice and practice—whatever simple piece Miss Henley assigned me. But, as performance day approached, panic took control. Dressed in some Sunday dress and shiny shoes, I'd grow sicker and sicker as my turn neared—nauseated, dizzy, chilled and sweating, my thoughts and my heart galloping out of control. I was twelve or thirteen when my worst fears came true: I sat down at the bench, my hands froze, and my mind blanked. A silence ensued, and when Miss Henley silently walked up to place the music before me, I burst into tears, fled the room, and could not be cajoled or bullied into playing piano in public, that night or ever again.

I don't recall my parents punishing or criticizing me for this failure. I don't remember if my father was even there but his presence or absence would have made no difference. What mattered was my mother. The embarrassment I'd caused not just her but everyone at the recital—I got that, from their averted eyes and tactful lack of comment. The shame of having earned pity from strangers added weight to the load of black sorrow I lugged with me everywhere by then.

My plight = my fault. I provoked it, so I deserved it.

A man lets a woman take his hand in the cab she's flagged, at an uptown street corner in mist and cold March rain at dawn. The video in this safe-distance clip is grainy and the sound quality poor. At a diner for a breakfast appointment she's cajoled him not to cancel, they could neither eat nor speak. The little he did say was exactly what she's told her therapist she has to hear to let go for good. *No*, and *never*. The man's voice was over-loud; it's the one audible line in the soundtrack. The harried waitress clearing their table, plates racked up her arm, heard it, too; her face went bland with pity. But for five hurtling minutes down an urban avenue still empty at this ungodly hour his hand snugs her hand against his warm thigh. So much is gray: the laden sky, the wet asphalt, the blind office towers, and yet: this little ray of contradictory comfort.

At the hotel portico V.T. gets out and flees. She pays the small fare, because she's offered to, and walks in alone, as she's expected to. It is her birthday; she is forty-nine. She takes what she gets. She knows she deserves it.

Forced daffodils bloom in concrete planters either side of the revolving glass door.

My mother conferred on me in my elementary school years a confounding pet, a parakeet, lime green and yellow, named Chirp. She and Sara had canaries or parakeets when I was a tiny child, but birds held no attraction for me. I yearned for a furry, affectionate, four-footed pet: a cat, a dog, a horse.

Chirp's color—fabulously unnatural, at least in the context of the fauna I was used to in Appalachia—did interest me. His hard, hooked beak—the sound and motion of it as he cracked seed; the fierce, bloodletting grip of it in the flesh of my finger—mesmerized me. His feces, black grains with a white-dot center, repelled me, especially when I found them floating in his water dish, or in my hair, or on the backs of the chairs in the den, where he lived on a table draped with a plastic tablecloth layered in newspaper it was my job to change. The door of his cage stood permanently ajar. That the bird should be allowed the run of the house was my mother's idea, one I could never quite accept but would never gainsay either. When we first acquired him, Chirp's wings were clipped but when the flight feathers grew in and he occasionally made swooping tours of the downstairs rooms, no one made any move to stop him. The necessity of trimming his tiny talons frightened me, as too close a clip made him bleed, and he had to be held firmly in a fist for the clipping, often with that beak hooked in the hand that squeezed him, drawing tit-for-tat blood. His twig legs and twig toes—naked and scaly, their color the blued pink of oxygen-deprived lips—repulsed me, as did scrubbing those feces off every surface he frequented.

That he ate celery leaves and bits of fruit encouraged me, in contrast to the boring bins of seed and grotesque cuttlefish bone wired to the cage. I gave him an exercise yard full of toys and equipment atop that round table—a honey-oak antique that would eventually, when I first left home, become my dining table. Chirp had bright plastic ladders, mirrors, balls with bells inside, objects to climb, perch on, peck, and preen before.

He died of some wasting disease, a creeping paralysis, growing weaker, thinner, and finally dropping like a leaf from his perch to the floor of his cage. He lay there inert but not dead for several days, trapped in his body inside a cage.

When Chirp expired, my sister Sara had long since left home, so his funeral fell to me. On my own, I boxed the stiff little corpse in a cardboard casket lined with some fabric scraps and dug him a grave under a half-wild rose trellising the wires of one section of the long grape arbor. My mother claimed the bush was the yellow rose of Texas referred to in the song; I had some attachment to the flower on account of the romantic lyrics associated with it, but also for the profusion of its buttery petals, showering the ground after rain. I found a flat stone, inscribed on it Chirp's name and death date in permanent marker, and pressed it into the raw dirt.

I remember that day as a Saturday, the sky bright blue and the rose in bloom. Saturday mornings I had ballet lessons; I loved ballet and for that reason Saturday mornings. But this morning, standing over a parakeet's grave, aware as of a parallel universe of the need to hurry inside and wash, to get in the car and be driven to the lesson, some ligature inside me gave way, and the curtain between my feelings and all the darkness, death, suffering, and sickness in the world tore open. Like a sharp scent or arctic wind, enormous reasonless sadness rushed me.

I returned to the house and got ready for ballet. For weeks or months thereafter I drew breath with difficulty and dripped tears for no reason anyone could see. I felt sad and utterly alone, and knew deeply and fully I would always be sad, and forever alone.

I was maybe seven years old when this first depression seized me. What seems remarkable now is the way the condition arrived instantaneously and full-blown.

Thereafter, for decades, depression arrived and departed without warning. "Green darkness" was my secret name for this trap door I tripped through sometimes, pitched headfirst and helpless down a deep well with slick walls, no light, and no ladder.

Down there I suffered. Down there I yearned. Where *was* my one and only? Why would not someone come to me and make my hurting stop?

The summer between junior high and high school, the summer puberty took hold—my menses having arrived, finally, that spring—Zefferelli's film of *Romeo and Juliet* enthralled me like a gateway drug. I saw the movie once, and could not quit. All that voluptuous, milky flesh pushed up and steaming at the necklines of stiff-jeweled renaissance velvet and brocade. A palette of dark green shadows, blood-red draperies, and gloomy stone sepulchers in decadent contrast to the arid glare of Verona's streets, teeming with testosterone-charged vendetta. The teenage love I longed for spouted from plump lips, amped up on writhing taut loins, borne skyward on flights of Shakespeare's poetry. Again, and again, I sat alone in the theater, fascinated, stimulated, fed, entrapped, pulled down, and disabled with melancholy.

My mother drove me to the little movie house downtown and must have been handing me the cash for ticket after ticket. At home, between viewings, I could barely speak. I sat and stared, or paced. She suggested I buy the soundtrack, something I was not aware existed. She drove me to the record store, a place I'd not been before. She gave me money for the LP, which I played and replayed for hours, day and night, until I had memorized not just the excerpts of Shakespeare but the exact sequence of dialogue and musical interludes. She meant to help, but I got worse. More and more obsessed, and sick, physically ill in some way I could not shake.

Sometime that summer we made a trip, my mother and I, to visit Sara in Madison, Wisconsin, where she was in graduate school. The year was 1969. In a photo from that visit I am taller than my mother, broad in the hip and thigh as puberty made me, wearing a pair of skin-tight, aqua-colored denim shorts and a white, button-down oxford cloth shirt I remember as a favorite outfit, but which looks pretty awful. Above the stiff collar my face is pale but my cheeks fiery red, as if I am feverish. I remember burning up, feeling fever-hot all that summer. I could not eat, and slept prodigiously. On this trip—much desired because I had never flown on an airplane before and never before left the South—I could not get up from bed to do the sightseeing my sister planned. I could barely talk, barely walk, barely function. I cried and cried, usually alone, but sometimes in front of my mother and Sara; I vaguely remember their worried responses but I never saw a doctor that I can recall. The tears welled up and poured out, for no reason. They could not be assuaged. Sadness sucked all the color from the world, pulling me into that black hole in which there was, at best, a numb nothing—the only possible *something* being pain too awful to bear.

Depression, again. I didn't know it by that name, of course, but I recognized it. It felt worse—deeper, longer-lasting, the suffering more intense—than in my first encounter at age seven. This time, though, I lucked into a savior. A ladder to the light. I met the boy I'll call Hen.

During the fall of my freshman year, I'd been out on three miserably awkward first dates, at my mother's urging. In October some girl I knew in the band said, "You should be Hen's girlfriend; he likes you." I'd never had a boyfriend, and I wanted one. From way down in the dark, glimpsing some possibility of relief, I said to myself not yes, and not no, but *okay*. On the unlit drive home from an away-game I sat down beside Hen, a junior, in the back of the band bus. We made out, I discovered the force of my sexual desire in collision with his, and that was that. Hen became my Romeo.

Just like Juliet, I was fourteen when I found him.

In the shrine room at the Tampa Dzogchen Buddhist Center, much is familiar. My cushion in the shrine room where I sit every Saturday and Sunday morning; a dull strain in my low back, noted and dismissed; and the stinging ache in my hips and knees, a warning I've sat too long and will pay with sharp pain when I get up. The pitted pale surface of walls I helped other sangha members repaint a few years back remains blank except for dusty sets of framed thangkas under mildew-spotted glass. The permanent scent of the place—citrus mold, candle wax, resinous Bhutanese red incense, and dust—envelopes me. Veils of spider web drape the unreachable uppermost corners of the high-ceilinged, rectangular room, once a Cuban dance studio, its still-lustrous hardwood floors a testament to better times in this inner-city neighborhood now gripped by dereliction and violence.

On the other side of the stuccoed cinderblock walls, the unfamiliar howls: a hurricane, the first of four—Charley, Frances, Ivan, and Jeanne—that will maul Florida during the summer of 2004. A Category 4, Charley is the strongest storm to make landfall in Florida in forty years. The wind grates on the roof like a grinder on a stump, the sound a continuous turbine roar punctuated with booms and thumps when the highest-speed gusts punch the building and shake its bricks. Only through thin oblongs of window flush with the ceiling on two walls can I see outdoors: a sky more green than black, and the nearly stripped tops of three palm trees canted hard left. The dirty glass is wet from horizontal rain driven so fast it's invisible until it hits, and the corroded aluminum frames leak humid hot air.

Thumbing beads, counting, sweating in semi-darkness—the power blinked off hours ago—I chant mantra. I work at paying attention to what I'm saying and why, because it's what I'm supposed to do when I pray but also because the effort it takes to concentrate pacifies me. I am grateful to have something to do when there's nothing I can do, waiting out this storm, alone but for my children's cat. Karma cowers silently beneath the several tables that crowd the front of the room, draped in red and heaped with scriptures, candles, and fruit offerings.

My teacher, I reason, would surely approve my motivation—to save the cat's life—if not the result—an animal, food bowls, and a litter box sheltered in a holy space.

My mother made the decision that I should be in the band. Lessons commenced in fifth grade. In some basement room at Thomas Jefferson Elementary, walls enameled and floors tiled with the vile industrial green of all public buildings in those days, I gazed upon the open boxes of beginner instruments. Clarinets, trumpets, and flutes, or drumsticks with practice pads on stands. I chose flute because somebody said clarinet would be easiest to make a sound on, and I didn't want easy, whereas trumpet, when I tried, proved completely impossible to blow.

Band practice in that basement room was not unpleasant. My used, nickel-plated flute pleased me with its complexity of keys and its right-angle position to the rest of the instruments in the room. I pitied the wannabe drummers, whose practice pads gave no noisy satisfaction, for whom rhythm and steadiness had to be all. I knew how to blow on a bottle and make a sound, and once someone explained I must blow across the flute's hole instead of into it, I had an experience of triumph: I'd learned to do something other people found hard. I could already read music, courtesy of the unwanted piano lessons, and playing flute allowed me to forget about the troublesome bass clef along with the mental and physical coordination challenge of playing two clefs at once. I practiced my flute every day and excelled, in a schoolgirl way.

Band was a wholly good thing until high school when my mother insisted I quit ballet to have time for marching practice every afternoon after school in football season. She was not wrong that ballet and band did not mix, but I knew why she really wanted me to quit. I had failed at ballet. Lanky and awkward with weak ankles, I was shy and tense, too. Easily rattled, and ungraceful. I loved everything about ballet—the disciplined movements, the romantic music, the pageantry of the performances—but I never got good parts in the company's recitals; my usual position was the back line of the corps. The ballet mistress disliked me, maybe because my mother aggressively accused her of holding me back.

My mother needed me to be popular. Socially successful. Or, failing that, a credit to her in some public way. We struggled a long time, crying fits on my part, hours of haranguing on hers, and she won. I quit ballet. But I exacted as quid pro quo the cessation of piano lessons, for surely the long hours she wanted me to devote to band precluded daily piano practice just as much as twice weekly ballet classes.

Once all my performance eggs were loaded in a single basket—band, she needed me to achieve and hold onto first chair. I didn't care if I held first, second, or third chair; this much success was in my range. But the annual try-out was agony, and the "challenges," necessary to unseat the rivals who'd placed higher up the line, tormented me, embedded as they were in girl-on-girl emotional vendettas.

Next, maybe because of my fixation on Hen, a fellow band

member, my mother decided I should try out for cheerleader. I refused; the chasm separating an A student like me from cool people with a shot at winning that popularity contest was obvious to me. She countered that I could become a majorette—requiring another tryout, of course, and a skill I did not have, twirling. I didn't want to wear a silly short skirt and prance along in front of the band. I liked my stern, unisex band uniform. I reveled in the precision of marching in formation. When I wanted to show off, I had the piccolo, allowing me to shriek descant during football season. But my mother won this round, too, at least to the extent of enrolling me in twirling classes, taught by a big-haired woman named Sonya, a former local beauty queen who'd been a majorette at a rival high school.

I sucked at twirling. I practiced, outdoors, at dusk, in the drive-way. I enjoyed the sight of the slender silver baton going end over rubber-bulbed end in the sky above my head but I couldn't catch it, and in class, amid popular and confident girls who liked the sequined unitards and gobs of eye makeup required by the obligatory competitions, I was a goon. Sonya made fun of me and encouraged the other girls to join her. The kindest thing she ever said to me was at a twirling competition where, on talent show night, I took part in a spoof on beauty queens. Wearing a polyester drapery from the motel room, hanging by its hooks from my largely unnecessary bra, I preened and vamped and got laughs. I was, very briefly, popular.

Sonya said, "I didn't know you had it in you."

—

The run-down house I own during my single-mom years, two blocks from sea-walled Hillsborough Bay at the fringe of a tony South Tampa neighborhood, stands just seven feet above sea level. Hurricane Charley's storm surge is predicted at fourteen feet. The Dzogchen Buddhist Center lies inland, at near peak elevation for the Tampa Bay area: eighteen feet. Evacuation maps, published each storm season in the local paper, band the peninsular city in concentric uvular zones. Once a hurricane watch turns to twenty-four-hour warning of its imminent arrival, the media announce police-mandated evacuation orders by zone.

When Charley bears down on Tampa in 2004, I've lived in Florida for twelve years. I know the hurricane-preparedness drill. Buy water and batteries *before* the pre-storm run that empties the shelves, sometimes for weeks at a time. Keep gas in your car; keep the Weather Channel on. When the red funnel of projected-path indicates your home lies in the cross-hairs a few days hence, decide whether to stay or to flee. Can you afford to miss several days' work, cancel crucial appointments, and live somewhere else in a motel—all for naught if the storm track shifts? Is there someone within a day's drive who would take you in—for days, weeks, even months if need be? If you wait for the probability of a hit to rise toward certainty, are you willing to risk riding out the storm trapped in a gas-less vehicle on a gridlocked freeway? It's hard to know what to do when the chips are down. It's easy to guess wrong and, no matter what you choose, there are consequences.

When Hen left for college in central North Carolina, three hundred miles from Bristol, I was sixteen. I announced my intention to follow him. I arranged to finish high school early in order to keep our separation down to a single year. I saw him every weekend his parents would allow him home—not a simple drive in those days, especially in winter, as the Appalachian mountains at the Virginia-North Carolina border are the highest peaks in the East, and no interstate highway yet crossed them. Still, "marriage" never figured in my single-minded pursuit of Hen, my first and only high school boyfriend, until my mother brought it up.

I lived with her but was lost to her once I took up with him.

Anytime Hen and I were together with any kind of privacy at all we smoked pot and had sex. The foggy bliss of oxytocin and THC obliterated the past and clouded the future; I abandoned myself so completely it would be twenty-five years before I'd perceive the possibility of an identity separate from the man, or the drug, of my choice.

I took the ACT and the SAT and wrote exactly one college application—to the little no-name institution Hen attended, the only place he'd applied because it accepted him without regard to standardized test scores. He was a math and music savant but because of severe dyslexia he had grave difficulty reading and writing. I received a merit scholarship offer so fat it covered almost the whole tuition, and that, I told my mother, was that. So drunk was I with the success of my plans that her sudden refusal to cooperate stunned me.

First, she lay down the guilt card. In wheedling tones she told me how much she would miss me. How she needed me. How alone she'd be, with my father and her illnesses, if I, who claimed to love her, left her.

When that did not move me, she remarked, causally at first, that it might be better if I stayed right there in Bristol, a good place to live, and attended one of the two girls' schools in town, one of them a junior college she herself had attended decades earlier.

Next, she appealed to the sense of entitlement she'd cultivated in me all my life. I didn't really want to live in a stinky awful crowded uncomfortable dorm room with just any old roommate I might end up with, did I?

When I still didn't bend, she played the family-superiority card. The college Hen was attending had very low standards. Nobody had ever heard of it. I'd never amount to anything if I wasted my talents there. After all, I had once said I'd like to go to the University of Virginia—

Then *why* was she suggesting the hometown schools, which no one in *the world* who wasn't from Bristol had ever heard of? I was just about to graduate from high school as valedictorian, I pointed out to her, and I wasn't going to go to any damn junior college.

Those schools were affordable, she replied, quite reasonably. Especially since I could live at home. With her.

Panic choked me. She *did* have the power to keep me home, a dorm room really did seem unbearable, and Hen's college *was* completely lacking in prestige. The reality of all she said made me wild, spurred me to fight her even though I knew she always, ultimately, won every struggle between us.

"Hen's school is free." My voice rose. "On account of that scholarship they gave me. It's huge."

"That scholarship doesn't pay room and board. And if you think I'll support you to shack up with him, you've got another thing coming."

She had for over two years put up so little interference with my attachment to Hen that I couldn't believe she'd balk now. She let us spend hours alone in the living room, entwined on the couch, making out, and more. She claimed she'd rather have us at home, "safe," than sneaking around and parking up top the aptly named Horner's Hill, an activity from which I was once returned home by the police.

My struggle to get my way played out, in grinding iterations of haranguing, silence, and outbursts in the kitchen—where she spent most of the hours I was home from school and band practice cooking, cleaning, and canning—or in the den—where she tipped back in the recliner watching television or sat upright at her tiny cluttered desk, squinting through her bifocals, paying bills, her back to me. Nervous and restless, I slumped or slouched nearby, biting my nails into the quick. She made me miserable and I couldn't stay away from her; that was the way we were, we two. My father never said a word to me about college nor Hen; I was that completely my mother's daughter.

Eventually, after weeks or maybe months of this, she slapped down her trump card. "If you get married, you can go with him."

I'd spend years of my life viewing that statement as spite, dressed in guile. At the time, I smelled guile because her sudden shift lacked logic—my getting married in no way addressed her concerns about the reputation or the price of the college, nor did it put me nearer to her geographically. But at that moment I mostly registered the yearned-for, unlikely acquiescence. I reeled, as one does when trumped.

"I won't be eighteen," I managed to say. My legal majority, the first station in my official individuation from her, seemed light-years distant from sixteen.

Licking and sealing the envelope she'd just addressed, or briskly stirring biscuit dough, or sealing the lid of a pressure cooker filled with jars of canning tomatoes, she said—her back to me—"I'll sign for you."

I gasped.

I almost choked on heady oxygenation from the powerful draft streaming through the exit door to my life as her satellite. Marriage at seventeen would make me an emancipated minor in the eyes of the law.

"Okay!" I said. "Yes! I'll ask Hen."

All summer and fall my mother canned beans and tomatoes and pickled cucumbers from the garden. She canned, froze, or made jams and jellies from peaches, blackberries, raspberries, and strawberries sought out in bulk at the end of long drives on winding mountain roads to orchards, fields, bogs, and roadside stands that were, for me, way stations amid hours of carsickness. Hundreds of dated and sealed jars stashed behind a curtain on a tier of deep shelves in a back corner of the basement attested to her compulsion. Beneath the deep and dirt-stained ceramic slop sinks in which my father gutted fish, her vinegary vegetable relish called chow-chow pickled in five-gallon crocks. Somewhere beneath some dusty drape in that basement was the enormous and witchy cast iron cauldron in which I'd seen her cook down several bushels of apples over a fire in the backyard, making apple butter the old-fashioned way.

These sweaty storehousing projects overlay her daily and seasonal schedules of housekeeping. Annually, during the years I was young and she was able, she took down every window treatment in the house—several dozen windows layered in 40s-style elaborations: lined draperies or ruffled, tied-back curtains she'd sewn herself, all layered over cotton organdy sheers. I was a teenager before an automatic washer was installed in the kitchen; until then she wrestled sodden curtains, the sheers dripping with bluing, from the three-legged tub washer into the electric mangle. Wash and wring, rinse and wring, then starch, then dry, then iron. And re-hang.

Born in 1910, my mother grew up spending summers on her grandparents' farm, a welcome contrast to her life in town where from the age of eleven she kept house for her abusive father, drove her two younger siblings to school, and nursed her mother, bedridden with permanent nervous breakdown. Early on, she set me to dusting, sweeping, and washing dishes, and I ironed for hours—in those pre-permanent press days, everything from bed linens to my father's boxer shorts. My father, born in 1907, raised on a farm, saw in me an available laborer—as he did in every human being with three or four functioning limbs and enough wit to take direction. By kindergarten age he'd assigned me the job of picking up sticks tossed down from our many shade trees by storms, and not long after, I began weeding, planting potatoes, shelling peas, and picking beans. I started mowing once my head cleared the handles.

My parents' angry, exhausting work obsession frightened and exasperated me. Briars ripped my mother's skin and hammers mashed my father's fingers but they kept on laboring. When my father's big gas-powered chain saw escaped his control and chattered up a log to bite him in the neck, my mother screamed and I felt faint but he staunched the gush with a towel, drove himself to the emergency room, and returned to finish the job bearing a four-inch row of coarse, black cross-stitches. The injury healed into white keloid X's, a Frankenstein scar visible for the rest of his life just inside his shirt collar—unremarkable to him; just one more scar amid his body's dozens—but disturbing to me: how near he'd come to sawing off his own head, and how much the scar made it look as if he had.

I never wanted to work like my parents did. I ran from the example they set: out of the house and into the bushes, up a tree and out on a limb—right into a marriage where I'd work the way they taught me all right-thinking adults did. When Hen and I moved into married student housing in August of 1972, I handled all the cooking, cleaning, laundry, and shopping solo, on a rigorous weekly schedule that emulated my mother's, all while employed at one or two part-time jobs and carrying an overload, twenty hours every semester and a full load every summer, in order to finish in three years and graduate when Hen did.

I never asked Hen to help me with any of this. When he had papers to write, I sometimes wrote them for him. Most days, after lunch, I got high to get some space from the responsibility of him. Afterwards, I got right back to work.

In my experience, running from a monster storm is less possible for very practical reasons, often economic ones, than it sounds on television. People who have ridden out a hurricane on an island—where there is literally no escape route—understand a truth as pragmatic as it is metaphysical: the most realistic response to a hurricane on the horizon may well be to sit tight, stay low, and—if you can—pray hard.

Hurricane Dean struck Bermuda on the night of J's fourth birthday in 1989. I was eight months pregnant with B. We'd lived on the island, expatriates transferred there for my then-husband's job, for less than six weeks, and our family energies during the days preceding the storm centered on the problem of the party J expected when we knew almost no one to invite. Her dad and I cornered some parents at the nursery she attended and begged shamelessly; acquired balloons, ice cream cake, and some hideously messy but exciting craft projects involving paint and glitter; and had almost pulled off the event to her satisfaction when the parents began to arrive early to pick up their children, pointing out with baleful British acerbity that the sky had turned bilious, the wind gusted already above forty knots, and we had maybe two hours to do whatever we were going to do to prepare for the hit.

We lived in a rented house on a cliff on the island's southwest side, the most exposed and most likely place for a hurricane to make landfall. I had lived all my life to that point hundreds of miles from any coast and had only a bookish familiarity with giant sea-storms. I looked at the chaos of paint and glitter, cups and cake, paper and ribbons and glue stuck to the floor, the counters, the kitchen table. I looked at J, contentedly grooming her newest My Little Pony.

I glanced to my husband for help.

And You asked *me* what *I* thought we should do.

I took in my watermelon belly, my sprung navel visible through a thin summer dress, my ankles swollen thick as fence posts. My pelvic floor ached as it did all day every day in the island's soupy heat. I found a roll of masking tape, crisscrossed the windows on the sea side of the house and opened the ones on the lee side, following instructions I'd read in the island's daily paper. I sat down, heavily and with relief, to read to my preschooler her favorite books.

The three of us would spend the next twenty-four hours hunkered down in the spare bedroom on the house's northeast corner, the one most sheltered by the cliff. Minute by minute the world grew smaller, darker, more fetidly humid, and brutishly louder—100-mph gusts set the wrought iron porch rail whining at high pitch and the windows clattered like a never-passing freight train in their aluminum tracks. As the hours slowly elapsed, J shifted from innocently oblivious to agitatedly fretful. Her father and I sank further and further into exhausted, incredulous wakefulness. I kept on reading aloud, turning the pages of *Goodnight Moon* and *A Giant Treasury of Mother Goose*.

I did not pray; I felt no right to petition some distant judgmental being, the God of my Methodist upbringing, to save me and mine from a great force of nature threatening everyone in its path.

But sing-songing familiar words, chanting out rhyme and meter known by heart since childhood—that effort to concentrate gave me something to do, a tether for my whirling mind while we waited and waited to find out if the roof would come off or the windows blow out, if we'd be fine or be injured or die.

When I popped the question to Hen, I said not, "Will you marry me?" but, like the child I still was, "Mama says we can get married, do you want to?"

You'd have been at the wheel of the hand-me-down Oldsmobile Vista Cruiser station wagon we cruised and camped and partied and petted in. Or maybe You were cleaning your trombone, or swigging some of the Coca-Cola we both loved so much. Could be we'd just had sex on the couch in the living room at my house or in your bed, if parents were out of the house.

I remember no setting at all. I remember, in fact, almost nothing about this fateful transaction.

It's possible I posed the question by phone. More probably, I wrote it in a letter; in those days long distance phone calls still cost real money, transacted on Hen's end at a pay phone in the hall of his dorm. Ink was the life line by which I held him tight; I wrote a letter every day. Sometimes—because of his dyslexia he could barely write, much less type—he answered.

I'm sure I felt conflicted bringing up the subject of marriage with Hen; well-versed in romantic novels and movies I knew the question wasn't supposed to come from me. I know I felt, in the aftermath, confused. And deflated.

You never answered either yes or no; this is the one thing I do remember clearly. You were agreeable, usually, to just about anything I suggested—either You liked me to lead or You didn't know how to resist.

You might have said, "Okay."

You might have only nodded.

I wanted more. I wanted more without understanding what that would be. More to push against. Something to lift me. No doubt I launched right away into an elaboration of the plan. The marvel of my mother offering to sign. The dream-come-true of our getting our own apartment—no dorm for me, no restrictions on drug use or sex, plus lots of non-sexual bennies for Hen: "I can help you with school."

I'd already helped him—or managed him—to conscientious objector status with the draft board. Voicing passionate opposition to the Vietnam War, I brought up the issue, and he acquiesced. I did the necessary research, writing letters, in those pre-Internet days, to pacifist draft counselors, Quakers, and clergymen all over the country. I found the names and addresses listed in books, magazines, and on bulletin boards in the public library and Bristol's brand-new head shop. I composed the appeal to the local draft board: letters and an essay appended to a government form. Hen went to the meetings he was summoned to, we gritted our teeth through several months of waiting, and it happened. The moral vision I'd authored prevailed, but all this effort ended up moot due to simple random chance. His birth year, 1953, was the last year subject to the draft by lottery, and his number was just high enough to miss the small draw taken that year—1971.

I haven't any memory of what I wrote in the pages he signed, other than that killing was wrong. I recall being lightly and occasionally troubled by the idea that successful C.O. status, in the instance he were drafted, would put him in the war and on the battlefield without a weapon.

Mostly, I didn't consider what Hen's life meant to him. Mostly I was caught up by the sense of mission the project conferred on me. The details, the timeline, the dire necessity of succeeding, all lifted me clear of myself, helped me feel successful and important—even though my real motive—anyone except me could see it—was not to preserve life but simply to hold on to what I felt certain I could not live without.

During our triumvirate years, my children keep a wary distance from my devotion to Buddhism. They are not oblivious; they simply decline to get involved. They sleep in on weekend mornings when I go to the Dzogchen Buddhist Center to chant prayers. They stay at their dad's on the infrequent occasions when I go to my teacher's properties to retreat. They allow me to tell them how I think the conflicts and problems they bring me should be handled from within a Buddhist view. B does not comment. J says, once, "I don't want to have to be that good."

I wonder if my commitment to participating in Buddhist practice makes me a good mother or a slack one. After all, I leave my children home alone all morning every weekend. I've given up drugs, depressive anhedonia, and suicidal ideation, but isn't it possible I've replaced those addictions with a new one: all those mantra, and adherence to the teacher's instructions?

A goal of Buddhist practice, a long-term practitioner will one day tell me, is to have no habits. Just clarity—awareness—about the way things really are. But until that goal is obtained, bad habits—deluded ways of seeing and being—obstruct clarity, and the antidote to bad habits is good habits.

This makes perfect sense to me. I need habits. I need to *know* what to *do* to be *good* or at least better. I need a ladder—a one-next-thing-to-do rung to reach for when I don't know what to do and barely have the strength to try. Buddhist practice provides that; it's that simple, for me. But to others it looks strange. I know it does.

At the end of some ordinary Saturday outing to the beach years ago with my children, a friend of mine, and her son, a departing tourist we encountered on the way to the parking lot offered B and the other boy two big bag of sand dollars. B was ten or so, skinny, crew-cut, and unmistakably earnest; the tourist no doubt saw in him a boy who'd value the prize he himself had reluctantly to give up in order to fly home. But the sand dollars had been collected from the warm Gulf waters, not the shore; they were still alive. Inside the five radiating slits that give them their distinctive star-like beauty when dead and bleached bone-white, the tiny feathers of the creatures' gills trembled, seeking water and oxygen.

When a bag of the sea creatures was placed in his hands, B ran full speed back to the surf and dumped them into the water, attempting to save their lives before it was too late. Everyone present—including B's young friend, holding on to his bagful—just stared, aghast with either incomprehension or umbrage.

I felt both poles of judgment and wavered between them: the Buddhist force of my son's wish to preserve life, and my old familiar shame—this time for complicity in my child's failure to meet the expectations of two friends and a stranger.

~

I spent my entire senior year of high school, Hen's freshman year at college, planning our wedding, on a small budget and with infinite attention to every detail—the music, the flowers, the engraved invitations. I convinced the youthful associate minister at the Methodist church to allow into the traditional ceremony my recitation of Desiderata and some other improvements of my design. I required Hen to recruit ushers matched by height to my chosen bridesmaids, and I sewed their dresses myself on the fancy new sewing machine (with zigzag setting!) my mother awarded me as early high school graduation present.

I stitched up my dream bridal gown, too, using a complex Vogue pattern instead of the Simplicity or McCall's I was used to. The look I sought was hippie-faux-medieval, in homage to the last days of the Age of Aquarius and my Romeo and Juliet obsession. The romantic style turned out to be grossly unsuited to the conventional and economical fabric my mother steered me to purchase from a remnant table: translucent white organza. The pattern featured long, fitted sleeves gathered into a banded puff at the shoulder, a square neck, empire waist, and a three-tiered skirt with no train. Rendered in lush velvet or brocade the result might have been elegant, but the unadorned organza—thin and stiff, slippery, fragile, subject to puckering if the thread tension deviated the slightest degree from optimum, each strike of the needle bursting its tight weave and opening a tiny hole thread would not quite close—was rendered lusterless by the thick white polyester underskirt modesty required. I tried dressing up the dress by bordering the bodice and each juncture of the skirt tiers with wide white cotton lace my mother and I both thought pricey at nearly two dollars a yard.

The cost of the dress before I added the lace was eight dollars. The completed gown puzzled me; the intersection of my resources, my skills, and my wishes ended up nowhere near as thrilling as I'd imagined. The dress was uncomfortable, too; it prickled my arms at the tight band and creased permanently at the elbow the first time I tried it on. My veil, however, pleased me mightily. My mother allowed one splurge, a ready-made lace cap that cupped the back of my skull in an appropriately Juliet-as-envisioned-by-Zefferelli manner. I attached to it several yards of tulle exotically labeled "French illusion," which I bordered, laboriously and inexpertly, in fake seed pearls.

I dressed Hen—who resembled James Taylor, young and dark and folksy in 1972—like the male escort of my renaissance-rock-fair fantasy. Black tux, rented, with a royal blue shirt, purchased at the head shop. This shirt was disappointingly prosaic as to fabric (cotton), but suitably romantic in cut (a densely ruffled front and cuffs). The color complimented Hen's eyes and set off to perfection his straight, shoulder-length black hair, worn center-parted, and his dashing, down-curved dark mustache.

You, spun by me into the spitting image of a dream: Sweet Baby James.

After sitting on Bermuda for twenty-four hours, Hurricane Dean, a Category 1 storm, lumbered off to sea, leaving the island slick with a mash of pulverized leaves and salt water. The power stayed off for over a week; we had no lights, no air conditioning or refrigeration, and only buckets to draw water from our cistern to bathe and flush. Miserable conditions for an enormously pregnant woman alone all day with a small child, but not oppressive enough, not really, to justify the rage I choked on long after those conditions were relieved.

The second time a hurricane drew a bead on Bermuda during our three-year sojourn there, my children's father was off the island on business. By that time we'd weathered several false alarms: dire warnings cancelled when the hurricane abruptly dissipated or changed course.

He phoned me from London—an unusual gesture at that point in our chilly association—to ask if I wanted him to come home because of the storm. Fury boiled up my throat like vomit; the island's airport had already closed, and I knew he knew that. Whatever was going to happen, I'd be on my own with it.

"I don't see how you could get here," I said tartly.

He agreed it was in fact impossible to get home. Bitterly I asked why he offered help he could not provide. He had no answer for that, and because of the safe transatlantic distance between us I didn't stop myself from saying out loud the undecorated truth of our position: "It will hit us or it won't."

From Bermuda his employer relocated us to Tampa, where for fourteen years, married and divorcing and single, I'd weather many a tropical storm and tropical storm warning, along with some destructive and unannounced winter gales. Each year I spent August through October, the peak hurricane months, grinding my teeth. Addicted to weather reports, pushing at the calendar to turn its pages faster, furious that geography and life circumstance I saw as *his* fault made *me* a sitting duck for the random possibility of destruction.

And yet, Dean in Bermuda, the storm he and I weathered together, would turn out to be my one and only hurricane—until the "Four of '04" hit Florida, long after we split up.

On the way to realizing my teen dream, the perfect wedding on a perfect June day to my perfect one-and-only You, I experienced a single and singular bad omen. In the photographer's studio a few days before the ceremony, near the conclusion of a long session of formal portraiture beneath banks of blazing lights, I fainted. My knees buckled; I hit the floor before I understood anything was happening. I'd never fainted before, and failed to take warning from a sudden shock of nausea followed by inky dark pouring in from the periphery of my vision, narrowing my focus like the aperture of a shutter abruptly twisting shut. I simply dropped.

Afterwards, seated in the bathroom, having my face mopped by the photographer's nervous assistant, I felt too sick and weak to be embarrassed by the scene I'd created. Numbly, distractedly, I resented the determination of the photographer to proceed, as he insisted on seating the two of us on a white satin bench, my bowed back propped against Hen's blue-ruffled chest. The quiescence with which I slumped there—in the photos that survive I am wan as a fairytale princess not quite released from enchantment, too ill to squirm, no longer even attempting a smile—carried me right through the ceremony.

Neither feeling nor thinking, I would execute perfectly the script I created.

Buddhists take refuge in the Three Jewels: Buddha, Dharma, and Sangha—the teacher, the teaching, and the community of accomplished practitioners. Sometimes it is said that the Buddha is the doctor, the Dharma the medicine, and the Sangha the nurse.

In essence, "taking refuge" is conscious recognition that death is inevitable and its timing unpredictable, and that nothing worldly offers any shelter from that truth.

The various traditions have formal ceremonies for accomplishing the taking of refuge, but I never participated in one. Instead, I stumbled into Buddhist practice in the early days of my divorce, through the odd luck of my divorcing husband's unintended steer.

Searching everything I left behind for clues as to how I could finally say no to him, he came across the books and magazines in which I'd underlined and starred and circled Buddhist views that spoke to me. It was he who somehow found the Tampa Dzogchen Buddhist Center and took some solace there; weeks later he went abroad and asked me to take our children to the Center's Sunday morning sessions. I did, and immediately, helplessly took refuge, even though I had no idea that was what I was doing. Despite the strangeness of the place, the people, and the prayers, I felt the possibility of finding balance there the moment I stepped through the door.

First the children and then their father stopped attending but I returned and returned because only the effort I devoted to speaking prayers gave me one single instant of calm. Our divorce was my fault; everybody, including me, thought so. The financial and physical terror that resulted, I deserved. I'd provoked it with my desperate need to breathe. The enormity of blame I had to shoulder was so great I wanted only to escape it by any means possible, but I had children to care for. I had to keep on keeping on. The cushion, the mantra, each weekend's scheduled sessions of practice, these were the rungs of the only ladder I could see. I seized it and climbed. One foot in front of the other, hour after hour.

I spoke the chants haltingly at first. My tongue would not form such foreign sounds easily. *Om Ah Hung. Om Mani Peme Hung.* I couldn't keep up with the blistering pace set by those with long hours of practice behind them. And the rituals—Tibetan Buddhism is full of smells and bells—baffled me. But I persevered.

For ten years—struggling to stay afloat with an ever-shifting mix of part-time and occasionally full-time teaching, writing and editing, child support, a few years' alimony, gifts from my mother and then an inheritance after her death—I kept coming to the Center, sitting down, and chanting, twice and sometimes three times a week. I made a shrine room in my house and sat there on my cushion for two hours or more every day without fail. Sometimes while I did all this my heart raced and tears coursed down my face. Once in a while I felt the dawning of a measure of acceptance about the disaster I was caught in.

At home and often at the Center, I chanted alone. Among the sangha members, large and small dramas erupted; some people left for good, others came and went in accordance with the rise and fall of their ambivalence. Spiritual tourists drifted in, sat awhile, asked questions, grew impatient with answers that suggested right effort is as good as it gets, and drifted elsewhere in pursuit of more abundant bliss. The teacher was almost always absent, at other centers or in India, sometimes for a year or more.

I kept at it because I vowed daily that I would but mostly because the self-imposed requirement to do the practice daily gave me something to do and someone—my own mind's calmly abiding awareness—to keep me company. Sitting and singing prayers tethered my mind while the pages of my life turned and I waited to find out if the storm that had seized me would ever let up.

~

When I was still a newbie volunteer at the safe house for battered women in upstate New York—and not yet a mother—the director sent me, because no one else was available that day, on a salvage mission. A woman who'd run away from a beating and a gun needed a ride back to the home she'd shared with her abuser to pick up her things. The law, public awareness, and the attitude of police departments toward domestic violence as a criminal rather than a family matter was still forming in the early eighties, and activists—resources for victims were not yet the province of social services departments—had learned the hard way what could go wrong. The director gave me careful instructions. Call the local police before driving to the woman's home, and ask them to meet us there—to observe that we observed the law, and as deterrence in case the abuser, who was supposed to be at work, got a tip from a friend or neighbor and showed up armed and angry. Stay in the car, no matter what, while the woman went in for her things, so that no one, including she, might later allege that I'd committed a burglary. Tell the woman to hurry, and remind her that if she insisted on rescuing a pet, we'd have to take it to a vet who'd agreed to provide temporary safe haven for non-human victims.

I don't remember the season. It presents in my mind as leafless, wet, gray and cold. I head up the Taconic Parkway—narrow, winding and slick, walled in by stones and naked trees—driving a beater belonging to the shelter. The trip takes an eternity and is conducted in rigid silence. My passenger is terrified and so am I, a fact that shames me. I also feel very brave, almost heroic, and this inappropriate, un-squelchable self-importance further shames me. I'm afraid, too, that I'll turn out to have been terminally stupid: I've been unable to bring myself to phone the police in the hamlet where the woman lives. I cannot bear to push myself that much into the faces of authority; I've heard many stories about the response of rural cops to the kind of uppity woman I'm pretending to be.

I pull up in front of the house, a sagging, wood-frame bungalow on a steeply pitched lot above a lichened granite retaining wall. The car idles roughly while I clutch the wheel, sweat, and scan 360 degrees repeatedly. This mission takes place long before ordinary people had mobile phones, so if we encounter trouble, I've no recourse but to stamp on the accelerator, or duck. When I am almost beyond my ability to bear this waiting, the woman—younger than me by a half-dozen years, lank-haired, her face puffed, one eye blacked, her cheekbone scabbed and stitched—reappears on the porch above me. In each hand she clasps a giant, distended garbage bag. She lumbers down the steps awkwardly encumbered by the load; I fight the urge to get out and help her. Back up the steps she scampers, and down she comes again with another bag and a cat.

"That's it?" I ask.

"That's it."

Her luggage, the three bulging black plastic sacks, fills up the back seat. Her cat in its carrier sits in her lap. I press the accelerator; her escape is complete.

I'm proud of her and I say so. I'm ashamed of how relieved I am the mission is accomplished without any gunplay, and I am offended to the depths of my middle-class soul that all she'll carry forward from her old life to her new is stuffed into garbage sacks. I'm also frustrated about the cat (and angry at myself for that lack of charity); I don't know where the volunteer vet is located and by the time I find out and make that drop-off I'll be in danger of arriving home late myself, something that may trigger my husband's dangerous anger. I complete the mission, doing everything that's required because I've said I would. The woman seems more depressed than grateful but I drive home feeling exhilarated and—to myself I admit this—definitely heroic. I have made a difference, and to do so I've faced down one moment of my own complex fear.

One week later I return to the shelter on my appointed day to volunteer. The woman I think of as my rescuee is not there. When I ask about her, one of the other residents tells me flatly that she's gone home, back to the guy who beat her bloody and threatened to kill her. He sent flowers, my informant says with only a touch of irony, so she forgave him.

He sent her flowers, at the *secret* safe house. He knew where she was. That meant she'd told him. She chose to go back: that habit of being caught just too hard to break.

In a picture I snapped of my parents in their eighties—ringside at one of those bonfires my kids loved so much—they are seated in a pair of metal lawn chairs likely almost as old as their marriage and shellacked with many layers of the silvery aluminum paint my father must have bought wholesale, in quantity. He looks at me wielding the camera, but her eyes are fixed on him. Her walker is in view just behind her, as are a row of those gloomy, shaggy hemlocks.

When I ended up divorced not once but twice, I quipped that my parents' long miserable union—"sixty-seven wedlocked years," I termed it—was the best encouragement anyone could ever have had to end a bad marriage. I knew by that point that he bullied her when no one else was around. She'd confessed to me by then the real source of her broken wrist. But I knew him to be bullied, too—relentlessly verbally abused by her. I thought, frankly, they deserved each other. All the years I knew them as a couple, she missed no opportunity to remind him and anyone else who'd listen how he was a shit. A liar with no taste, no culture, and nothing to give her but trouble.

After they were both dead, another photograph from another time in their union came into my hands. A black-and-white from the forties, the two of them posed side by side at the front steps of their newly completed home. The house is a bald box, one window each side of the door and a little brick chimney like a stem up top, exactly the way a first grader might draw it. To get the whole house into the frame of a simple fixed-lens camera, the unknown photographer has had to step way, way back. A broad expanse of foreshortened, utterly naked lawn dominates the composition, and my parents are minus-cule, standing straight as soldiers at attention squarely in front of their front door, adorned with a Christmas wreath. They're dressed to the nines. She wears heels, a cloche hat, and a fur stole over her coat. His overcoat is folded on his arm, revealing his nice tailored suit, white dress shirt and wide tie. The smart fedora on his head is the one detail of this picture that is completely familiar to me; until he turned to bill caps in retirement, he wore grey felt fedoras everywhere, long after they'd become anachronism.

In my snapshot from their final married years I've filled up the frame with their lumpy bodies and fallen features. My mother gazes at my father with frank distaste. Beneath his bill cap's brim his expression harbors a subtle smile, as if he's aware of something she and I are not. This effect is purely illusion, I know. The slight compression of his lips is due to the absence of his teeth, left behind in the house in a jar on a shelf above the kitchen sink.

When the minister gives us the cue, Hen and I kiss. The organist, my childhood piano teacher Miss Henley, launches with professional gusto into Purcell's Trumpet Voluntary in D, my choice for the recessional. Together Hen and I turn to face the people packing the burnished pews of the chapel, the smaller, warmer, and less bland of the two sanctuaries inside the enormous, plain-vanilla Methodist church I've attended since pre-school, and the full reality of what we've done, what *I* have done, strikes me like a punch to the kidneys.

Hen and I are *married*.

Till death do us part.

The blow emanates from the happy expressions on the ordinary faces facing me: the-not-particularly-attractive but gussied-up and sweating, pink and overweight and acne-pocked faces of people I've known all my life. I've directed the whole force of my being since kindergarten toward escaping these people and their ways—I am, after all, as my mother has insisted as long as I can remember, smarter, prettier, and better mannered than anybody else in town. Now they smile at me with goodwill because I've joined them. I am married, locked down into hometown culture at seventeen, barely one step ahead of the majority of my high school classmates who'll do the same thing at eighteen or nineteen, and right in stride with those who've married as minors because they are pregnant. I stretch my mouth into a wide, frightened, insincere smile and take the arm Hen offers.

Up the aisle we strode, the organ's enthusiasm rushing us like a tailwind toward the door, Hen's Vista Cruiser, the reception in my mother's flower garden, and the opening act of the "ever after" I had never even attempted to imagine but could now, my back to the altar, foresee in Technicolor. I'd go on doing exactly what I'd hated most about my existence to this point: attempting to placate my mother while striving to get what I wanted, whatever that was, from her and now from Hen as well—an affable but passive nineteen-year-old.

The shock of so much sudden clarity was akin to fainting. At the reception I made conversation with difficulty, writhing about the fuss being made over me, all these people pretending I'd not made a terrible mistake. My mother's face was thundery, and I worried obsessively that one of my friends or Hen's would do something—spill grape juice, leave a watermark on a table, say the wrong thing or anything at all —and ignite the wrath—explosive inside You, Mother, and cancerous inside *me*—invisible to anyone but You and me, spilling through our tangled veins like toxin.

I sipped punch, nibbled cake, and smiled, poisonous and betrayed.

My mother told me I'd better marry, so I said I would. She threatened repeatedly on my way to the altar to renege, so I took a stand; I refused to let her stop me. By my wedding day I'd shown us both who was the boss of me.

Her fault. My fault. I couldn't tell the difference.

I hated You because I hated me.

Praying my way through a hurricane nine years into my Buddhist commitment, I understand clearly that I am practicing being okay with what is, no matter how I feel about it. Again and again, I lead my wandering attention back to the attempt to make peace with *nothing I can do* except observe my own mind. *See own mistake*, my teacher has so often admonished. My heart gallumps, my stomach knots, the wind-engine outside grinds and thumps and shrieks, never letting up. Eventually I am so exhausted and bored and physically uncomfortable from the stuffy heat and the posture of sitting that I have no energy to feel fear.

I eat from time to time; I've brought fruit and peanut butter and bread from home. I feed Karma, change her water, and scoop the litter box each time she uses as if that lessened the offense of its presence in a temple. I turn on the radio at judicious, battery-conserving intervals hoping to hear that Hurricane Charley is leaving town. For a long time, there is no news. The authorities are battened down in shelters like everyone else; communications towers and power lines are down; neither news nor news gatherers are traveling. The telephone land lines, because they are buried, never go out, so I call my children at their father's house, across town on the sheltered, lee side of this storm. They are restless and hot, but okay.

Later my teacher phones me from her home in New Jersey. I am surprised and delighted; I've asked permission to ride out the storm in the Center but did not expect individual notice of my situation. She issues instructions—which prayers, and how many—in her familiar rapid-fire idiosyncratic English. She does not promise to save me nor tell me I'll be fine, since no one could guarantee that. She wishes me good luck. I feel guilty that I do not tell her I've brought Karma with me, and I feel comforted, too. I know what her "good luck" means: she sincerely wishes that I will indeed be fine, and for the meantime she's given me what she can to help with that: a reminder to stay focused, remain calm, and repeat the prayers that aspire to beneficent outcome for all sentient beings.

During the darkest nighttime hours, I lie down on the sleeping bag I've brought and try without much success to sleep. The wind and rain never stop. The damp dark that presses my eyelids is anxiety that also does not let up. When a weak daylight returns, I sit up, sweaty, bleary-eyed and aching in every joint; I am much too old to sleep on the floor. Right effort at prayer is much harder this second day; I want so much to go home. Assuming home is still standing. The air in the Center is stale and hot. The pages I turn are limp. By late morning, I decide—judging by the sound of the wind—that its speed is diminishing. The light at the narrow windows seems less green, too. Abruptly I lose patience with the attempt to be patient. I fling aside the effort to concentrate and give in to irritable striving to make things go my way. I want to get on with living since death is not, after all, happening today.

I ease the back door open a few inches, less worried about the weather on the other side now than the people I might encounter. The neighborhood surrounding the Center is a blasted place the well-off drive through fast, refuge to crack houses, registered sex offenders, the mentally-ill homeless, and the truly desperate poor. Anything remotely pawn-able left visible in a car parked in the Center's sandy lot invites a smashed window or punched out lock, and I once answered a knock on the front door to find two big boys with baseball bats; they turned away without comment when I told them they were visiting a church. This time what greets me is a cloudy but clearing sky streaked with innocent blue, and an astonishing number of lid-less trash cans rolling loose in the street. A gusty, sodden breeze pushes at my face. The air smells of salt and bruised vegetation. Door step, sidewalk, and pavement all wear a slip of pulverized palm fronds, live-oak leaves, and sand. A decoupage of paper and plastic litter pastes the sagging picket fence dividing the Center from the decaying bungalow next door.

The couple who live there sit on their porch stairs smoking cigarettes. The man, barefoot and florid in a dirty undershirt, low-slung boxers, and the thick gold chain of an alpha thug, calls out a friendly hello. The woman, usually stone-faced and occasionally visibly battered, watches him impassively. Usually my neighbor eyes me coldly as I enter and exit the Center, and because I respect his hostility— sangha members' cars, clothes, and skin color cannot but make us either marks or antagonists in the eyes of this neighborhood's disadvantaged denizens—I usually make my way from outside to inside in the urban safe-passage mode: brisk steps, alert demeanor, and no eye contact. But this morning this normally sullen man with no prospects is glad to be alive, just like me. Spared by a killer storm on account of what he must feel is his very own good luck, he's enjoying life. Feeling likewise, I meet his expansiveness with some of my own. I smile and ask if he's come through the storm all right, and he asks me if I've got enough bottled water, because he's just heard on the radio that we're supposed to boil what comes out of the tap. I thank him for the news and wish him more good luck. I load my parcels and my cat into my car and drive home slowly through deserted streets that look just like the movie aftermath of natural disaster: standing water, uprooted trees, and runaway shopping carts blocking the city thoroughfares; chunks of roof, broken drywall, and wind-tossed lawn furniture making obstacle courses of the residential lanes.

Charley, a compact, fast-moving storm, predicted to strike Tampa dead-on on Friday the 13th of August with 150 mph winds and storm surge that would put downtown under fourteen feet of water, has veered south a mere one hundred miles, at the very last moment, to flatten and flood the retirement community of Punta Gorda. My luck is good. Theirs is not.

I understand I have learned something from what did not happen—although I have no words to label it. I know I ought to be ready to start my life over, with greater clarity and resolve. I have, after all, taken refuge and been spared. But all I really feel is wonder: my own open-ended amazement about how much we can't predict, how surprising life is, what happens to us, and what does not.

One night in the yearning years I dream of a bone-thin man, barely clothed in rags, poling a disintegrating raft through deep, unbounded sea. His plight is hopeless. Gaunt already, every rib visible, he has no water, no provisions, and no shelter from the sun. Surely the force of his emaciated arms applied to that frail, bending cane, swallowed almost to the hilt by each ocean swell, cannot possibly propel him more than inches with each effort. He is You, V.T.—inside the dream I know this with strange certainty—making your way to the place You will find me.

From a different angle, a longer view, I discern that the sea You pole yourself across is inland. Wholly contained in a vaulted, flesh-pink cavern. Stalactites and stalagmites are everywhere, as rosy as tonsils. Somehow present also are my teacher and her teacher, their faces benign, their calm reassuring.

~

Midnight on New Year's Eve, 1973 turning 1974, I stood in an open window on the top floor of a small hotel in Heidelberg, Germany, assessing whether and how to kill myself. The window stretched floor to ceiling, as I recall: French doors, flung wide, with long dusty curtains swept aside to let in the frigid, gusting night air and a cacophony of pealing church bells. In the room behind me were some number of my college student companions—I have no memory of how many or which ones—on this winter-break junket to Europe.

My boy husband Hen must have been among them. It's inarguable that much hashish was being smoked to see in the New Year. We'd all been toking as often as possible for five or six days, ever since some daredevil cool-fool among us scored big in our port of entry, Amsterdam. I was eighteen, almost nineteen, a stoner among stoners to whom I had no other connection. I'd had great affection since high school for any form of downer drug but I'd never had hash before this trip, and instantly became enamored of the aromatic honey taste on my palate, and the sticky-sweet resinous smoke in my hair, and the languorous drone to which it reduced my twitchy consciousness. But by New Year's Eve I'd had so much I couldn't take any more. All I wanted was oblivion. As doped up on Baudelaire and Jim Morrison as on hashish, I summoned death to take me. Shut me up, just please oh please shut me down in orgasmic, obliterating, pain-ending embrace.

Problem was, the top floor of the small hotel was the third floor, and I was not too stoned to reckon carefully whether the fall would be fatal. I looked straight down at the ink-black pavement: insufficiently far away. I leaned out, bowing slightly into the burning cold, and felt a swell of glacial joy almost take me, the way the big waves threatened to, too far from the shore at Cape Hatteras. The wild Dionysian clanging of the church bells—only once before in my life had I heard real bells in real belfries—urged me to cast aside reason, and fling myself freely toward divinity and insanity. With wind searing my skin and delirium budding in my brain cells I could believe that no difference, no boundary, existed between the pain that threatened to burst me and the sensory chaos of the night that beckoned.

I stepped closer to the edge and lifted one foot off the sill. I gazed down again, torn, uncertain, assessing. The drop was just not that far. I visualized my broken body on the pavement below: alive, bleeding, hurting. I did not want to hurt more than I already hurt. I imagined angry, upset people staring at me, shouting at me, handling me. Fear flooded me. Fear of pain, fear of death, and fear of the pain of more shame. I would be sent home from college, maybe locked up in an institution, certainly subjected to my mother's judgment and blame. I would be, very publicly, what she had taught me most to fear becoming: a public failure and embarrassment. Scraped from the street in a foreign city, shipped home with much fanfare and injuries, maybe even lasting disabilities that might place me, indefinitely, inside her control.

No drama came down that midnight in Heidelberg, except the crying jag into which I fell when I closed the window and sagged into some chair. I cried myself sick, without explaining why, and everybody who knew me was quite used to that.

~

When I officially became a serious writer, an MFA student at the age of thirty-nine, I announced myself to my peers in workshop with what I thought of as a powerful display of passion and creativity.

I gave my character my own first name, the one engraved on my kindergarten loving cup and repudiated in first grade. I made this character blond (because I wasn't) and richer and more privileged than me. I let her live in Greenwich, Connecticut, where I'd once house-sat for old money. I gave her the ability to play the piano pretty damn well, so she could be better than me in that way, too. But I let her mother be the real pianist, maintaining a balance of power I understood in my cells.

I gave my character my entire accumulation of depression, self-hate, and self-pity. I made her a victim of her husband's ego, and of her only child's over-nurtured dependence. I laid her out on her back beneath her mother's baby grand Steinway in the glass-walled living room of a beautiful and expensive home, paid for by her husband's commitment to his job, situated on a large and handsome acreage of hardwoods decked in gorgeous fall foliage. I put on her stereo Pachelbel's Canon in D, familiar to me from the soundtrack of the suicide film *Ordinary People*, and I opened her veins.

I accomplished all this on pages one through five of the manuscript I submitted to my workshop for discussion. Writing this scene, I exorcised something. I felt better for having done so.

My workshop peers performed on me an intervention that is sometimes necessary and sometimes merely a committee's reflex to Apply The Rule. You cannot, they told me, kill somebody on page one and expect your reader to care about that character. Big drama presented too soon grabs at emotions that don't yet exist.

They existed for *me,* of course, those intense feelings I tried to write. But even at nearly forty, I couldn't tell the difference between my emotions and other people. I'd lived in blind, solitary enclosure with my feelings so long—depended for so long on nothing but my keen ability to *feel* my loss and loneliness—that the derision of people I thought I was one of left me gasping with shock.

When the workshop was over I sat by myself in the hall, no doubt whiter than a blood-drained corpse. My newly-assigned writing mentor happened by, took notice, and asked if I need to talk. I shook my head hard. Later, though, I told him in short-short form what had happened. "Ah," he said, nodding sadly.

My actual near-suicide in Heidelberg, it's not something I have talked about. I'd failed to really try. I was gutless. That embarrasses me.

My teen marriage to Hen is another thing I haven't talked—or written—about. The whole relationship was a mistake I edited out of my official backstory, never mentioning it when summing up my personal history for new friends. I didn't tell my children, either. When B found out, from his dad, somewhere in his mid-elementary years, he was terribly shocked—what other secrets might I be keeping? It may have been his distress that first impelled me toward awareness of how much I habitually hid from myself and others.

The facts are these: there are many behaviors from the drug-addled depression-dogged three-and-a-half years of my first marriage of which I remain bitterly ashamed. There were other half-ass attempts at suicide, too. I wanted not death but relief—from the intractable pain of clinical depression. I wanted Hen's attention, or *somebody's,* to make me stop hurting. One day I swallowed about half a bottle of an over-the-counter sleep-aid. When I felt sick and strange, I got scared. I walked the half-mile to the building where Hen was attending an upper-level math class. I sat on the hard tile floor beside the open classroom door, my back pressed to cold cinderblocks, crying quietly and listening to the professor's voice rise and fall. I was too polite and too ashamed to even think about interrupting class. When I couldn't stand to wait anymore I walked the half-mile back to our little rented house on the shore of the campus duck pond. I lay down on the couch and waited to die. I didn't. Hen came home and was not sympathetic but he did act responsibly; he got us an appointment with an off-campus counselor recommended by student health.

We went together to the counselor. I told my story. The counselor turned out to be a Baptist minister. He talked to me about our savior's suffering. He told me to pick up my cross and bear it. Although I'd given up on religion when I took up sex at puberty, I had at age twelve earnestly absorbed Methodist doctrine in a series of confirmation classes, joined the church, experienced a sort of emotional vision of Jesus's goodness, and set out to be a good Christian. The minister-counselor's admonition struck in me a deeply engrained chord: my *fault*. My misery was my mistake to fix. I resolved to do as the man said, tried ardently, and failed.

Hen and I completed our bachelor's degrees and entered graduate school at a state university. The depression got blacker. I couldn't breathe, couldn't eat, couldn't stop crying. The recurrent impulse to accelerate my car off a bridge or into the concrete pillar of an overpass finally landed me in real therapy for the first time.

That and anti-depressants helped me leave the marriage. I was twenty. I dropped out of grad school and took a job for $125 a week as an untrained secretary for three recently graduated and barely solvent attorneys, one of whom would sexually harass me at the office and, when I finally agreed to a supposedly compensatory dinner at his house, drug and rape me. I lay pinned beneath this ugly and obese man on his couch while he did his quick, dirty business. During and afterwards, I hated him but despised myself. *My fault,* not just the stupid naïveté that put me in his clutches, but the fear and drug-induced paralysis that blanked my will to fight back, that made me easy prey.

My divorce from Hen was simple; we had no assets and no children and no fight left in us; our puppy love had long since run its course. I typed up the papers myself at work, and the one woman among my employers, sympathetic to my plight, filed them for me at no charge.

What wasn't simple were my feelings. The mistake I'd discovered at the altar and hidden for four years was now nakedly public. I was a failure everyone could see. To stay alive thereafter was almost impossible. I clung to therapy, the therapist, anti-depressants, Valium, and pot.

You sold me out for spite, Mama. In years of twice-weekly therapy, that's the blame I pieced together to explain the humiliating fact of marriage at seventeen and divorce at twenty-one.

You knew you'd lost me, so You made sure I lost, too.

During the last years of my mother's life, when I brought my children to visit every six months or so, I understood that she was in genuine danger from my father. I knew she feared him even while—and maybe because—she continued to abuse him verbally and emotionally. Once she began to confess her terrors—the broken wrist, and his threat to shoot her and himself—she told more of it every time I visited. I coached her on the law and psychology of domestic violence; I called the local women's shelter and had them visit her; I taped the hotline number to the bottom of the phone and made her promise, over and over again, to use it.

By this time I'd had more training and more experience; I was volunteering weekly at a domestic violence shelter in Tampa answering hotline calls, and I recognized her situation clearly. I knew she'd never call for help, and I knew she'd never leave my father. I understood he might kill her. What I didn't know about and never considered—an extension, I suppose, of a child's willed blindness to parents' life in the bedroom—was the sexual violence.

The fact that he regularly raped her became public through the intervention of the nursing staff at the assisted living facility where they ended up after her broken hip finally forced them to leave that house where they'd been so long enclosed together. I will never know whether the fall that broke the hip was a genuine accident or not. But there's no doubt about the non-consensual sex. One night, during a routine bed check, he was caught in the act. My mother was eighty-nine, incontinent, and crippled—her hip, despite surgery and painful physical therapy, never fully healed.

Fifteen years had passed since I first volunteered in the battered women's shelter movement. Public attitudes and the law on domestic violence had evolved. A social worker arrived to tutor my mother on her legal right to refuse sex, and my father was removed, very much against his will, to an adjoining room. Every night the door between them was locked with a deadbolt, to enforce my mother's right, since she—despite spewing all that vitriol at him for all those years—could not speak up for herself in this matter. My sister Sara and I, reeling from the revelation delivered by phone, were called in by the facility's management, like parents summoned to the principal's office, to receive fair warning of our father's possible future expulsion.

Seated on a floral couch in the formal parlor, stewing in guilt and amazement—why hadn't I guessed? What could I have done to prevent it? How could he be capable of such a thing, morally *or* physically?—I watched my ninety-two-year-old father be admonished by a policeman less than one-third his age that "no means no." My father's demeanor was defiant, defensive, humiliated—exactly like an adolescent called on the carpet—but he was also uncomprehending. He'd have clocked that young pup of a cop if the man hadn't been wearing a badge and a gun; I know my father wanted to shout out what was, as he understood it, the truth: "She never says no."

I knew enough of his family history by this point to guess that most of the emotional connections in his life had been forced. He'd been required, with fists and a belt, to respect a distant, imperious father, and driven by guilt and manipulation to attend to his mother's complaints. Pigs, slopped and cared for through a season, he shot when told to. The pet chicken he once mentioned to me that slept on his pillow and was warm against him, ended up dinner like all the rest. His older half-brothers, four of them, derided or ignored him and his full siblings as a second litter, not on their par. His mother fought for scraps for her four children who lived past infancy—out of the six she bore and the several others she conceived and miscarried. Her husband may have beaten her, likely derided her, and surely ignored her except when he desired some rough connection.

I could imagine my father's take on conjugal rights. In fact, some years later, at a public reading of an essay in which I shared this story, a kindly-seeming elderly man in the audience explained to me, in a confidential, embarrassed whisper as the audience dispersed, that I'd overlooked the obvious: my mother was my father's *wife*; ergo, she belonged to him. One flesh, the Bible tells it so. When he wanted her, she was his for the taking.

My mother, from her side of the locked door, told me once and tearfully, "I *can't* say no. Something comes over me, like a caul." She made a motion with her hand, of a hood drawn over her face. "I go away," she explained. For that reason, she could not say for sure whether he raped her or not. "I don't know," she told me, "I don't remember. It *could* be someone else. He says it's somebody else, maybe it is."

You are what I perceive You to be.
You'll do as I say, or You'll cease to be.

The spring I finally grow bold enough—and desperate enough— to tell my children's father I have to leave, just temporarily, in order to draw breath, in order to maybe get still enough to guess who I might be without the non-negotiable need to please, he tells me it's my job to tell J and B. This is the equivalent, in my heart, of requiring me to disembowel them.

It's the perfect punishment for my temerity in challenging your hold on me. I agree, tacitly, it is your right to demand this.

We stand side by side in the kitchen. My hands in the sink, washing dishes. Dizzy, suds dripping from my fingers, I walk out of the big beautiful house, across the lush patio, past the crystal-blue swimming pool into the back house, a guest suite and rec room where our children are watching television. I interrupt their viewing; they are miffed. I gather them to me. I am their mother, so they come; they trust me. I sink the knife of my truth deep into their small vigorously beating hearts. I don't implicate You; it wouldn't be right. What is befalling all of us is *my fault.*

I still hear B's scream and J's stony silence: unceasing reverberation from the carnage of cutting ties.

~

In the aftermath of Hurricane Charley, I arrived home to a house unbroken and unflooded. A huge jacaranda tree downed by the wind filled the entire backyard. But the roof had not come off nor been punctured, and even the rickety screen enclosing the sagging back deck still stood, spared from the fallen tree by inches.

The power was on, too, making me one of the truly lucky, since many people in Florida that summer would go weeks or even months without electricity. One sprawling brittle bough of jacaranda did lie on the drop line linking the main power cable to the house, pressing a tangled cat's-cradle of branch and live wire nearly to the wet ground, inviting explosion or an electrical fire. The power company refused to touch it; once I got through to someone there after days of trying, they told me without even the facsimile of sympathy that the drop line was my private property and thus my private problem. It would be six weeks before I'd locate a contractor—a woman—brave enough and rapacious enough to charge me eight hundred dollars, twice the normal rate, to put a chain saw to that mess.

But, during those intervening weeks, three more hurricanes

would strike or threaten Tampa. Charley had been only the beginning; Frances, Ivan, and Jeanne would follow in short order: the Big Four of '04. With Ivan, I'd guess correctly that its crazy start-and-stop path would veer west of us in the last hours before the predicted landfall; that storm savaged the Florida panhandle. When Jeanne made a U-turn in the Atlantic to cross Florida a second time, this time east to west on the 26th of September, only five days after Ivan's threat, I again retreated to the Dzogchen Buddhist Center but came home early in the midst of merely torrential rains, anxious to find out if the wire-and-branch knot in the backyard had burst into flame. Between Charley and those two near-misses, however, I would ride out Hurricane Frances inside my house, the fallen jacaranda bouncing on the live drop wire, because I had no chance to run.

Frances—big, wet, and slow—plowed across the state from the Atlantic to the Gulf during Labor Day weekend. She'd been downgraded from hurricane to tropical storm and dismissed by the media as already over when she stalled for twelve hours in Tampa Bay, pumping so much storm surge up the urban peninsula that when the wind finally subsided, crazy kids drove jets skis up and down the bayside boulevard on sewage-fouled "black water" several feet deep. The night before, I'd turned off the Weather Channel at midnight and gone to bed, assured the storm's center was over water and moving away from Tampa.

I snapped awake before dawn on the powerful sense that something was very, very wrong, and confirmed that intuition when I turned on the porch light. Water lapped at the first step of three that raised my house eighteen inches off ground-level. Between me and my across-the-street neighbor's front door stretched a dark lake, its surface lightly rippled by the storm's fitful last breezes. The only way to leave the house would be to wade—or maybe swim—through black water.

Inside, B and the cat were sleeping. J had left for college already, out-of-state. Awake for less than two minutes and uncaffeinated, I strategized blearily. If we placed Karma in her carrier, B and I could float her out on the boogie board we used at the beach, he on one side and I on the other to steady it. I pictured us doing this. Judging by the flood's height on the Norfolk pines in the yard, I estimated the water would be waist-deep. We'd better leave quickly, before the water got higher. I stumbled back inside to dress, heading first toward the bathroom from force of early-morning need. I stopped short in the doorway: as I watched, sludgy water gurgled up into the toilet bowl from the sewer, rose to the rim, and slopped over the side.

To be flooded with unpredicted storm water from the street was one thing, but to watch my house fill with other people's sewage via my own toilet was another. Without thinking I flung towels at the spreading puddle, snatched the phone book, and called the city water department. At not quite six o'clock on Labor Day morning, the phone was answered immediately by a man genuinely and gently sympathetic. The pumps that raised sewage from the pipes into the treatment plant were without power, he said, and the resulting back-up was crawling back along the paths of least resistance into individual toilets at the lowest points on a given line. I took this in, blinking: sheer random bad luck that my house was affected. The solution, he told me wearily, was to go out into my yard and, if I could find it, open the trap on the sewer pipe linking my house to the main line, releasing the pressure, and the sewage, into the street.

The cap atop that trap had recently been broken and replaced by a lawn contractor so I knew exactly where it was. But, as I told the kind man way too sharply, I'd have to snorkel to get at it, given the flood. Enraged and helpless, I stumped back out to the porch. Water now lapped the second step. We had to go.

I turned to find B standing behind me. Fifteen years old then, a hard sleeper and late riser, he was bed-headed and barely dressed but very awake and rattled by what surrounded us. I recounted my escape plan, told him to find shoes and not to flush, eat something fast and get ready to go. I had no idea how far we'd have to wade or swim to find dry ground, nor where we would go afterwards—on foot, homeless, soaked in sewage, and lugging a cat.

I hurried to the utility room to retrieve the cat's carrier stored there. Reaching it down from the shelf, I glanced into my writing room, at ground-level in the converted garage, already flooded several inches deep. I stepped into galoshes and waded through the flood to lift my laptop, repository of all my past and present writing, including the unpublished and maligned novel, from the desk to the highest shelf just in case we got to come back and salvage anything. I remembered I'd better shut off the pilot light beneath the water heater—a gas leak is an explosion hazard in a flood. I was on my knees in muck fumbling for the knob when I noticed a tide line on the carpeted stairs leading down into the writing room. The water level had dropped a quarter-inch from the mark of its high point.

I stood up, confused but pushing at my foggy brain to process data and figure odds. Our block had inadequate storm drains; it flooded briefly in every hard downpour, obliterating the pavement and occasionally lapping into the yard. I knew from ten years' residence there just how fast the water could rise—and fall—in sync with the tide in the nearby bay. The storm drains emptied into the bay, and when they were rain-gorged at the same time the tide pushed in, our street could fill and empty in less than an hour as the tide turned. I snapped on the television—the electricity powering it and the trip wire in the backyard would remain on throughout the storm; this would turn out to be, on balance, a lucky thing. Impatiently I awaited the Weather Channel's Local on the 8s for tide data. High tide at our point on the peninsula had occurred in the past quarter-hour. Complacency about the storm on the local news channel suggested flooding in Tampa must be localized. It was just possible, with the storm once again moving away from land, that the flood outside my house would recede with the tide, and quickly.

But there was no way to know for sure what would happen. No way to be certain what to do.

I told B, now dressed and holding a cereal box, wide awake but speechless, my theory. He looked doubtful, not about the data I'd gathered nor what I deduced from it, I think, but about the not-knowing. The raw risk we had to take—stay or go, dangerous either way, the choice essentially a hunch. I wanted him to help me decide. He wanted no part of that responsibility. His mute misery made me miserable, and he didn't help me with that either; he was so deep inside himself, he could not even look at me. So I decided.

Defaulting to what I knew best about what to do when I had no idea what to do, I waited. For five minutes, to see what would happen. And five more, and then fifteen. I could not sit and I can't remember if I chanted any prayers. I paced: something to do. Years later, V.T. would ask me did I not fall back, at that point of most grave uncertainty about survival, to petitioning the Methodist God of my youth to save me and my son. Did I not at least feel the temptation to do so? I did not. Only some minutes earlier I'd demanded, in outrage, that the city's water department intervene to stop my toilet from pouring sewage into the house. But something about their incapacity to help me—in so-close conjunction with my inability to spare my son his suffering, and the still-resonant memory of my teacher arming me, from within the jaws of the earlier storm, with the simple clarity of *good luck*—made me a good Buddhist, at least for the duration of that moment. No one except me had responsibility or ability to save me and mine. I could face the question squarely, do what I could, and accept the outcome. Or I could panic, do nothing, blame someone else. My choice.

I walked circles through the house, pausing again and again on the porch to eye the water where it lapped the steps. It definitely wasn't rising. I thought it might be slowly dropping. B stayed in his room, door shut, Karma for company.

Most of the day passed before our fate resolved. Frances, by that time a mere tropical depression, wallowed sluggishly north-westward, and gradually the storm surge that overfilled the bay subsided. When the water in the yard dropped below the first porch step, I waded out wearing my galoshes and a pair of rubber gloves to open the sewer line trap as the nice man with the city had instructed. With chagrin and distaste, I watched a dark gush disperse into the standing water, our household's contribution to the befouling of South Tampa.

In a dream that has visited me more than once, I wear a very heavy hat. A black tricorn of tremendously exaggerated scale. Its hue, and its density supersaturated. The hat weighs so much I can hardly balance my skull upright atop my spine, and the prow point rides so low on my brow, extends past my nose to such a distance, that my vision is compromised. Without a great effort to tilt my nose up, I see only the ground in front of my feet.

That's all there is to it, this dream.

It's while I'm awake and walking about, thinking of something my teacher has said about right view, that the dream, or actually the hat, teaches me something: I can see what's before me, with or without the heavy hat's obstruction and tedious weight.

The angle of my vision is my choice.

B and I were lucky. Our house remained habitable, neither of us got ill or injured, the millions of words stored in my computer remained mine to call up and stir around, and even my car, parked in the neighbor's yard at six inches greater elevation than mine, survived the storm; the water at its highpoint rose two-thirds the way up the wheels but stopped just short of entering the engine (a terminal form of damage) via the exhaust pipe.

By the evening of that long day life returned to what passed for normal in Florida that summer. The broken tree lay quietly on the live drop-wire in the backyard; the cat once again ventured out beneath it to patrol our perimeter for trespassing felines. The lawns and streets around us were coated with black-water mud that dried and cracked and then stank in the sun until sanitation workers arrived to chip it loose with shovels and pressure-wash it down the storm drains into the bay. Out-of-state power trucks and tree crews moved in convoy from job to job around the city, leaving behind on the curbs mountainous piles of chain-sawed debris that would take the city until nearly Christmas to clear. But schools and workplaces re-opened right away, and grocery stores and gas stations sold what they had available at the jacked-up prices the market would bear.

I could not then foresee the shocking images of people marooned on rooftops and drowned in attics that would emerge from the Katrina disaster just one year later. Sitting ducks, those people, stuck with what fate handed them, no matter if they guessed wrong about whether and when to leave, or simply had no means to flee. When I did see those pictures, I felt my good fortune all the more keenly, of course. I felt my mortality, too: I could so easily have guessed wrong. The water from the bay might have kept right on rising, fast, and B and I might have climbed to our roof with the cat in our arms to wait for hours and perhaps days in stifling heat with no shade and no water to drink, the world become a filthy seascape graveyard surrounding us horizon to horizon.

Instead, our lives went on as if nothing dire had happened. I had the carpet in my writing room steam-cleaned, tossed out ruined books and files, and carried on teaching, editing, and writing. B recommenced being a teen among teens at school and after school. We each vowed to get out of Florida, away from hurricane alley, and we did, separately, though it took us several years and much effort to accomplish that.

In the days immediately following Hurricane Frances' departure, I tried privately to hold on to the impact of my brush with death.

Feeling new and amazed and jazzed with the need to share that wonder, I emailed everyone in my electronic address book a little note: we were flooded, we have electricity and food and water, and we thought you might be worrying, if you watch the news, that is, if you remember—*do* You remember, V.T., who I am and where I live?

I might have died but didn't and still it's mostly my yearning for You, my one and only, that proves to me I'm real.

B to my left, J to my right, the three of us are sunk deep in the too-soft cushions of a scuffed and scarred blonde leather sectional, a hand-me-down from the affluent parents of J's roommate, centerpiece of a living room in a rundown apartment complex—makeshift home to college students and immigrant service workers—in Greensboro, North Carolina. Heaped around us on the worn beige carpeting are binders and dried-out highlighters; discarded takeout containers; laptops, printers, and iPods in a tangle of cables and chargers; and, spread lightly over everything, three black cats, their toys, and the kitty litter they've tracked from the box in the closet. Our three pairs of feet—B's long and narrow in Chucks, mine in socks-and-Reeboks, J's petite, callused and bare—line up on the smudged glass top of the coffee table.

Each of my children holds a beer. My hands cradle a glass of white wine. We have full stomachs; they have just taken me out for Thai food for my birthday, and they have paid.

The large-screen TV we stare at plays a DVD made by a workers' collective in Venezuela, celebrating Chavez and the socialist revolution there. The year is 2007, and J is just back from spring break in Caracas, clowning in hospitals and communing with Marxists beneath the wing of compassionate provocateur Patch Adams. In only seven weeks she'll graduate from college. B and I, on spring break ourselves, will hit the road in the morning for a victory lap visit to the nearby university he'll attend in the fall.

I've escaped Florida by means of a temporary teaching fellowship in Asheville; J and I have lived, this year, just two hours apart. Tonight, like one of her cats, she curls warm against my arm. B's sinewy fist rests on the couch near my thigh. For nine months he and I have been separated by more than 700 miles, sharing just a weekly phone call while he finished high school in Tampa, grubbing the necessary grades and wearing through his dad's resistance to an out-of-state school, orchestrating a three-in-N.C. togetherness that won't happen after all, now. J's broken up with the boyfriend she thought she'd make a life with; she'll return to Tampa and wait tables until she figures out what's next. And me, I tell my children, against a backdrop of revolutionaries' cheers and testimonials, another knife-edged truth: the elusive and problematic V.T. is suddenly mine for-real. I've just committed to this man they've heard too much about but never met. Unilaterally, I'll be making our threesome some kind of four.

The words are barely out of my mouth before others rush after them: "Don't tell your dad."

That reflexive fear, maybe necessary, maybe not, twelve years past the divorce, spikes my blood pressure and sets my stomach churning. I apologize to my children for putting them in the secret-guarding position, again.

B speaks immediately with protective, manly prerogative. "It doesn't concern him."

But I can't stop the outpouring, now that I've pulled the cork from my bottled anxieties. I blabber on to my silent children: how far we three have come and how stuck I still feel, how much it troubles me, my flawedness and especially my need to share it with them. What an improper parent I am, how my failings have shaped their lives....

When I finally stop, J says: "What matters is that you don't lie to us."

B commences a rationalization: "It's more...." He pauses, searches,

searches more, and offers his answer, a non-answer that nonetheless assuages me some: "It's more *real,* this way."

That's when we get to talking about our Christmas tattoos. We lift shirts and J's pants' leg and refresh our memories of each other's marks. We share satisfaction and disbelief that we actually got that ink. Settling back into cushions, sitting tight between my children, I say, "This is good." J shifts fractionally closer. B gives an adamant, eloquent nod, then lets his head loll back in slightly tipsy relaxation. We are all a little bit buzzed.

We could take hands, but we don't. We could talk more about what's next for each of us, but we don't.

We are linked not just by the lines scarred into us but by the spaces—our balancing, ballasting silences—bridging what we are, and what we are not.

I asked my mother once, in her last days on earth, how she and my father met. What I wanted to know, of course, was how in hell two people so unsuited ended up yoked together for nearly seven decades. Her answer—a blind date—made me remember I'd heard the story before. A blind date on a double date with Arthur Lyons and Evelyn Goode, in Arthur's car. The car sounded shiny and exciting; in the telling I recalled from girlhood, my mother sounded much more approving of Arthur's car than of my father. In her deathbed version, much briefer, her evaluation rode her lip, curling past contempt into incredulity. Utter astonishment. Recollected folly. She had done *that* thing. The outcome had been...*my goodness*...what the cost had been!

Did they ride, that afternoon, that evening, sometime in the early 1930s, in a rumble seat? I put them in one in my mind. She'd told me in my childhood about rumble seats; it was clear they'd been the very edge of daring for her in her youth.

From where she sat that day, a few doors down from the grave, she could at last appreciate, without pain or outrage, the irony of her life. Oh, the consequence of that simple act—saying "yes" instead of "no," an impulsive decision, perhaps a rebellious one, and daring.

~

A Buddhist teaching instructs practitioners to carry every form of mental or physical suffering onto the path. The diligent effort to see one's affliction clearly and to mindfully experience its "one taste"— the bitter with the sweet—this *is* the path.

The together part of V.T.'s path and mine began on the day I'd decided I would dare to tell him I could hang on no longer. I would say no, and make it stick. But instead, he told me, by phone, that he was gravely ill. There would be, under our circumstances, no venue except this telephone call to process this news. Seated on the floor—I had to ground myself to stay conscious for this kind of talk—in the laundry room-foyer of the un-insulated and buggy bungalow where I did purgatory for the one sin I grew up certain I'd never commit, I said yes instead of no. I couldn't quit now, I was his life line.

There was dirt on the floor. I pushed at it with my fingers. A bone-chilling damp seeped beneath the door and through the thin walls. January. Nearly February. A season when everything dies.

Promises were made. Love was vowed. And luck fervently invoked. The phone went back into its cradle. What came next for him was surgery and for me, blackout, weeks of it.

~

When I legally severed my tie to my boy husband Hen, the real divorce was between my mother and me. How many years before I discerned that truth? How many more until I accepted it?

In the early months of my teen marriage I fought her, not Hen, over money, visits home, clothes, the minutiae of my daily schedule, matters no business of the mother of a married woman but which neither I nor she could separate from the birth tie that bound us. The thick letters I wrote her every week brim with self-justification snarled in childish efforts to ingratiate; after she died I found them, having forgotten for decades I ever wrote them, bundled in her desk. I tossed out the whole stack as if the envelopes leaked poison—or an elixir of truth I refused to taste. I couldn't bear to re-encounter, word by silence-breaking word, that clinging, enmeshed girl I had revised, over thirty years, into an abuse-survivor yearning for autonomy.

In 1972 when I married Hen my mother was already over sixty. When I divorced him at twenty, she was pushing seventy.   I had, like most teenagers, no ability to imagine what a parent's life felt like. Only at midlife myself, world-weary and bruised single mother of two healthy adolescents, could I speculate with some clarity about my mother's situation in my teens. The way she'd depended on me, not my father, through the ordeal of her cataract surgeries and the daily struggle to wear the contact lens that granted her sight. The twenty-five years, by the time of my wedding, she'd managed Betsy's illnesses and intractable social maladjustment, all alone: no government help in those days, and no interest, ever, from my father or the extended family. The stigma of mental retardation that was so potent she did not allow Betsy to attend either my wedding or Sara's. The back trouble that more than once landed my mother in the hospital, in traction. The constant pain of arthritis in her knees that would cripple her completely in just a few more years. And my father, forced into early retirement around the time I married Hen, hanging around the house angry, frightened, and humiliated, feeding her depression and setting off battles. The both of them drinking, a handle of cheap vodka or grain alcohol stashed under the kitchen sink alongside the cleaning supplies.

After the wedding she cut me off financially—it was Hen's family that supported us—and I cut her off, too, at some point in the therapy process. Amid a shouting and sobbing two-sided tear, I packed every object I ever expected to have from her house into the used, powder-blue VW Bug I'd bought myself with my first debt, my first tangible gesture toward self-definition, and drove away to North Carolina. Done with her, at twenty-one. But when I returned to grad school, the following year, I had to ask her for help. She rallied, even though she was, at that point, some distance down her path into agoraphobic self-isolation and self-destruction. She left the house, as she rarely did by then, to travel over the mountains to Chapel Hill, bringing money and furniture, driving with my father in the tired family Rambler, pulling an open trailer better suited to hauling fire-wood, painted silver with my father's trademark aluminum paint. When she arrived at my rundown, roach-infested apartment, I was glad to see her.

From where I stand now, it's easy to see that she loved me, and tried to show it. That she also could not stop herself from confusing herself with me, from expecting me to bring her the prophesied joy, and resenting me when I didn't—that's clear too. When I had to tell her I would marry again, at twenty-four, I was frightened sick of doing so, and she raged at me for not knowing better and not caring what she felt. Her expression, in the photos of my wedding to the man who would be my children's father, is identically as sour as her demeanor at my first wedding.

Never mind she was right about the mistake I was making with that second marriage; neither one of us could name it accurately.

Sixteen years would pass before I could see and say what I did do wrong: when I married him, my second husband, I married her. The fit so familiar, and the outcome much the same.

During the two years of divorce war that closed out the second marriage there arrived a single moment of open-ended closure when I could see what I had done to You. A space of one minute or two when your guard dropped while mine was down, and we sat down, exhausted, flank to flank in settling dust on the floor of a house where

You would begin again, surrounded by the cartons and the chaos of moving house with—for the first time in two decades—not a lick of help from me. So many familiar objects once ours, now yours, surrounded us in profoundly unfamiliar disarray as if earthquake or explosion had ripped the world we built and defended to shelter our children, the one and only value we always agreed on. I faced one direction, You, the other. We touched only along our femurs' lengths. Beaten dumb by despair, we cried together about our now forever separate losses.

I felt synced to You these few moments with purity I never felt while we were married. We met at last and fully only in finality: no more common ground, not even in our yearnings.

You needed me to be whatever it was You could not name as missing.

I required the very same of You.

How lucky, to ever see such a terrible thing that clearly: our shared delusion burned to ash.

~

I make a second retreat to Harris, four years after the first one. It rains almost every day, spring cold and late that year. For the entire two weeks my socks and my toes, my sweatshirt, and the mattress beneath my sleeping bag are forever cold, always damp. I work all day each day clearing out junked cottages on the teacher's instructions, alone. At dusk, still alone, I circumambulate the property, reciting mantra. I walk without a light on mud through wet night-chill in an Adirondack hardwood forest. Preparing to lift one foot, I see path toward which to direct it only as the other foot finds ground and sinks.

Inked into an interior door frame of the crumbling, unplumbed, unheated shack I sleep in is this cryptic message from an anonymous prior retreatant:

> *Up* ↑
> *Down* ↓
> *Touch the ground.*
> *Knob* →
> *Open the door—*

I do not understand what this means but copy it into my journal because it *feels* like some kind of directional indicator, for aspirants seeking balance amid cross-currents of clarity and confusion.

On my nightly circumambulations I pass a dump repeatedly. A thousand or more guttered candle glasses carried over the years from the shrine room lie open-mouthed in rotting leaves, dark with beetles, grubs, and soot: what once was light and scent and holy now burned to exhaustion and housing insect dung. My shoes slide on slick dirt. Fern fen peels down a slope on my left to an unseen but rilling brook. Tree-ears, fungus the size of plates, tier the trunks that flank my path; the venerable forest drips and sighs. My prayers rise visible: pale breath-mist drifting up, dissipating as it forms.

Each step, I thumb another bead, my rosewood mala a circuit of syllables imploring release from the circlings of samsara. All beings circle, trapped in cycles of existing—arising, dissolving, manifesting again in different form. Clinging to any being in any form creates suffering. I aspire, in this solitary retreat, to comprehend this truth clearly.

But, in my pocket in the hand with no mala, I clutch a cell phone, talisman of a tie I cannot cut, my link to V.T. I do not know at this point if we will ever meet face-to-face again but we are talking. And I will not willingly miss any chance to do so. I pass the holy dump again, and then again. Counting, concentrating, and waiting. Aware I am gestating inside emptiness fresh attachment and fresh pain.

The phone quivers, lights, trills, and I know nothing but You, V.T. Your name on the screen, your voice in my head. Steel towers scar mountains, squat in fields, blight skylines across a continent—only so that I may pull You from empty air.

The path exits the forest to enter a black meadow. Rain-laden grass soaks my jeans to my thighs. I sight the stars above, through cloud cover now dissolving. I raise the phone in the dark to offer You the peeper frogs' chorus.

You give me back June bugs in the desert, and wheeling hawks that snap them midair.

You ask me for silence, together. With two thousand miles between us we look up. One sky encompasses all.

My knees give way. I sink to the ground, your gasp flying from my throat.

Careening through his first semester of college like a hot car with burned brakes and loose steering, my lanky son B phones me to say, "Mommy-o, I think I need another tattoo."

I'm at my writing desk, elbows parked on the same plank balanced atop the same metal filing cabinets that comprised my work space as MFA student fifteen years earlier, in a breakfast nook of the little rented dump in Tampa where my children and I lived when B was in elementary school and we were newly divorced. In my new little rented dump in Black Mountain, North Carolina, a teacher of writing students now, but an adjunct just as poor as I was as single-mom student, I'm engaged in another morning of not-writing my own pages when I have carved out the time to attend them. B's call releases me from flogging myself forward in a place where no path appears.

I sigh out my unspoken wish that writing were easier. I let go of a dusty eddy of impatience that his grades aren't what either of us wish them to be, that he's not returned a half-dozen of my calls, and that

I feel angry—no, the truth: I feel frightened and hurt—our relationship is not what I want it to be. Is it what *he* wants it to be...?

But, he's called. He's called!

But, the subject of the call is that which I do not want him to have, and he knows it: more ink.

What I need he's offered in a form I don't want.

What does that mean *he* needs?

I try nonchalance. "What are you thinking about getting?" I smooth the misaligned edges of a pile of file folders, phone squeezed tight between my ear and shoulder.

"Compassion mantra," I hear him say. "Om Mani Peme..."

"Hung." I finish with him—reciting mantra in unison with others as reflexive for me as breathing.

Om, the perfection of generosity,
Ma the perfection of ethics,
Ni the perfection of patience,
Pe the perfection of perseverance,
Me the perfection of concentration,
Hung the perfection of wisdom.

I mouth the words for comfort while my mind rides its habitual squirrel wheel, spinning anxious propositions. Tattoo = sketchy. Mantra = spiritual seeking. Not so unusual an association after all... but...would it not be something akin to sacrilege to permanently ink the six syllables of the enlightened mind on the body of a young man with no official devotion to Buddhism?

"I need you to help me find the letters," B tells me. "The Tibetan script, I mean. You have it, don't you?"

"Sure I do." I screen doubt from my voice. The minute the call ends, I'll go on line, jettisoning my writing day, to find him the mantra displayed large in exactly the right script, contextualized with the right commentary from a right lineage of teachers.

But first, grasping at him when he's clearly ready to go, I ask where he'll put this new tattoo. I feel him straining toward whatever presses him in his life beyond me. He says probably the new tattoo ought to go on his chest.

"Heart chakra?" I breathe, tapping my own sternum involuntarily.

"Off to the side." He bristles and bustles. "But on my chest."

He hangs up. Done. We've talked of nothing I want to know about, and nothing has been resolved.

Om.

Mani.

Peme.

Hung.

In some closet or drawer amid the mounds of papers and possessions my sisters and I sifted through, emptying our parents' house for sale, I found a small, unlabeled black and white photograph of a woman I am nearly sure is my mother, standing on an unpaved county road behind a thirties-looking car. Its rumble seat, open, is right behind her. Slender and young, she's looking at the ground, or maybe avoiding the sun, eyes downcast and hands clasped demurely behind her back. Her long hair, thick with corrugated waves like mine, is parted in the middle and tied back. Most of what's visible is entirely modest, but the car—big, decked out with running boards, that rumble seat, and a convertible top—it's no farm car. And despite the white dust of the road and the obvious country setting (a farmhouse up ahead in a bend; sumac straggling over a fence alongside her) my mother is decked out. She's wearing a white low-waisted flapper's dress that bares her arms and nearly exposes her knees. She's got on white stockings and pale high-heeled shoes cut low to expose her arches, laced around the ankles with useless, jaunty bows.

I like to think this photo dates from the blind date. I like to think this is how my father saw her: what he saw, when he decided he had to have her.

For he *did* decide. He tells me so in seven letters he wrote her during the last months of their engagement and the first months of their marriage. I found these letters in the bottom drawer of that desk of hers, banded together with a short length of black satin ribbon. They lay atop a stack of paid bills, household account books, and contracts from her job, in the years before she had children, as elementary school teacher.

My father shoots the pig twice in these letters. The first time, in October, the one I've reported already, he's matter-of-fact; it's his job and it's always been his job, and it's the pig's job, too, to be food. But in November, "full of tenderloin," he gloats about his ability to kill. "I shot the critter right smack between the eyes, and down he flopped."

During the weeks before their Thanksgiving wedding he's sometimes cocky, flaunting bad-boy grammar and dismissing punctuation: "Do you still believe we will not be married you always said we never would be and now we practically are. How do you like them apples?" But just as often he's pleading and holding the line: "I didn't do a thing Sunday but wish for you...hoping and praying that things would be alright with us...I hope you will be marrying someone worthy of you."

Just a few days before their wedding, he writes, "Do you still think it wrong for us to marry?" He says he knows she cannot answer that, so he answers—softly, I imagine—for them both. "I guess we'll just have to try."

Two months into the marriage, in January and separated from her by fifty unpaved miles for a job he's been damn lucky to find in rural east Tennessee in 1937, he writes: "Remember I love you. and <u>I am trying hard</u>."

His underscore is thick. It's decisive. No more pleading; she belongs to him now.

~

Are you <u>sure</u> that you want to go ahead with it. I <u>promise</u>

I'll never ask again. I'm just afraid that this time I really did push you. Maybe if I hadn't gotten so hurt, you would have gone ahead and changed your mind. Honest to God, I didn't do it on purpose, but I'm afraid that all the same you feel trapped, since you said it was 'the only thing' you could do. Please don't be trapped. I'm really sorry I got so upset, 'cause I really did want you to make up your own mind freely with no shit. I would absolutely die if I ever thought you regretted it <u>at all</u>. Be sure! Now I won't ever ask again.

There, in giddy hormone-ramped fast-forward skidding, is my mind at sixteen. This sprawling paragraph covers part of one 8½ x 11 page among four, each one typed edge to edge on a manual typewriter in tiny, Elite font, replete with streaks of asterisk and pound-sign strike-outs. The paper is cheap and loud, printed in a tie-dye effect of hot pink, bright orange, lurid yellow. This letter is but one of the hundreds I sent Hen, from the fall of 1971 through the spring of 1972 when we married in June. The entire stack of letters, bundled with crumbling rubber bands, housed in a shoebox, turned up in a crawl-space closet of my old attic bedroom during the emptying out of my parents' house. Why my letters to Hen came back there when the few he wrote me have disappeared, I do not know.

I've promised in that letter that I've said all I'm going to say, but that promise is empty. In letter after letter I cajole and cling and harangue:

You <u>do</u> still want to get married, don't you? I hope so, after all this preparation I've been working on. I feel so alone...please still love me...I'm bored, lonely and terribly, terribly nervous. Please help me out by finishing your guest list. I know you don't want to but it has to be done and I can't understand why you won't cooperate. It will only take a minute.

I never seem to notice that I am making him responsible for assuaging my neurotic "nervousness"—in the same guilt-tripping, goading, and frankly flaky terms my mother used on me.

~

On Thanksgiving Day in 1936, wearing a wine-red dress, my mother married my father. She had no attendants, not even her sister or her best friend from that double date, Evelyn Goode. No one stood up with her, except him. Evelyn played Liszt and Handel, Schumann and Mendelssohn on the piano and some tenor sang; one-third of the newspaper's wedding notice is an exacting description of the music that began and interluded and ended this ceremony held at "an improvised altar before the fireplace" in the home of the bride's parents. "Only a few close relatives and intimate friends were present," the newspaper confides, as if there were need for secrecy, haste, or the extraordinary and protective privacy of the very rich or the thoroughly infamous.

The article, brittle and sepia-toned now, is written in the breezy false intimacy of thirties' social-ese; everything that anyone would want to know is there to be inferred between the lines detailing the names of the flowers and the shapes of their arrangement, along with the number—and the number of branches—of the candelabra. The headline reads, *Miss Edith Darter Is the Bride of Smith Douglas Hale of Rogersville.* The picture beneath it, a head shot of my mother—a yearbook picture, maybe, but so unflattering as to be nearly a mug shot, unsmiling and squared off to the camera—is cracked across one eye and the nose with a diagonal white line. A second, meandering white line runs downhill beneath the first, bisecting her cheek and her chin.

The effect is of a framed photograph that has been flung against the wall, or perhaps into that fireplace. The flaw might have occurred in the printing of that day's newspaper, or maybe the negative was scratched, but whatever the cause, the result was the most unbride-like likeness possible.

I've re-read the clipping a hundred times but the unanswerable question persists: Why *did* she marry him?

~

The shoebox of letters to Hen I pulled from the attic crawlspace resided untouched in my possession for nearly ten years. I thought when I carried them home with me that I'd take a look at them some-time, but I didn't. Finally reading them, an act of self-examination the writing of this book forced on me, felt like breaking open sealed sarcophagi.

Ninety percent of what fills hundreds of pages of eye-rending stationery or regimentally lined notebook paper is the minutiae of an academically successful and not completely friendless sixteen-year-old. I complain about being ostracized for my grades and my weird parents even though it's clear I would not have been caught dead prostituting my socialist and elitist "principles" simply to be invited to the right clubs and parties. I detail the hours I devote to band practice, Keyette projects and Tri Delta Tri Hi Y meetings, football games, pep rallies, and shopping (I buy short boots, a midi skirt, a purple crushed-velvet car coat). I shave my legs and report that; I wash my hair and report that; I write letters "under the dryer"; my period is late, arrives, goes away—an undercurrent of tension always on this topic. My preoccupation with band challenges—to achieve and hold on to first chair in the flute section—is omnipresent. If I make dinner, I report the menu, dish by dish. I sew and sew, stitching hippie headbands of brushed denim for Hen and his new friends and offering to make him a "jumpsuit" I assure him will look "tuff" and that never gets mentioned again.

I mythologize marriage: *I dreamed the wedding and everybody there. Oh God, I was so happy, 'cause at last we were married forever and you were all mine and nobody could take you away,* and I cling to him like a barnacle: *I dream about you every night.* Sometimes I sound to my present self like an abuser, rationalizing unforgivable behavior:

> *I was nearly hysterical when I called and I just got worse. Please try to forgive me and love me anyway, I know you will because you are so good and loving and FANTASTIC! I just feel so lost and I'm so scared...I go wild, absolutely, when anybody threatens to upset the balance...it seems like I am forever apologizing for something, why, oh why, can't I ever treat you good?*

There's no evidence in these letters of Hen's participating in any of the decisions, choices, or shopping expeditions leading up to our June wedding; either he meant to let me do everything my way, or my mother and I gave him no chance to assert his way. He was a college freshman, coping with courses and dorm life amid the enticements of the psychedelic 70s. He coped that year with something else, too: his father's untimely death. Until I reread the letters, I completely forgot that salient fact. In all those pages I wrote him there's no mention of it. What is evident is the presence of my mother's strong arm in the negotiations between the families:

> *Mama says to tell you that she has decided not to go see your mother...she will wait 'til you are home and we three can talk about it and maybe work on another summit conference. Things seem to be pretty stabilized as of tonight...so maybe it will work out yet....*

Hen's father, an apparently healthy man in his forties, completely opposed our early marriage. But he fell ill abruptly and in short order was diagnosed with cancer and died, at home. Nursing her husband through terminal illness sapped the small energy Hen's mother ever had for life beyond her day bed and the stack of books beside it, and she put up no real resistance.

If his father had lived, Hen and I might not have married. Maybe he would not have regretted that. I have no recollection of ever wondering how Hen, an eldest son, was affected that year or thereafter by the sudden early loss of his father. At the time his father's demise struck me as sad but surely a *sign*: my Romeo and I were meant to be, 'cause heaven and hell both moved to bring us together.

~

What made my mother keep those letters my father wrote her? Those seven—and only his, none of hers—out of all the letters they might have exchanged?

Did she re-read them, sometimes? Did she want a record she could hold in her hand, of the chance she once had to say no?

I wonder if she wanted someone—me?—to find them. Maybe she handed them down, consciously or not, as instruction in how much can go wrong. How insubstantial, after all, the place we stand when we decide, or don't.

Through all our we-two years I understood my mother had married down, to a country boy barely better than white trash. As a young woman she'd escaped Appalachia and its ways, temporarily, for college in Macon, Georgia, deep in the Old South where the Confederacy's sense of entitlement, and defeated bitterness, lived on. The Great Depression forced her home to Bristol to finish college and then teach fourth grade at the same Thomas Jefferson Elementary School I'd one day attend, but she'd absorbed from those Georgia belles tastes and desires that defined her. Her degree was in chemistry but she could lay a fine table and preside over it with social graces. She aspired to be *somebody.*

My father was not uneducated nor without prospects; the newspaper write-up of their wedding is able to cite his degree in electrical engineering (albeit from a college in Indiana no one in Bristol had heard of), plus membership in two fraternities. He began his work life in a blue collar—as a lineman, climbing poles and stringing wire up and down the rugged slopes of the Blue Ridge and Smokey Mountains for the Tennessee Valley Authority—but his industriousness and an affinity for the miracle of electricity were apparently in-born; his father and half-brothers were entrepreneurs as well as farmers, building and operating the first electric power grid in their corner of southeast Tennessee. He worked his way up the ranks to assistant manager of the city utility, and as far as I can tell, he made good money all his married life, even if he preferred to save most of it.

When my mother wed him, she was twenty-six, an old maid in those days. Did she settle? Did she take what she could get before she got permanently relegated to the shelf?

I asked her just once why she married my father. It was during our last hours together, as I sat beside her hospital bed watching her wake and sleep. Her answer: "Daddy liked him so much." She meant her father approved. She meant, I assume, that he pushed. She said, other times, that her father always got his way. Overbearing, and abusive, were the words other relatives applied to him. My mother reminded me, on that death bed, of something I'd heard once before. There'd been a boy in Georgia, a *nice* boy—her voice lingered on and turned the adjective, drawing it long into impenetrable but tantalizing mystery. Her daddy, she said, "got rid of him." Why? I asked. How? He came to the door, she said. He told the Georgia boy to clear out and leave her alone.

Her daddy ran that one off, and her daddy agreed to my daddy as her husband. Did he have reasons? Or were his no and his yes equally capricious, the result of his overbearing mood on a given day?

I think my mother knew better than to marry my father. I think she couldn't say yes but didn't say no. I think she failed, like I did when I married the first time and the second, to confront an uncomfortable truth. I had no idea who I was.

I gambled, instead, on You to complete me—so I wouldn't have to see what I was really missing.

Once in his last years my always-reticent father surprised me with the story of a boyhood crush on a grade school teacher. He was, he reckoned, about eleven, and his feelings—I pushed him a little to describe them—made him "go all juicy inside."

That glimpse into his emotional innards so amazed me that I asked him what it was about my mother that made him want to marry her. Right away he said, "She was *so* pretty." After that, a pause. The pause got long. Then, his eyes faraway, on some vision of her, he added, "She could *work*. Lordy." He shook his head, with wonder, and respect.

About a month after my mother died, he fell in love. A woman I'll call Bonnie, eighty-eight to my father's ninety-two, turned up at his dining table her first day in the assisted living facility. My father was shrunken and depressed; he seemed completely lost without my mother to bully and bear; we all thought he was dying. But Bonnie took a shine to him, and he to her. Bossy in an irrepressibly cheerful way, she talked *all* the time and was, as Sara accurately pointed out, uneducated and utterly without class pretensions.

Two times a coal miner's widow, one of a dozen children raised on a subsistence farm way up in the mountains, she'd lived hardscrabble all her days and was determined, every day, to find her glass at least half-full, if not running over. Her closet bulged with pastel pantsuits lavishly appliquéd with sequined birds and flowers, and for every suit she owned a matching pair of flats. She wore make-up and nail polish every day. Her hair was always styled. She was utterly different from my mother. That, I think, is what my father found in Bonnie:

the stunning revelation that a woman—and a relationship with a woman—did not have to be hell. He did not have to be a shit.

Every word out of Bonnie's mouth erased the persona he and my mother had built for him. Bonnie said over and over, in his hearing, "Everybody brags on him all the time. How good he looks. How good he is." I think she meant it. To her, he did look good. He had some money and a full head of silver hair and, in those months he was Bonnie's beau, he still had all his marbles, a driver's license, and a car he would not give up. He *was* good to her. He bought her presents. He took her out to dinner and such shows as were available in the area—things he never, ever did for my mother.

Bonnie taught him to bowl. She taught him to dance. He introduced her to literature, reading aloud from Rudyard Kipling's collected stories. On Valentine's Day, their peers at the facility—the other "inmates," my father called them—elected Bonnie and him queen and king. I have the photo in which they hold hands, wearing gold paper crowns.

When we were just beginning to catch on to my father's renaissance and the reason for it, Sara asked him if he and Bonnie were "a romantic item." He responded with a sly grin. "I guess so," he said, laconic. But spark crackled in his voice, his gaze, and the curve on his lips whenever he talked about Bonnie. Soon, he and she had an arrangement. Single rooms adjoining a shared bath, like college suite-mates. Separate bills, paid by their separate pairs of grown daughters. They spent all their waking hours together and nobody ever inquired who slept where. As the director of the facility said, about them and other happily re-coupled couples their age: "Whatever works."

I know my father knew joy. As he once explained it, he felt content that every day he knew which pants and which shirt to wear because he and Bonnie, together, laid out his next day's clothes each night before they went to bed. He knew himself blessed. He never uttered the word but the astonished tenderness that transformed his face when he spoke her name gave that import to what he did say—that with Bonnie he had "remembered so many things."

~

V.T. called me to talk about tattoos one afternoon from a phone booth at a Fina station in the desert. Homeless and wandering, everything lost on his way to find me, he confided he'd spent the whole afternoon in a tattoo shop in a gritty little town spitting distance from a military base. I heard big motorcycles revving in the background; sometimes their super-macho chortling drowned out his voice.

He described with an artist's precision and passion the ink he envisioned for himself—its lofty price and the hours, two sessions, the inking would require. The part of the description I understood was "blue" and "waves," to be rendered in the style of a certain Japanese painter whose work V.T. admired. He knew exactly where he wanted the mark, too: garlanding his thigh, high up: "Right where the string on a gunslinger's holster ties."

We laughed out loud over that because carrying a gun is the last thing anyone would ever imagine V.T. doing. I laughed inside, too, over this odd choice of lark amid a pilgrimage of cuttings and tearings. I cheered him on because that cheered him up. I was certain he'd never get a tattoo, mostly because he had no money to spare. Freeing himself, he was, by dreaming and drawing, jaw-boning with bandana'd vets the way he could with just about anybody about just about anything.

He was exhausted and hungry and cold in that phone booth. Broke, disoriented, and hemorrhaging pain. A divorce attorney we called the Death Star had him locked in her sights, and already toxic smoke from the Armageddon of a lifetime's way of being choked his lungs, seeding tumors we would find out about later. We didn't speak of these dark things. We joked a while about the dregs of beer and malt liquor standing warm and backwashed in bottles discarded around the phone booth, and the cigarette butts under his shoes, a puff or two left, probably, in some of them.

What a concept, I thought, when the call concluded. Gentle, gentling V.T., hounded by the furies and friends of a woman scorned, holstering himself with an imaginary tattoo. Proposing to ink his flesh when ink on the page was already the very juice of him.

⁓

Just once that fall of B's freshman year—I exercise restraint in the matter of questioning, always, on any occasion my young adult children take my call or return it—I ask, "Still thinking about that new tattoo?"

"Still thinking."

I push the littlest bit. "You got the script? I emailed you the link to a website—"

"I found it myself."

"Oh."

The beat it takes me to register and suppress the wounding news of my wasted effort registers on him. He is sensitive. He backpedals, the littlest bit.

"You and me," he says, "we found the exact same website. How weird is that."

"Weird," I say. "Yeah."

Call and response. My call, his response, our connection slack, holding a charge but leading nowhere.

At fifteen, he'd left my house, put up a wall and lived alone beyond it inside his father's house, loosely orbiting the patriarchal wealth and power. Until I moved out of range, he visited me dutifully on Sundays, treating me kindly but keeping his guard up.

In his brief and rescinded tattoo-tacit *I need you,* I thought I heard what I longed for: a rusty grate in his defenses sliding open, offering me a glimpse inside him.

So. I hold tight to this new tattoo B thinks he just might get. I know better than to cling to words or pictures or anything else, but—force of habit—I clutch helplessly at possibility. This might mean something, all this talk of ink, if I can only wait long enough to find out.

> *Om* the perfection of generosity,
> *Ma* the perfection of ethics,
> *Ni* the perfection of patience....

Rereading my letters to Hen, to force myself toward clarity about who I was when he was my one and only, I start to wonder if he read them all the way through. I have to hope, from where I stand now, that his dyslexia and his schedule caused him to glance at their length and heft and set them aside. The awful, disturbing, hindsight import of that shoebox full of my past self's language is this: the girl on the page is needy and narcissistic, a confused and crazy me I recognize but don't want to claim.

When I suspect Hen of distancing I grovel and disintegrate, but task him with the power to destroy me: *Please please don't be mad at me...it kills me, tortures me to feel mean thoughts from <u>you</u>, my angel, my lord...my god...my soul.*

I cultivate my depression but name him as its source: *I feel dead... there is something very very wrong...You haven't written me in a long time, the letter I got today was written <u>Thursday</u>.* I stake my pride on my differentness and woundedness—*it's in my nature, this self-destruction urge*—and romanticize suicide and my dependence on self-medication: *I don't belong here, my mind struggles to cope and one day it will break down...I'm not sure what the little white pills are, but they are definitely downers.* A large arrow comes next, pointing way down.

Then I beg him for insight he surely did not have, right before demonstrating my complete lack of it: *How do you know your true feelings from impulses and other emotions like pity? I wish there were someone to tell me how I feel!* <u>*What did you mean when you said I was never happy?*</u>

In just one of the letters there's a surprisingly calm burst of effort to see what is really happening to me:

> *I am doing all this for some reason. It seems to center around you, but I cannot grasp it…I am very much scared of the future, the past is <u>gone</u>, and the present is but a second and rapidly turns into the past. I am being hurtled forward at a dizzying rate of speed. Don't worry about it, it is part of me that is new, not known to you, <u>or</u> me for that matter. I love you…it is only the weekends that are long and that is when I think these thoughts.*

But again and again I default to blaming him; he is so often guilty of insufficient consideration for my need of him:

> *I debated not writing you at all for a few days, because I don't have anything much to say to you. I had one of the worst days of my life yesterday. I was shitted at all day about how awful you, your family, and friends are. How you use me, don't really care and how she will not come to the wedding. She wants to call it all off. I was extremely dizzy and nauseated. For the <u>first</u> time, I really reached the final point, I really did decide to and tried to kill myself. Fortunately or unfortunately, as the case may be, it didn't work, but it came damn close. Then when you called I was sicker than ever. I've never been so hurt or disappointed by you. Just your attitude. Giggle, giggle, chuckle chuckle isn't it funny. And for you to be in such a hurry to go. Why wouldn't you talk to me for a minute. You were just playing, paying no attention at all to me. I worship you. And you, the last one, my refuge, you treat me so hard…I'm so completely crushed and hurt. I thought you were god. I'm sorry I hung*

up, I guess it was rude, but if you ever cared at all, you ought to know how I felt. I fought for you and loved you all day, then you kicked me in the teeth. ...You're horny. Always goddam want want want. Why don't you <u>care</u> about me. See if you can't force yourself to think about me as other than your piece during the next three weeks. Because I love you and I'm too weak-need [sic] and gut-less to tell you to fuck off. ...

That is my mother's voice. That is the way she tore at me when one of her tears took her. Her diction—*I've never been so hurt*—her tone—*See if you can't force yourself*—and her withering, self-righteous rage.

Poor Hen, poor boy, You had to marry a manipulative shrew who would forever find You wanting: my mother, replicated in me.

From the window of my newest writing room—the desk facing sky, as it always does anywhere I can have it that way—I observe the lazy loop of a hawk riding thermals on a blustery day, autumn falling fast toward winter. Unbroken cloud cover, occluded light. The highest limbs stripped, leaves sifting down like peony petals in a greener season of breeze. Dogwoods and poplar framed in the glass. A sugar maple sapling. Banks of haw that were crimson not long ago. The autumnal palette still intense but dulling: rusty iron, blond leather, and russet now, every hue declining toward pewter, the gravel in the drive.

That hawk. Mote in the eye of god, I once wrote, after lying on my back in an October field still green, stretched aching head-to-head with a man who, wisely, did not want my need for love. Today's hawk slides and tilts so much closer to the earth; I sit a little closer to the sky. The home I share with V.T., my third husband, perches part way up a steep wooded ridge facing its twin at close quarters, with the Swannanoa River—beautiful, sluggish or muscular by seasonal turn, and dead, poisoned by industrial run-off—winding through the cleft.

I aspire to be this time the wife I could not be the first two times I married. To not want so much. To be willing to let go when his time, or mine, runs out. I make no claim that I have been a good mother. A better mother than mine was to me: I aspire to that. I so feared failing to do better than she did that I might have avoided mother-hood altogether had I been allowed to. I knew too much about habits of abuse passed down, hand to hand, across generations. At each of my children's births I vowed afresh to get it right. Put their needs before mine. Love them unconditionally no matter what it cost me. Get for them what they needed to grow in body, mind, and spirit. Encourage them to become what their essence made them, and give up my attachment to the outcome.

I wanted them to be like the parts of me I liked. I wanted them to not be, ever, the things I hated about myself. I knew all this but could not track, amid the flux of my feelings and our paths' twists, the effect on my children of my vows and my back-slidings. I made rules. I yelled. I badgered. I apologized, tried harder, and screwed up again.

J told me once, in desperation, "Your big love, it's *too much*." More than once B referred to me, maybe affectionately, as his "tita-nium mommy." My children made me a better person. But I wasn't easy to live with. Nor all that easy to love, either, I suspect. Still, they succeeded; I do know that.

During the complicated year preceding my third wedding, J told me this story, apropos, it seemed at first, of nothing much. With some other members of her class, she went to dinner at the home of her biology professor, J's biggest booster on her path though hard sci-ence toward medical school, a woman whose discipline, confidence, pragmatic feminism, and kindness she has clearly chosen to emulate. Over dinner, J met the professor's husband. Her third husband. J summarized a backstory I had to wonder when and how she'd been given. The professor, approximately my age, married in high school and soon divorced. Married again, badly and at length, a man with whom she had only children in common. After a rough divorce and a long stint as single mom, she married again. To a good guy, J said. She added, "It took her three tries but she finally got it right."

After this came a pause until we located the next thread of conversation. I couldn't read my daughter's face because we spoke by phone but I did know what I was receiving. Absolution by indirection.

The Christmas before the spring I left my second husband, my children's father, the bomb we kept buried between us almost blew. I can't remember who set the fuse, what off-hand remark struck the match, but we stood a-tremble in the kitchen on the cusp of losing our cool and our marriage, I stirring the pancakes our tradition for that day called for, our agitated glances flickering from one another to the children emptying their stockings in the den. Intent, self-absorbed, innocent, our children were.

I bit down and You bit down; we just couldn't spoil their Christmas. They exclaimed and examined and chattered, aware or not aware of our eyes on them and the force of rage and resentment our clamped-shut jaws barely retained. Somehow we moved on, ostensibly past it, through breakfast and phone calls with relatives, and, in that dead space that so often elongates a holiday afternoon, a first attempt to fish, as a family, from a nearby pier, catching nothing but a cold chill.

Once it began, that divorce, it could not be stopped. I kept the letters You rained on me. I made myself not destroy them. To write this, I have made myself read them, to be sure I have done as right by You as I am able. Here is the one thing I'd forgotten You ever said among so much that is harsh, generous, desperate, confounding: "I hope our separation will help you to strengthen your spirit as a person. That hope is the basis by which I gain strength to let you go."

You *did* release me. At least that once.

Does that mean that our end could have been different, less lethal, less lasting, if I'd been smarter, or softer, or stronger sooner?

When V.T. arrives in my end of the country, on the run from the napalmed ruins of what he and so many others had thought his life would always be, now on his way into his first Buddhist retreat, the exact tattoo he described to me from the Fina station is needled into his left thigh.

I already had evidence, of course, that he does do some of the most improbable things he proposes. His body's in-born disregulations have taught him to disregard all manner of conventional limits, just to keep out of the tomb. But, still, I'm shocked. We've neither one mentioned the tattoo since the day I privately dismissed it as life-forwarding fantasy.

With a fingertip I trace round the garland of waves. As cerulean as real surf in real sun, as glossy as fired enamel. A thin band of breaking swells, slightly stylized, simplified to their essence in the Japanese way. The foaming curls embellished sparingly with delicate droplets of spume, each one shaded toward three dimensions.

The circlet remains open at two points, in the center of the outer and the inner thigh. The outer gap is a blank he tells me he'll fill some day, when he knows what belongs there.

When he says this, we are lying on the floor so we can fall no further. The circle's inner break is completed already: a wheel of fire, blue-black spokes streaming rampant red flame. An angry, colorful whorl in the tenderest flesh of the upper, inner leg, this one part of the whole tattoo has as yet incompletely healed; it oozes and is shaggy with thousands of miniscule scabs.

For this beautiful expiatory wound V.T. has spent money he did not have for food. I know this for a fact, and we do not speak of it.

At Harris, on retreat, V.T. and my teacher do not get on well. Within hours of our arrival, an electrical fire breaks out in the first cabin we are assigned. A bad omen. To me, about You, she says tartly, *Must be you karma.* After that, she gives me the cold shoulder. To You she says things You do not share with me, and in my hearing she suggests with her fierce attachment-destroying wit that You might, should she tell You to, spend your entire two-week retreat in the dry hole of the abandoned and drained swimming pool—once the summer escape of Hasidic city kids, now an attractive nuisance surrounded by a sagging fence posted with stern admonitions not to trespass.

And yet, she gives You refuge. And instructions: *Clean inside, clean outside.* She means: Clean your karma. She assigns prayers, and prostrations. Me, she keeps busy, and at a distance from both her and You. For most hours of most days, You and I are separated. There is stress all around and between us. Every day I rise too early from the inflatable mattress on the dirty floor of the little frame house we share with another retreatant and rush to prayers and the teacher's bidding. When I run in at midday with a bowl of food for You, or drag in exhausted after dark, You have spent the day sequestered in the cottage's cluttered, spidery, makeshift shrine room. You are not happy, with me or anything else, and that looks to me like my fault.

You karma.

Having volunteered for all this, there's nothing we can do about it, except endure. The teacher prescribes equanimity. With acerbity she commands us: *Be happy.*

There is for me a single point of joy in this retreat, near the end, on the full moon day, Saga Dawa Duchen, the day of the Buddha's enlightenment. A set of liturgies conducted over several days culminates in an ancient ritual rarely performed in public, a particularly passionate plea for release of all beings from the sufferings of *samsara*. Amid a hundred or more of my teacher's followers, I watch her sing and chant. Through the drum play, the clashing cymbals, and groaning horns, she offers a prayer of great, melancholy beauty and power. At the ritual's conclusion the full moon—a potent symbol of enlightenment in Buddhist iconography—is high and white and perfectly round in an ink-black sky. When I get back to our cabin, at nearly midnight, I am high on bliss, but the place is dead dark, and You lie burrowed under blankets—exhausted, hungry, and cold. I tell You to get up, come outside, and look at the moon. I have to insist. Then I point.

I worry, that night, You are too angry, or too deep in despair, to see my finger or the moon.

But I do not know that, not really. You are not me; to see *that* is to see You clearly.

Into the solitary confinement his retreat turns out to be, V.T. brings the death throes of a life he's lived for thirty years, along with a deviling dilemma: given the path he's now taken, is it possible—is it *permissible*—to go on living? Excluded all day every day from the rituals and festivities the great crowd of practitioners attends, he chants prayers, as instructed. He prostrates. And he cleans. Scrubs the tub, the walls, the floors, the toilet—all filthy when he begins, and gleaming when he's done.

The weather during this retreat, every single day of it—late May, high spring—is glorious. Bright and warm. Wild flowers rampant in the tall grass, red-purple rhododendron in heavy bloom. One day, seated on the steps of Cabin #9 at Harris, all alone in the sunny breeze, everyone elsewhere chanting long prayers in a hot and airless shrine room, V.T. discovers his cell phone has snared the always elusive signal. He calls up voicemail, gulps the poison stored there for him—more than enough to kill a man. Amid the windborne dandelion fluff he's pressed between the pages of his journal, he writes a poem:

Pool Instructions

Empty in the Deep
End—empty in The Shallow.
Die here. Drown. Swim.

V.T.'s tattoo shed its last scales on retreat but, kicking hard to stay afloat, I've forgotten it is there.

One Memorial Day weekend—wet and cold but very green—my two sisters and brother-in-law joined me in the final hectic effort to clear out every last closet, crawl space, and drawer of our parents' house, from basement to attic. We had only the weekend left before the whole place had to be empty and broom-clean for the new owners. Late the second night, when I was bone weary but the living room floor was still hidden under piles of things to keep and things to toss and mounds of boxes incorporating both, and I was sure we would never, ever live to finish, one sister opened a box and the other exclaimed: *Look, do you remember, I was there, it used to always look like that....*

The yellowed shirt box bulged with black-and-white snapshots of Sara and Betsy as toddlers, our mother and father as newlyweds and young parents, the house un-obscured by shrubbery, uncluttered by my mother's hoardings inside and my father's built-ons outside. My sisters dimly remembered seeing these pictures before, in their childhood but I, who had dug through all the troves of family photos for years looking for clues about how we ended up in the mess we did, I had never seen these snapshots before.

The moment felt like lifting something holy from silk wrappings. Anyone would have thought, sifting through the contents of that box, that ours was among the happiest of "normal" families. My mother is smiling, not just with her mouth but with her eyes. There is light in them. She and my father hold hands, sit near each other, look each other in the face. My sisters are giddy kids building forts and wearing fairy costumes handmade by the lovely mother and lovingly photographed by the doting father. The scenes and the people and the feelings evidenced in these pictures seemed both real and unreal, but really they are simply gone. Used to be, but are no more.

We three sisters dubbed our find "the happy pictures." They made us happy, at midnight, filthy and exhausted with hours of work yet to go. They gave back something I, at least, didn't know we'd ever had.

When the three-day weekend ended and they left for jobs and home, after the Salvation Army truck pulled away with the last of the shabbiest lamps and couches, I filled two dozen jumbo-sized black plastic garbage bags with the junk it seemed nobody, not even for free in the last hours of the yard sale, would take. With the help of Margaret, my childhood friend and supportive companion all the way through my parents' last days, I lugged the bags to the curb and lined them up, two rows deep and two bags high. I took a broom to the seven echoing rooms that once defined the whole hard and confusing world to me, and methodically moved dust bunnies, dead insects, and scraps of trash out the door. A steady rain fell. When I was done sweeping I photographed all that emptiness, as if I could hold onto it.

The next morning when I came by for a last look, trash pickers had ripped into the sacks on the curb, the mystery of what might have been inside too great to ignore. Some of the bulk was indeed missing but most of what they'd pawed through lay sodden in the street. Resentfully, I re-bagged it. Picking from the pavement waterlogged scraps of paper bearing my mother's handwriting or my father's— grocery lists, planting instructions—made me queasy, as if what I handled were bits of their flesh, their remains desecrated by strangers. Then, sodden myself, I dropped off the keys at the realty office, and drove away to my other life in Florida.

The happy pictures disappeared. Sara is certain she took the box of them to her house in Maryland, but they've yet to turn up again. It may be they went by mistake to the curb, and from there to the dump. Surprises continued to surface, though. Betsy, always tightly emotionally attached to our mother and uncomplainingly loyal, spontaneously spoke in the first months after her funeral a short, crystalline list of the injustices done her, like the beating she took for ruining the monkey costume Mother sewed for the kindergarten circus, by forgetting to remove the mask before drinking from the water fountain; and her exclusion—"Mother say I couldn't come to your wedding"—from Sara's one and only, and my two to that point.

Every time I saw Sara, she'd list out loud the many things our parents had done *right* raising us: the work ethic, the books, such attention to history and culture, and their epic frugality—permanently inoculating us against materialism. She brought up examples, too, of their simple kindnesses: our father uncomplainingly carrying box after box up flight after flight of stairs to her top floor room in an old dorm when she left home for college. About the rest, though— the guns, the rape, the police involvement it led to, the hoarding, the venom our parents stewed in, the hulking bitter ruin of their bodies, their hopes, and their minds—she could not stop grieving about this. More than once she said—rhetorically, I knew—"Somebody should write about this."

The second time I heard it, I confessed: "I am."

I only ever got that single glimpse of the happy pictures, in a late-night rush, exhausted. I meant to look more carefully, another day, when I felt better. I never imagined there'd not be time to revisit them in less harried circumstances. I assumed what was lost, once found, would remain.

I was wrong. Impermanence, you know?

Years later, more pictures from the past drop into my life. DVDs, this time, given me by my children's father's new wife. She has salvaged many hours of video from old camcorder tapes documenting J's and B's early years, long before the divorce. Birthdays, holidays, visits from relatives, visits home. So many Easters and Christmases. I watch these alone, late at night, on V.T.'s and my brand new flat screen television. There I am, the me I used to be, living a life that used to be the only one I could imagine. My children are plump babies and opinionated toddlers. Everyone in these videos adores them and patiently caters to their every whim. We all look so admirable. My sisters, who bore no children, lift mine up to swing seats, crawl around with them on the rug, hunt Easter eggs beside them, and cast with them for fish.

Both sets of grandparents are in these moving pictures, too, of course. What a shock, to see my parents alive. The clothes they "always" wore, my father's elderly stoop and the odd way he carried his hands in his old age, stiff as paddles alongside his hips. My mother's decrepitude—a dowager's hump so pronounced she looked like a hunchback; the pathetic way she clung to appliances and cabinets to make her way around the kitchen; and her constant, repetitive mind-numbing patter about *nothing* but who had done what and why. How amazing it is, their—and my—insubstantial substance on that screen: we could not look more "real" than we do in those pictures but my parents are vanished from this earth and whoever I was in those days is someone who looks familiar but is a stranger to me now.

How did we get where we are, from where we used to be? A question common as dirt—and unanswerable.

So many times I have heard my teacher's followers repeat *her* teacher's admonition: *You do not know what may happen.*

I repeat these words sometimes, to soothe and to chasten myself, but only silently, because hearing them makes other people uncomfortable.

They sound way too simple—too obvious—to be so powerfully true.

In the summer of 2007, I put my much-rejected, eight-times-re-written novel manuscript in the mail one last time, in the complete absence of hope, and departed alone amid a group of strangers for Tibet.

J, a newly-minted college graduate, waitressed in Tampa between long hours cramming for med school entrance exams and unpaid work as a nurse's aide. B was a brand-new high school graduate shocked by my teacher's presence, in the wings, at his commencement. I'd invited him to come with me to Tibet, and after a while he answered in kind tones, by email. He had a chance to make some money. All summer long he would detail cars and boats in Florida's syrupy heat.

V.T., back in the desert after our retreat at Harris, longed to go along to Tibet but of course he could not. The furies, the machinations of divorce, questions and wounds, so many things tearing and gaping.

That any of these loose ends added up to anything or ever would no matter how long I waited—that black hat of resentment sat heavy on my head when the jet lifted off for Beijing.

When my dance dream comes true, the beat's a box-step, not a waltz, and the Bliss is in a bottle, a brand of chardonnay, on ice. My third wedding, the only happy one. In photo after photo, I glow like a lamp, my gaze fastened on You.

Your blue tie. Your sky eyes. Our home, on a ridge. Bare windows and naked trees. Mullioned November light.

I am marrying at Thanksgiving, just like my mother did. The irony stings, but pragmatism overruled superstition; amid many complicated calendars only this date would work. Faces lit with mixed emotions turn round us as I turn and You turn. Loyal friends, shards of family, encircling me clasping You. My dead parents look on from separate frames on the mantel garlanded in autumn foliage: wine-red asters, bronze lilies, the bright berries and dull leaves of the bittersweet vine.

In a random cut from the nuptial mix, Bonnie Raitt croons a song called "You"—

the only one that mattered—

My mother.
My father.
My daughter, my son.
My husband, my husband, my husband—
You.

Part 4

Walk Fast, Keep Going

My mother died alone in the hospital in the middle of the night, from pneumonia. She stopped breathing, and sometime later a nurse found her. This was not unexpected. Her doctor had advised us—my father, my sisters, my children and me—that her end was very near.

My father sat with her that night as he had most evenings since she returned to the hospital. When it got toward his bed time, she suggested he go back to his room at assisted living, to get some sleep. When he called me before dawn to say she was gone, I was lying awake in my bed, more or less waiting for the phone to ring. What surprised me was the single fact he shared about their last evening together. "I kissed her," he said.

That he had done this and that he told me, I saw it as his simple benediction to their sixty-seven-year marriage. I have no memory of ever seeing them embrace in all the years I lived with them, and the few kisses I observed him attempt to give her she dodged, or bore with flagrant distaste. In the decade since her death I have often wondered what that last kiss between them was like. Did she flinch? Did she allow it graciously? Is it possible she welcomed it? Was there, at their very end, a moment of warmth and acceptance? Even gratitude?

My mother, in the final six months of her life, was not the person I'd known her to be all of mine. She softened. Admitted mistakes, and asked for forgiveness. Sara and her husband told me she apologized to each of them for the way she'd shut them out, and vilified them to their faces and behind their backs, for decades. This dramatic change in her nature came about like this: convalescing in a nursing home from a surgery, she coded. Resuscitated by staff, she remained to the end of her days sweetened and mild. Often silent. Eerily calm. She never described any kind of near-death experience—no white light, no voice of God, no feeling that a savior approached. But nonetheless and for whatever reason, she completely, profoundly changed.

Deep in the attic closet I feared as a child—where the glass-coffined, undead man from *Twilight Zone* somehow lay according to Betsy's sly, indelible suggestion—there stood a treasure: a big, black steamer trunk with arched ribs of smooth blond wood. The lid was heavy and sharp-fanged; the tin rim could bite like a guillotine when dropped by accident on small fingers. The locks had teeth too, pointed tabs inside round cavities meant to be closed by hanging thick tongues secured with a key no one ever possessed. Once the ordeal of lifting the lid had been passed through, the tray beneath it—thick cardboard, green with a fleur-de-lis pattern like the backs of playing cards, lidded with flaps of that same cardboard replicating the curve of the trunk's lid—held jewelry and hat pins, feathered cloches and beaded handbags. In the hold below were long-waisted, narrow dresses of slick or shiny or gauzy fabric, flapper clothes that must have been my mother's finery from her college days in the 1920s but which were, to my little-girl eyes in the early 60s, as fantastically other-worldly as the suits of fairies.

Sometimes I pulled dresses from the trunk and wiggled myself into them willy-nilly; I had no reference point for how such exotic garments had been worn. Mostly, I handled them for their mysteries: their mildewy, moth-balled scents, their scaly or tissuey or slippery textures, their faded, fabulous colors. A whiff of strong story clung to the lot of them—a past unknowable, a significance undeniable. My mother put a stop to this play; I can't remember why. Eventually, I'd learn the trunk originally belonged to my mother's father, her "Daddy" whom I knew as a frighteningly dour bald-headed old man, dead when I was still very young. Only as an adult did I find out, from relatives, how he had beaten and bullied my mother and her mother. For me, the trunk was simply romantic and alluring. At some point in my early adulthood my mother allowed me to have it. The dresses, the hats, the jewelry were no longer inside it. I refurbished the trunk and moved it with me from place to place for years before passing it—an attractive antique stripped of its charge—to Sara, who has it still.

The first day I re-entered the house of my childhood with the pending necessity of emptying it for sale, I harbored a deeper, secret intention. My mother had been dead for just over a year, and I could not shake the notion that her house, minus her darkly complicated presence, held answers to questions that dogged me about her, about me, about who I had been growing up and might yet turn out to be. I believed—although I told no one this—I could claim this information through my senses by living there, temporarily, again. I feared the house in an obscure, inspecific way. I dreaded going there, as I had all my adult years, because I associated returning home with the fresh onset of depression.

It turned out that the intersection of the closing date with the end of the semester I was teaching left me only ten days to re-inhabit my past.

I climbed the steep stairs to the attic bedroom; its familiar scent seized me and made me small again. When I approached the walk-in closet's door, blank and dark as ever, its ancient iron doorknob still a-kilter, my heart accelerated. I laughed at myself—my fear of the boogey man still alive after forty years—and opened the door. Dust motes, heat, mounds of boxes and long rows of zippered hanger bags greeted me. The steamer trunk's absence instantly excavated a long-buried memory: the sensation, in my body, of closing myself inside the trunk, or letting some playmate close me in. I recalled in my fingers and shoulders and lungs the tense excitement of permitting that interment, the suffocating mothball-and-dry-rot smell of the chest and its contents, the blind weight of its lid, the dark possibility it might never re-open.

I remembered something else, too. Alongside the trunk, beneath a small four-paned window, there had sat for all the years of my youth a behemoth air conditioner draped with a cast-off slipcover. Some years my father installed the air conditioner in that window; the house had no other cooling, not even an attic fan, to beat back a summer's intense heat gathering there beneath the roof. Most years he did not do this; frugality had higher value than comfort in that house, always. Some winter afternoons in my childhood, though, the sun fell just so on that strange window seat, the green cover lit up with gold sun partitioned into four rectangles. The old air conditioner was as gone now as the steamer trunk, but I felt all over again the sweet solitary pleasure of sitting atop it, high up, close to blue sky latticed by the bare branches of the elm in the yard and the wooded flank of a hill across the street.

How many layers of experience—nightmares, risk-taking, the solace of loneliness—crowded that single dusty place. I really had feared that closet. And I really had played there, finding refuge and release. I cannot sort out which feeling dominated which years. Scanning back across five decades, I cannot make my memories add up, line off, make sense.

My trip to Tibet made no sense either. I went without regard to expense; I had no job at that point and no prospects for future full-time work. I had the summer off from teaching as an adjunct, and I had some money, an inheritance from my mother—fruit of her strong attachment to what was hers; she'd fought my father for decades to keep his name off the money her father left her. I didn't make the trip with my teacher or to please her; in fact, she strongly suggested I not go. Tibet, whence she had escaped more than thirty years prior, crossing the Himalayas on foot, was dangerous, she said. I traveled instead with a group of college alumni led by an Asian studies professor who happened to be both ethnic Chinese and a Tibetan Buddhist practitioner. I went to Tibet simply because the opportunity presented itself. Arriving in Lhasa, I attained a pilgrim's circumstance minus a pilgrim's intention.

In the Barkhor, the cobblestoned marketplace encircling the seventh-century Jokhang Temple, monks and lay practitioners circumambulated Tibetan Buddhism's holiest site, some of them in full-body prostrations. Locomoting like human-sized inch-worms, they planted their thickly callused bare feet at the spot where their foreheads—also callused—had just touched ground, then slid hands and torso forward to stretch out full length and face down on the stones. They pulled their feet toward their heads, stood up, and lay down again. They covered miles with their bodies this way; some wore squares of tire tread bound to their knees and their palms. They offered this devotion single-mindedly, parting waves of gawking tourists pointing cameras, while the locals gossiped, bought vegetables, and policed with friendly, hands-on insistence the necessity that all human traffic in the Barkhor move always clockwise around the temple—because to circumambulate counterclockwise, the "wrong" direction, is unthinkably inauspicious for everyone. Inside the temple, Tibetans standing in an hourslong queue to touch the revered statue of Jowo Shakyamuni Buddha let me cut line simply because, at the urging of our leader, I asked. My feet slid from beneath me more than once on greasy black soot laid down by scores of butter lamps before I pressed my forehead to the Buddha's hem, an awed and nervous poseur pilgrim wondering what, if anything, might result.

Food poisoning. Just before dark, that very first day in Lhasa. Nausea, with vile sulfurous burps, gave warning in the afternoon, and although I went along with the group to dinner at a vegetarian restaurant run as a fund-raising venture for a monastery, I ate almost nothing. Nibbled some rice, sipped some green tea. People asked later if the fiery seasoning of the food on that table had been the culprit but my best guess at the source of my sickness was the two or three leaves of fresh, inadequately washed cilantro floating in the tasty and familiar sauce of some Indian curry I'd eaten with relish at lunch time, in a roof-top restaurant in the Barkhor, an eatery already vetted by an earlier group of American travelers as "safe."

By bedtime, the ferocity of the bubbling and boiling in my gut, and the hideous smell and taste of first the reflux and then the vomit, left me no doubt what I was in for; I'd had food poisoning before, in Cairo and in Manhattan. I settled in to wait it out. Alone in the dark comfort of the Kyichu Hotel, a westernized oasis catering to European and American travelers (yak burgers and yak-milk mac-and-cheese on the menu; flush toilets; two computers in an alcove off the courtyard offering slow but reasonably reliable internet access), I tried to be a good Buddhist and a good sport, dealing patiently with the shakes, the convulsive dry heaves, and the violent diarrhea, even running a bath (that was hot, as the next one would not be) to clean myself and wash my sweat pants in the aftermath of a particularly foul and uncontainable purge. I did feel grateful for my prior experience with food poisoning; it gave me confidence the misery would pass.

As the night wore on, I noticed more and more trouble getting out of bed, more and more difficulty balancing on my feet long enough to reach the bathroom (very fortunately a private one, inside my single room). After a while I lay down on the floor by the toilet. But the unheated tile gave me shivers I could not stop except beneath all the blankets on the bed. I fell to bargaining with myself about how much longer I could stay in the warm bed with clamped sphincter, risking an accident I'd not have the strength to clean up. Eventually I diagnosed my accelerating weakness as dehydration and prescribed myself water, by the sip, which usually came right back up.

I knew something about dehydration. J, at fifteen, threw up for so many hours in response to an infelicitous antibiotic that I had to lift her from the bathroom floor and take her to the ER for an intravenous drip. The part of my mind that was now calm and becalmed—running slow for lack of fuel and balance—noted fear feeding like kudzu on that memory. It sprouted chains of reason tangled with unreason: the dehydration process had gone too far too fast; I could never stop the slide with the tiny quantity of water I could keep down; I'd have to miss tomorrow morning's bus to the Potala Palace; what if someone took me, instead, to a hospital…a *Chinese* hospital, a Chinese hospital in *Lhasa*. Our presence in Tibet was neither illegal nor fully legal; our visa applications listed Xining, not Lhasa, as the intended destination because Chinese officials were known to be squirrelly about westerners visiting Lhasa, especially westerners like us with ties to the Tibetan Buddhists the Chinese government was so particularly determined to repress. Who knew what medical or political consequences might befall me if my illness thrust me onto Chinese radar inside a Chinese institution? The more my body's energy drained away, the faster my mind whirred until, just before dawn, an enervation unlike any I'd ever known overtook me. I gave up on fear. I gave up on life. That I would die quietly in this bed seemed reasonable, a simple fact, nothing to fight against.

My mother lived less than two weeks after I last visited her, the millennial New Year's weekend I flew up from Florida to wait beside her for the death she'd told me all my life she meant to welcome.

Every time I left her hospital room, for a soda or a trip to the restroom, she fell away from the shore of the living on which she was barely snagged. Re-entering her room I'd be momentarily shocked by the sight of a skeleton barely covered with translucent skin—my mother's skin, my mother's *face*—propped in a lounge chair. Before my eyes she was turning into a corpse, the fullness of flesh, the elasticity of life, dissolving.

Her mouth open, she'd be snoring—a glottal gasping for the next breath. The sound was ugly, like the smell of stale urine always faintly present beneath the powder, the soap scent, the bleached sheets, the hygienic plastic wrappings.

When I spoke to her, or touched her, she returned with a startled jerk from however deep she had sunk away. Each time my presence summoned her back she was glad to see me, but each time it was apparent she'd come a distance, with difficulty. My face, my corporality, maybe even my existence, surprised her, to use her term, "no end." I was a fresh wonder, every time. She made me feel it.

Later, during the days intervening between that visit and her death, we spoke once by phone. She was weak and could barely talk; I heard the pneumonia's congestion clogging her chest and her voice while a nurse held the receiver to her ear. I said we'd had a good visit, hadn't we? She said, rallying to a fervor that surprised me, "It was something. It was...*something.*"

That word in her lexicon meant...indescribable. I understood, from my long familiarity with her and her words that for her that quiet, inconclusive weekend was something she'd not expected nor known she needed. A friend of mine, hearing me tell of the visit, its tenor and my mother's death soon thereafter, remarked with confident clarity, "She was waiting for you."

If she was, she did not say so, and I'm sure she never expected me to come. So much had been torn up between us by then, and for such a long time.

My father lit a candle for my mother when she'd been dead nine months.

The Methodist church where for years he'd attended Sunday school but never the service, declared a memorial Sunday for all its members who'd died that year. My mother's Daddy had been a pillar of that church, and she'd remained technically a member, never removed from the roster during the decades she boycotted, religiously, the church and its ministrations. When she was dead, the ministrations continued: her name on the list of the deceased generated an invitation to which my father responded. He took his new woman with him.

It was she who told me about the event. Bonnie said, sensibly enough with respect to issues of tact and public perception in a small town, "He wanted me to go with him, so I did. He didn't want to go by hisself."

She told me how he'd walked right up and lit that candle, sweet as could be. How nice he looked. Dressed in a suit, and a white shirt, and a new tie he'd bought at the mall.

The purchase of the tie seemed to surprise her. It sure surprised me. My mother would have been shocked, no end. None of us imagined my father capable of shopping for himself.

Bonnie's plain old love worked miracles, large and small.

In the Kyichu Hotel, blankets wrapped round me snugly, the mattress supporting me comfortably, I lay quietly in utter dark and silence, slowly rehearsing certain corollaries of my death. Bills left unpaid. Emails unanswered, an out-of-date will. My apartment back home a mess. My underwear lying befouled on the hotel bathroom floor. Karma the cat, chronically ill, a plague of sores, in the care of a sitter who would not know what to do with her when I did not come back and who would never be paid. I'd leave behind so much untidiness. And...*oh*...the ten-year life-or-death struggle to find a publisher for my novel would simply end, and...*ah*...I would not see V.T., my one and only, ever again.

You, V.T.: still recovering from surgery, and We: still a year short, best case, of a moment we might truly be together. And...You, my children, who kept me alive when I had no other reason not to die... and You, my ex, who needed so bad for so long to destroy me...and Hen, the other ex, written out of everything...and You, the dead parents, persisting in my dreams and my habits of being.

All you other-halves I'd clung to, resented, warred for, warred against, the long line of You I'd rejected yet internalized, in whose glance I sought myself, by whose response I weighed my worth—I was going to die and You would forgive me, forget me, or not; take spouses, have babies, find jobs and lose them, acquire honors and new tattoos…or just evaporate when cell death erased my brain's encoded memories.

All this clearing out and cleaning up was going to happen without my lifting a finger.

Hmm.... I sighed at the marvel, and let go of You.

Late in his first college semester B's plan for a second tattoo resurfaces. By this time I've forgotten all about it. His call, and my response: searching out the exact, right Tibetan script for the compassion mantra only to find he'd got it already, without me. Just days before I pack my car for the ten-hour drive south to a Christmas beach holiday wherein V.T. will meet my children for the first time, B phones me. When, exactly, will I be in Florida?

I stiffen. The question feels coy. He knows the dates; I've persisted in insisting he and his sister be there to meet the man I'm about to marry.

He overlooks my harumpf when I reiterate all that.

"Perfect," he says. "Lefty's moved, but I found him. He's in a new shop in Ybor." B names a date and time, already booked, when he'll get this new tattoo. "J will be there. You'll come, too, won't you? Be with me when I get it?"

All I can feel is how this blindsides me—not a word about the tattoo, for months—and how much I dislike being force-fed that much surprise.

I restrain myself from mentioning my feelings. I stammer, instead, "But V.T. will be with me. Will it be okay if he comes?"

The nexus of my husband-to-be with my children's and my longtime party-of-three is plenty awkward already; I imagine trying to explain to V.T. he'll have to sit alone at the rented beach house while I take off with my kids for another chapter in a family ritual.

"He's *supposed* to come." Loving exasperation at my mom-ish denseness floods B's tone. "Me and J, you and him. The welcome thing, you know?"

Geez. I swallow a wad of astonishment. Together-tattoo, redux.

"Okay," I say, all breezy. "Sounds like a plan." Then I remember my role.

"You need me to pay?"

~

In my bed in the Kyichu Hotel, my death upon me, the lifetime of effort I'd devoted to wanting some things so badly while striving so strenuously to keep at bay the things I didn't want, the struggle seemed, oh, just sad, and a little laughable. Ah...well...hmm.

So much clarity about such a plain old truth made me very happy. I giggled a little. I remembered that at death I was supposed to remember the lama. Lying on my back in the dark, tucked up in bed like a child, I visualized the guru and said *sadhana*, the daily essential meditation liturgy, speaking aloud and slowly with mistakes and restarts because my mind kept dropping the thread.

I made it all the way to the end of the prayer with bursts of *dren-pa*, remembrance, and calm pools of *shey-zhin*, mindfulness. I felt proud that at the threshold of the bardo I had the presence of mind to remember what to remember.

Maybe dying was not such a big deal, after all.

~

I remember my mother happy and relaxed—and myself connected peaceably to her—in only one place: her flower porch. There she tended in silence her flocks of orchids and violets, watering, pinching dead blooms or overgrowth, examining leaves and stems and roots for signs of health or disease. Warm in winter when the rest of the house wasn't, steamy in summer, the sun beating the three walls of casement windows my father had used to enclose an ordinary porch. Fecundity simmered there year round in the quarter-inch of water always standing in vast metal trays (constructed by my father from sheet metal, the rims bent with pliers and the corners spot-welded, since ready-made aluminum ones, purchased retail, cost too much) and many smaller glass baking dishes and molded resin trays lining wooden shelves that tiered the walls floor to ceiling, three feet deep at the bottom and narrowing as they climbed. My mother's calm inside this womb felt palpable. As a small child, anytime she allowed it, I joined her there, playing quietly within her sight.

The concrete floor's radiant heat and the long ranks of fluorescent light tubes mounted above each shelf kept the water in the trays constantly evaporating, hyper-humidifying the air, generating a swampy micro-climate in which hundreds of orchids, their terracotta pots raised atop a second, inverted pot, formed a rain forest. African violets wedged pot-to-pot on the lowest shelves, their thick nests of velvet-furred leaves interlocking to form a seamless forest floor. The highest, narrowest, driest shelves wintered houseplants ordinary and exotic, some ferns and succulents decades old, handed down to my mother from her mother and her aunts.

A tin washtub half-filled with water and aerated by a circulating fountain created a broody electric hum overlaid with burble; water-loving plants like philodendron and a vine she called Moses-in-the-bulrushes for its cradle-shaped blooms grew around and into this deep dark-water pond in which, in the room's well-tended heyday, goldfish or guppies swam. Jobs assigned me, ones I do not remember resenting, were the feeding of the fish and the replenishing of the trays. Several three-gallon buckets of tap water stood always on the warm floor, uncovered to allow the chlorination to rise off. I dipped a plastic watering pot into a bucket, pulled it out dripping, and inserted its long narrow nose into some gap amid the leaves and pots, pouring to exactly the old fill line, taking great care never to wet and thus spot the leaves of an African violet; I kept a tissue in one hand to dab up my mistakes before my mother could notice.

She protected her place as well as her plants; I was never supposed to enter the flower porch without permission. But I did. It was leafy and cozy, an outdoor place I could enter indoors. It smelled good and felt safe, no matter what roiled in the rest of the house.

I couldn't stop myself from introducing characters and their stories into this paradise—plastic alligators, appropriate to the setting, but also buffalo, giraffe and dinosaurs from dime-store packages labeled "zoo animals." Silently, I moved these actors through the water or perched them on the tree-pots, nestled them inside the V'd sheaths of the orchids' foliage or left them peeking from beneath white, fleshy air roots terminating in blind green nubbins. Inside my head I narrated plot lines I felt, knowing no necessity in those days to translate sensations and understandings into words. My mother fussed and fumed and forbade me to play out there but ultimately she gave in, leaving the plastic animals where I'd parked them while I grew up and moved on, so that I found them again, some few survivors, decades later during the emptying of the house, the trays long dried out and the last remaining orchids shrunk to desiccated skeletons.

Sara rescued the orchids that still harbored life, and takes comfort now in their blooming which, for her, is a sign of positive connection to our mother. When I buy orchids, I overwater or underhumidify, and they die.

My imagination, applied to reconstructing the flower porch as it was, remains damp and green. Through its lens I find my mother easily. I smell moving water and healthy mold, the slight bitterness of the violets' leaves overlaid with vanilla-sweet nectar oozing from Catalina orchids' big, showy blossoms: white with yellow throats, or lavender with rose-purple throats. The air's moisture beads on my forearms and my face, and I study her, Mama, seated on one of the two small wooden stools perpetually living on the bare concrete floor.

One is stained maple, a flat rectangle with splayed legs fatter at the feet, the pegs anchoring them to the seat visible at its four corners as blond circles in the maple's russet. The other stool is a wooden box, four sides, a top with a hole at its center and an open bottom, painted with many coats of white enamel, resting on its side because the top is the smallest and least useful of its surfaces.

I wonder distractedly, again, what could have been the original function of that odd creation, obviously homemade, its cavity stuffed with a wad of rags and plastic grocery sacks. My mother's thighs rising up from the stool seat dominate this amalgam memory built of many years of loving, needing, fearing, and despising her; they are enormous, the thighs no less than the feelings. Bared by her hiked-up house dress, they are tracked with twisting purple varicose-river-veins. The thighs angle up because the stool, dwarfed by her backside, is low, and they gape apart, probably for balance. What is between them, dark, I do not imagine. Her belly, also huge, distended, lumps into her lap like a parcel. Her hair, dark brown, almost black like mine but gone salt-and-pepper, like mine beneath its dye, is sweated to her brow and twisted on her head in crisscrosses of bobby pins. Her mouth hangs open slightly, for breath rather than speech. One of her upper front teeth is broken at an angle.

I don't think You ever looked exactly like that, Mama, in the days the flower porch still gave You, and me, some refuge. It's the way I can remember You, now, reconstruct You, now, love You and never know You, wish I could have known You better, wish I'd known then how to make things different, have no hate left, now.

⁓

Maybe the easy generosity of B's backhanded invitation to V.T. to join the family tattoo party encouraged me to imagine my children, at this point twenty-two and eighteen, warmly welcoming their stepfather-to-be into their lives. I could not have constructed a more unfounded delusion. Even the logistics of getting all four of us in one place long enough to conduct a formal introduction prove daunting: my presence in Tampa, much less V.T.'s, must remain prudently veiled from J and B's father and his new wife, at whose waterfront home on the other side of the sprawling city my children are spending most of their winter holiday.

The meeting takes the form of lunch, in the privacy of a public place, under a shelter at the bayside park where I often took J and B and their school chums to play, both pre- and post-divorce. The little green space is a vestige of Old Florida—a long wooden fishing pier jutting into Tampa Bay, massive live oaks and skinny palm trees, a concrete boat launch and cement-block bait shop, a scattering of heavy tables paired with metal grills on kiltered stalks arrayed round the swing set and seesaws—boxed in these days by high-end town-houses and a glittering yacht club. In the decade since my kids and I frequented this park, gentrification has arrived. The refurbished gazebo; the absence of junkies' cast-off needles and glassine wrappers; the brand-new, brightly-colored, downsized-for-safety playground equipment, all give our picnic a visual boost.

But the weather, a touch too cool and windy for comfortable al fresco dining, is a downer; this Christmas season will be one of the chilly, cloudy ones that disappoint snowbirds. J and B have volunteered to bring lunch, Cuban sandwiches, hot-pressed, from our family-favorite source of them, a hole-in-the-wall bodega across the road from J's old high school in a blue-collar, ethnically diverse neighborhood.

A good deal of history sits down with us at the picnic table. I feel on the lifted hairs of my forearms the tense breaths of the Christmas past when—a barely-still-intact family of four—we fished from this pier. Specters of the bottle-rockets I allowed J and B to illegally fire from the mangroved shadows of the shoreline, in compensation for a lost and angry father our first Fourth of July as family of three, whistle accusingly past my ears. The butter-skinned, meat-stuffed sandwiches slicking our fingers are foreign food to V.T., heavy in his stomach, but they conjure in my taste buds the now-inaccessible comfort such greasy sweet food once granted our threesome *in medias* divorce apocalypse.

My mind fills up with that static but the silence among us is solid; conversation proves actually impossible. Every brave sally V.T. undertakes dead-ends. My attempts to stoke interaction sound like sitcom chirps: the mom saying mom things while the children roll eyes and pick at food. Everyone is relieved by V.T.'s and my urgent need—we are middle-aged and coffeed-up—to march off to the restrooms behind the bait shop. He and I find nothing to say to each other as we hustle across thin grass, but I *feel* B and J talking fast behind our receding backs.

V.T. will gamely state, in the car as we leave the scene, "I don't think that made things any *worse*." I will have nothing to add. Too flustered to feel angry but suspecting betrayal: why would my children so readily agree to meet, and then be so pointedly unsociable?

It won't dawn on me until much later that I've just lived a replay of what so many family meals have taught me: what You need, my children, is so often something other than what my menu offers... except...You do seem ready sometimes to try and retie our old ties.

I didn't, of course, pass away in Lhasa. My chummy relationship with Death turned out to be just one more delusion. Soon after dawn on the morning following my collapse, Julie, the group's second-in-command, came to my door, letting herself in with a key from the hotel desk because I called out, when she knocked, that I could not get up. I hadn't tried recently, but only because I knew the effort would be pointless. I was finished.

Standing by my bed, she looked down at me with concern. I told her I didn't want or need a thing. Water, now mixed with the Gatorade powder another group member donated me, was at hand.

Food was out of the question. So was tomorrow's three-hour bus trip to the mountaintop monastery where the group would camp for two nights.

"You'll have to leave me here," I told her flatly. "I can't get up."

She didn't argue with me. She left and I lay back in weary peace. Very soon Julie let herself in again. The hotel desk, she said, insisted that I was suffering from altitude sickness. Oh, come on, I thought, prodded from my languor by their stupidity. Their prescription, which Julie had carried to me, made me genuinely angry: oxygen, delivered through a nostril tube from a rubberized inflated pillow I was to squeeze beneath one arm, and a bowl of steamed rice.

Irritably, I sent Julie away and took up the rubber pillow, inhaling the tendril of oxygen the full slight strength I could muster pressed out of the pillow and into the plastic tube. The oxygen stank of rubber. I felt absolutely no better, but already, on the back of my anger at the interruption of my death-embracing bliss, a ladder of rational thought was spontaneously forming. With no intention to do so, I trudged it step by step to the reluctant conclusion that the Tibetans downstairs were probably right: altitude sickness now trumped my food poisoning.

I'd had experience, only two days prior, with altitude sickness. But until Julie and the desk clerks made me see what they saw, I'd forgotten how much I'd learned, the hard way, about the physical and mental consequences of oxygen deprivation, and the Diamox I'd been taking to counteract that.

The drug is a diuretic used to treat congestive heart failure and a certain form of glaucoma. At high altitudes, where oxygen is thinner than a given body's accustomed to, the heart's pumping slows from lack of oxygen, and fluid can accumulate in the lungs or the brain, leading to death. Diamox reduces the load on the heart and gets to the brain more of what little oxygen is available. The drug is "recommended" to travelers who are "concerned" about altitude sickness, especially at elevations above 10,000 feet. The catch is it must be taken prophylactically, beginning twenty-four hours before ascent, and tapered off thereafter as the body acclimatizes. Simple instructions, but very difficult to put into practice when one is traveling from place to place, ascending and descending unpredictably. Drug-phobic in my upright middle age, and impressed by a list of possible side effects that sounded exactly like altitude sickness—headaches, dizziness, nausea, lethargy, confusion, shortness of breath, a racing heart—I obtained the medication as part of my trip preparations but intended not to take it.

Lhasa's altitude is just under 14,000 feet. In order to acclimatize gradually, our group had planned to travel to Lhasa not by air but by train, a twenty-four-hour ride from Xining, in China's Sichuan Province. After a thirteen-hour flight from New York to Beijing, and a hot, packed, bumpy flight from Beijing to Xining, we waited several desperate hours in our bus outside the train depot while our guide negotiated inside. Next came a hasty, short-sticks lottery among the group to decide who'd get a shot at the first seats that *might* be available; then a race, literally, dragging luggage, to the track where a shopping bag of liquor and cash bribes changed hands before *some* of the tickets our travel agent had paid for weeks ago were pulled from beneath the hat of the minor official to whom the sack was handed. We claimed bunks with our bodies and our bags. I and the group's youngest member found ourselves in a four-berth cabin with a Chinese mother and daughter amused by and friendly toward our American mal-adaptation. They offered tea and sweets, and voluntarily dialed down the volume on the piped-in propaganda—the glories of Sino-Tibetan unity—available in a choice of Chinese or English.

I drew a top bunk, on which I could not fully sit up, but which did allow me privacy as long as I was willing to lie down and stay put. That I did, once I'd made an obligatory and miserable scramble—the swaying of the train threatening to amp my low-grade nausea into full-blown motion sickness—to the toilets, one with a seat, and the other what the group had dubbed by then a squatty potty: foot-shaped depressions on either side of a hole in the floor.

In the bunk, I turned my face to the wall and tried to surf the building waves of anxiety that rocked me worse than the train. I feared the Chinese because we were Buddhists on the way to Lhasa; the political tensions that would erupt there in riots, arson, looting, and murder less than nine months later, in the spring of 2008, were quite palpable any time Chinese and Tibetans were in proximity. I feared my nausea, because I'd been prone to motion sickness since childhood, and an outbreak of vomiting would be impossible to hide or relieve for the duration of the twenty-four hour ride. I feared our destination, because I wasn't really sure I wanted to visit such an exotic and spiritually charged place, and I feared more than anything else the road there: its highest point—a fact I learned accidentally, from another traveler—at 18,000 feet.

The train would cross that high pass deep in the night, so I decided to try to sleep through it. Jet lag, sleep deprivation, and cultural disorientation exhausted me sufficiently that I dozed off despite hunger and noise. I awoke in full dark and complete stillness. The train had stopped moving, and I could not breathe. My heart punched my chest wall like a crazy, random fist desperate to break out of a box. Pressure in my temples suggested I'd held my breath too long under water. I sucked in air, under-oxygenated and unhelpful, and instructed myself to be calm. I assessed the frantic effort of my heart with dismay. I felt both keenly nauseated and absolutely inert. Terror zoomed round and round a racetrack in my mind, enlarging itself on every loop—why had the train stopped?

Had Chinese soldiers—omnipresent, gun-toting, humorless—boarded? Were they searching car to car? Our Tibetan guide, a devout Buddhist who lacked the permission papers necessary to lawfully accompany us, had been imprisoned and tortured already for anti-Chinese activities. I feared for him and the wife and child he'd told us about. I feared for us should anything befall him, as no one in our sub-group, split away from our Chinese-speaking leader by the lottery for the train berths, could communicate with either the soldiers or the locals. And I feared shamelessly for myself—that my aching lungs would burst, that my laboring heart would quit. *Move move move move*, I begged the train. Darkness and stillness answered me, my panic a tiny pebble swallowed up into vast indifference.

I lay there a long time on the motionless train, my mind in a frenzy, my body paralyzed. I had just enough clarity of thought left to gradually reason out that my body's distress created my mind's unrest. My cognition was impaired because my brain was as confused and stressed as my heart and lungs. I wrenched myself up off the mattress, closed my hand on the flashlight I'd wedged between mattress and wall, and in its small, yellow moon-circle of light dug laboriously through my backpack for a water bottle and a first-ever dose of Diamox.

Paralyzed silence—at the table, in the car, in the den while the television prattled: the default soundtrack of my childhood. On the infrequent occasions my parents did speak expansively, they told and re-told Southern Gothic tales of people they'd known—now tragically dead—and places they'd lived or visited—now ruined. A scree of nostalgia rubbled every story's surface. When we traveled, we toured graveyards, battlefields, antebellum mansions. Much of what I saw was sealed inside glass cases. Everything that mattered happened in past tense—way past. All of it reeked of loss. When I was very small we still visited relatives. They were old, wrinkled, eccentric, infirm or alcoholic. The "children" I was told I would see turned out to be grownups who sometimes had children of their own—babies, useless to me. I coped just as I did at home: I went outside and sat under bushes or climbed up trees. I wandered into weedy gardens and out to sagging barns, alone, collecting beggar-ticks on my pants legs and mud on my shoes while I worked to befriend my solitude.

By my mid-childhood, we no longer went calling, and the people who stopped by my parents' house—people who'd been their friends in that long past I had no part in—came only as far as the chest freezer on the back porch, to leave off buckets of tomatoes or foil-covered pans of yeast rolls. Something kept them from coming farther into the house or staying more than a few minutes. Accepting their offerings—since my mother would not come away from her recliner or her bed to greet them—I watched these visitors shift from foot to foot with duty and nervous restraint. From the kitchen window, I observed my father chatting with them in the driveway, sometimes for thirty minutes or an hour. I did not catch on until I was a teenager that it was my mother—her determined, passive-aggressive aversion to all social overtures—that kept them at bay.

My sisters, eight and ten years older than I, remember different, more engaged parents. A mother—high strung and manipulative— who nevertheless played games with them and threw card parties for friends. A father demanding and critical, but in charge of the family and his career. By their late forties, when I was born, my parents had thoroughly defeated themselves and each other. They'd been born defeated by their origins, the land where their people had always lived: beautiful and backward Appalachia. They'd launched their adult lives in a time of constricted hopes: the Depression years in a South already downtrodden by Reconstruction and embittered by Jim Crow. By the time of my birth, they'd been beaten down by hard labor and hard knocks I could sense but never comprehend. My parents passed their defeat directly on to me; I didn't just inherit it, it was cultivated in me.

In my childhood vision, the whole world was bleeding. Everything, even the tall grass waving in the fields and the unfettered birds hanging in the sky, hemorrhaged sadness. Nothing could be done about it; a mute offering of vegetables or bread was the most that could be attempted.

For years I thought everyone, everywhere, was expected at all times to act with that kind of dignified and hopeless resignation. I didn't know until I left Appalachia for college that it was possible to react to life's blows and limitations with the creation of art, or the seeking of a spiritual life.

~

My initial dose of Diamox—or the descent of the train from the high pass to a valley—pulled me through that first rocky night in Tibet. In the morning, after a breakfast of tea and a banana (I bought three from an on-board vendor for the equivalent of $1 each and offered one to our guide, who despite his usual gravitas accepted it eagerly and ate quickly, confirming my worst fears about his destitution), I parked myself on a rock-hard jump seat half-blocking the aisle outside the compartment. I had to be in a different position—sitting up—and a different location—out of that narrow berth—than the coffin-like claustrophobia in which I'd spent the night.

For hours and hours central Tibet in full summer passed by the broad window glass. Naked, arid mountains stratosphere-high, fringing a permafrost steppe textured with small rocks strewn on crazy-cracked hardpan. Neither vegetation nor snow covered anything; the relentless wind scoured away whatever traces of snow ever fell in that desert. Here and there a faint blue-grey cast turned out to be lichen, which must have been some kind of food for the yaks and the sheep we occasionally passed, the yaks roaming free and the sheep loosely herded by nomads astride Korean-made Harley-style hogs, the motorcycles' seats draped in prayer-seat carpets secured with bungee cords. These strange sights, the train's multiple unexplained stops and starts, and the many Chinese surrounding us, some armed and in uniform, some tourists, like me, struck me as exotic but benign. My night's panicked suffering appeared, in this light, very clearly the result of a brain starved for air that had abdicated, by biochemical cause-and-effect, its habituated responsibility for regulating the body and the will.

Inhaling rubber-tainted oxygen through the tube in my bed at the Kyichu Hotel, my mind worked its way to a second generation of that same insight. Vomiting from food poisoning, I'd missed or ejected three consecutive doses of Diamox and gradually become more ill from altitude sickness than from bacteria.

So, once again I jerked myself up off a mattress, swallowed a pill along with a couple of teaspoons of rice, and within twelve hours I was, amazingly, more or less all right. The outwardly chipper, inwardly uptight self I recognized as "me" was back, as was the revved-up heart rate, the slight lightheadedness, the deficient stamina, the dull headache, and a buzzing tingle in my lips, cheeks and fingers—all baseline symptoms of altitude sickness capped by a disagreeable drug.

And You, all my yous, were far, far away, and knew nothing of what had befallen me, and could do nothing to help me—but I reached for V.T. anyway, and took tight hold. I could not phone but called him to mind, many times every hour, and, lacking internet access, I wrote a letter of many scrawled pages I could not mail until weeks later, stateside. Dying, I had so easily turned all of You loose, but living, I could not be without at least one of You—for how else could I recognize who I was and had always been, if not in the mirror of my long, tangled ties to You?

In the basement of our family home history mounded up, in sagging damp boxes and unboxed piles muffled in old bedspreads, all of it veneered in ancient dust, sticky and opaque. Junk bulged from the shelves and hung from the rafters; my parents never willingly discarded any broken or orphaned, emptied or outmoded container, appliance, or piece of cracked plastic that might ever have another use. Ten years' worth of seed store calendars hung in chronology from a single long nail at the foot of the stairs, as if time itself could be hoarded.

The basement was my father's place. My mother worked down there when her household chores required it, and she sent me down the stairs on errands, to fetch leftovers or produce she kept in the 40s-era Frigidaire demoted from the kitchen when its 60s update arrived, or to bring up some potatoes or onions or apples stored in burlap-covered bushel baskets in a chilly corner doubling as root cellar. But my father lived down there when he had to be home and could not be outdoors. He reloaded spent rifle cartridges with pneumatic equipment that cracked like gunshots. He ripped lumber on a table saw shrieking and flinging sparks. He glued, welded, and rewired things from upstairs that broke or malfunctioned, and tinkered endlessly with tube and transistor electronics, the electrical science he'd studied in his college years. When forced retirement at sixty-two canceled the refuge his job at the city utility had given him, he installed a phone, a recliner, and a television in the basement. In the early years of my sister Sara's marriage, after I'd left home for college and my parents lived alone, a Thanksgiving visit she and her husband attempted transpired thus: my mother, immured in one of her black rages, would not allow them into the house, so my father entertained them in the basement while she lay upstairs in bed. Before driving back home, an eight-hour trek, my sister and her husband ate their holiday meal at a Denny's, without my father, who stayed in his underground bunker.

During the ten days I re-inhabited the home of my childhood, excavating memory while sorting and selling, giving away or tossing out the stuff that filled it, the basement still housed my father's banked anger—at my mother, and at the world that made him irrelevant despite his dogged devotion to work. He remained alive at that point, at assisted living, but mentally he was mostly gone; when his late-life love Bonnie died, without warning, on his ninety-fourth birthday, he began losing his mind to despair.

Emptying the basement, I put my hands on some fraction of the thousands of dusty objects signifying his abilities and interests.

More items than I could name that plugged in, cut, and abraded. Implements for wiring, coating, connecting, sealing, digging, and planting. Radio and television tubes, and the semiconductor boards he'd obviously been trying to puzzle out. Loops and tangles of bright copper wire; flexible coils of silver solder; piles of hammers, hasps, screw drivers, wrenches, and pliers. Buckets of nails and screws and clasps and brackets. Clutches of steel traps, multiple fishing rods, box upon box of tackle. He'd been electrician, carpenter, farmer, plumber, bricklayer; I can't recall anyone ever hired to do anything more than help him do what he already knew how to do.

But all those things were barely the surface of him, the slimmest evidence of what his life meant to him, or might have meant to me. At the end of the third and final day of the "estate sale" my old friend Margaret and I conducted in the house, trying to winnow down what we didn't know what to do with to what we could justify throwing away, I just waved the men who drove up in pickups and misfiring beaters right on down the stairs, to pick out and pay for, or just plain walk off with whatever they figured they could make use of.

I don't know if he'd have been horrified at the waste of what he'd valued, or relieved at a mess finally cleared up. He mostly hadn't fought the deal life dealt him. He endured. He loved the land he belonged to—the southwest Virginia mountains, the east Tennessee river valleys, the dark turned dirt of his gardens. He'd grown vegetables by the acre, prize-winning dahlias, and dozens of rare and common gourd varieties. He gave away this bounty freely. He enjoyed birdsong and could name the singer by the song; he built dozens if not hundreds of birdfeeders, birdhouses, and boxes for squirrels to nest in. When my mother's broken hip forced the move to assisted living, he got in trouble the first week, threatened with eviction for hooking his TV to cable for free—he knew exactly how to do that; he brought in the necessary tools from his basement—but he soon made up for the transgression by setting up and tending birdfeeders, and a dahlia and tomato garden, in the facility's arid central courtyard.

He always observed nature closely, and as his senses dimmed—and the world moved on, disengaging from him—he projected his alienation outward. Many times I heard him say how the songbirds must have all died off and the sun had gotten weak, never quite burning through the clouds anymore. But until his mid-nineties, when his dissolving mind got the better of his stoic will, he mourned his inner losses just once in my hearing. We were in the basement, near the table saw. Measuring and marking scraps of timber for a birdhouse he was building for J, who played nearby. She was maybe three years old; that would put him at eighty-one. He wrote dimensions on the wood with a thick carpenter's pencil, the way he always had. Then, to his shame, he couldn't add the fractions in his head.

You said, Daddy, "I'd be no kind of boss anymore." Your confession winded me. It must have been the first time I understood You really were going to die. As ever, though, I could think of nothing to say, no way to continue a conversation You might have been trying, bravely, to begin.

My father loved my mother and he also hated her. He stuck by her for seven decades despite her craziness and her meanness. That he also bullied her with emotional and physical violence when no one else was looking, that he broke bones and took sex by force, this is not okay with me but it is also not surprising—at least from the angle I look at him now.

~

Late in the day following my night-long bout of food poisoning and altitude sickness, after a long drive from Lhasa on winding, barely paved, sometimes obstructed or washed out roads, our group reached a campsite below a mountaintop monastery. I disembarked the bus in the odd, exalted state of aftermath—wan and wobbly, lit up with having survived. The world into which I stepped was stunningly austere—a mile-wide valley at just over 14,000 feet, bounded by two chains of tall, barren peaks and etched deeply through its center by a narrow, winding river canyon. Everything everywhere around me was some shade of brown, except a cluster of nomad's tents, canvas-white appliquéd with bright blue eternal knots, and the sky, a different blue, clearer, purer, so undiluted by atmosphere it assaulted the eyes. Our group would, in days to follow, donate hundreds of pairs of used sunglasses for distribution to impoverished Tibetans, who go blind from cataracts and macular damage; and I would—wearing new, pricey UVA/UVB filtering shades and doused in #30 sunscreen—dab my hand cream on the lips and cheeks of nomad children, chapped cherry-pink and raw from wind and sun damage. That the attention pleased them, and that my gesture, pitted against natural forces so huge and harsh, was futile—this would be obvious to me, and disturbing.

But in that first moment I was innocent and wonder-struck. Even more remarkable than the colors and the light of the stark landscape was its emptiness—the enormous capacity of its silence to swallow up all endeavor. The voices of our group of twenty, the hammer blows of the five-man mountaineering crew pegging down the mess tent (Chinese army surplus) and the dozen double-walled pup tents that would house us, the bus engine revving and relaxing as the driver executed a tight three-point turn on the rutted dirt track connecting the campsite to the two-lane blacktop "highway," none of this amounted to significant scale in the earth-sky bowl that cupped us. All of us together plus all our efforts were no more forceful and barely more sentient than the shale and lichen and round river stones on which we set up camp.

We had a free hour before dinner. And the weather, always mercurial at this altitude, waxed momentarily beneficent. The sun shone, the wind stilled. Toddling on rubbery legs, I carried toothbrush, toothpaste and water bottle, journal and pen to the river canyon's rim.

I peered over it, and the boom of wild water beating boulders nearly knocked me down. I took a single step backward, into absolute quiet. Fascinated, I tried the move again, several times, enjoying the impossible dichotomy of sound/silence, sound/silence. With almost equal pleasure, because I'd lacked all day the clean water to do so, I brushed my teeth, swigging merrily from the bottle and spitting hard into the canyon, experiencing a child's glee at my skill in staying upwind of my spittle.

I sat down to write, every detail of my life delighting me: the precipice into which I swung my legs, a straight drop of several hundred feet from the table-flat earth beneath my backside; the young yaks gamboling down the slightly-less-steep opposite bank for a drink, twirling their cow tails like awkward, happy dogs; the monastery perched four-square and gimlet-eyed like a medieval fortress on the rock face 1,500 feet above the campsite; the infinitesimally tiny but fully formed daisies growing under and between the pebbles near to hand; the sun heating up my back like an open flame although the air temperature was nearly freezing.

Even the hailstones that would mound up at my tent's flap door by morning thrilled and humbled me. I experienced the world from so deep inside my own senses, and at the same time with such freedom from the tight bounds of my usual worried self, that when I happened to glance up at the precise moment a fellow traveler fifty yards away dropped like a rock in mid-conversation to lie vomiting on the ground, my reaction came to me both through my cells and from way across that great yawning gulf of placid silence.

I watched people near her bring water and help her sit up. Enormous tenderness toward this near-stranger washed through me like my own blood. I thought: she is sick like I was, poor woman, that is hard; and, this is what happens to people like us, in places like this.

~

In the days following the un-festive picnic with my children, V.T. and I set ourselves up in a rented house at a small and lovely beach town on the placid, turquoise Gulf an hour south of Tampa. A fisherman's haven on a skinny sandbar island, this town is a holdout from Old Florida, its bohemianism and grit persisting amid the Sun Coast sprawl of cheap tract housing, gated golf communities, and super-sized shopping meccas. During our tripartite years, J and B and I often spent a few days or a summer week in a low-end mom-and-pop motel at the island's tip, floating in the pool, collecting shells from the tide line, wave-boarding the surf, then tracking in sand and boiling up mac-and-cheese in our efficiency's kitchenette. The three-bedroom house where we'll attempt our trial family-of-four Christmas stands across the street from that pink-and-teal cinderblock motel, looking down on it because, by code, all newer construction stands on stilts. When I booked the rental, its angle to the motel was coincidence, but when we move in I suddenly remember how I fantasized year after year about inhabiting this very house; its ample, wraparound screened porch looked like shady paradise from the burning sandy back patio of the motel.

V.T. and I put up a tree. Sorrow for all he has lost and will never again have brings him to tears, and I project my distress on his behalf at the tree: I hate it, along with the season of expectations it symbolizes. J and B drive down from Tampa for a couple of dutiful appearances, sleeping over only because I insist this is what I want. Every moment of their company feels like a fresh hitch in a straitjacket of social stiffness. J is bristly and B slippery; they are themselves, familiar, much loved, and baffling. Pancakes and syrup in the kitchen, walks on the beach, dinner at the fried-fish place we always ate at on the pier: someone sullenly goes missing from every group. J leaves the room if left alone with V.T. B brings a girlfriend he's almost already broken up with, as shiny, shallow buffer. I am tied up in my ancient quandary: no way to decide who's right and who's wrong one moment to the next, and no way to cease trying to make everyone happy no matter what. Before the end of the holiday week, I'll have taken to my rented bed with strep throat that is agonizingly painful, lying sleepless with suffering the last two nights of my vacation. On the final day, Christmas Day, I'll drop V.T. at the airport at dawn, and spend the rest of the morning in line at an acute-care clinic, acquiring a prescription for Cipro.

Here is a plain truth I seem unable to keep no matter how many times it is taught me: *you cannot have what you want.* Because, when you get there, it's not what you were sure it would be, or it's moved, like the mirage slicking a desert highway, forever just a little way away. It's the wanting, not the thing wanted, that drives us, for as soon as you grasp the object of your desire, it's something you already have.

There once was a Christmas, recollected now through the dim and narrow small-child lens, when my parents went away and did not come home. They'd driven 250 miles from southwest Virginia to Chattanooga in south-central Tennessee to attend an orchid show—something my mother, not my father would have wanted—and a sudden snowstorm delayed them on the drive back. Our parents never went away overnight. They never went anywhere without us, period. On Christmas Eve, my sisters and I waited by the fireplace where our empty stockings dangled above licking orange flames, the house growing colder as darkness fell. Then the phone on the stand in the hall rang, and my mother told Sara they'd have to spend the night in a motel and not be home until morning. After that I sat in Sara's lap while she read Betsy and me Christmas stories from a boxful of Little Golden Books and we all pretended we did not feel frightened. And abandoned.

That's the way I remember it. My memory can't be right. Sara kept the furnace going and the house warm; she remembers shoveling the coal. And surely an orchid show would not have been scheduled for Christmas Eve. Still, the feeling that Christmas could turn dangerous instead of light-filled, could threaten irreparable loss—its promise of joy and satiation as fragile as a glass ornament brushed carelessly to the floor by someone's too-exuberant sleeve—persists. And displeases.

~

For two nights I went to bed on the ground in Tibet, inside a tiny tent pegged to the hardpan plain between the booming river canyon and the blank-faced monastery atop its sheer rock promontory. Both nights, the wind blew at gale speed while I did not sleep, shivering inside every stitch of clothing I had with me, including hat and gloves, clutching V.T. in letter-form while zipped to the nose in my zero-Fahrenheit-rated sleeping sack.

On the first morning, we ascended to the monastery by bus, on unpaved hairpin switchbacks amid throngs of pilgrims on foot and day-tripping nomads on motorcycles, to watch the monks in an intricately costumed and choreographed ritual dance performed only once a year. That day of multiple once-in-a-lifetime moments ended with a rare audience with a young English-speaking tulku, but in-between we sat for hours on cold stone on a freezing day, lacking food and toilets, amid obvious surveillance by the Chinese. Several uniformed officials, including a chillingly beautiful young woman in severe olive drab set off with patent leather spike heels, arrived shortly after we did to digitally record the ritual—and everyone watching it. Paranoia from the long night on the train resurfaced and seized me; I knew our leader had brought to this monastery money and messages from exiled Tibetan religious leaders. When the Chinese abruptly followed him into the monastery and no one emerged for more than an hour, I grew painfully agitated.

On the second morning, having not slept for two days nor washed more than my hands, and having squatted above a latrine (inside a foul-smelling, wind-whipped tent on the verge of lifting off the earth) as infrequently as I could bear, I crawled out of my tent aching and angry, dizzy, nauseated, and reeling from a stabbing headache. Despite a daily Diamox dose, I had altitude sickness, again. That and the fine, cold rain that soaked me on my way to breakfast ruined my appetite for the day's extraordinary plan: a hike, long and steep, ascending over several miles to a site, at nearly 17,000 feet, normally forbidden to westerners, a sky burial ground.

We had specific permission from the monastery authorities to pass the sign, large, square, warning in black and white and red characters, Chinese and English, that non-Tibetans must proceed no further upon penalty of law. Pausing there, our leader admonished us once again to take no pictures, keep cameras completely out of sight, and give way to Tibetan pilgrims circumambulating the burial ground. "Stay on the path, and keep moving," he said, and set off briskly.

Leaving the path struck me as no option. To my left the mountain dropped away, affording an unobscured view of the river snaking through the valley thousands of feet below. To my right rose the sheer rock face into which the path, sometimes less than a foot wide, was worn. Obeying the command to keep moving was problematic, too. I pulled in each breath with difficulty, my lungs burning, snatching at air deficient in oxygen. I shuffled my feet diligently, but to small effect. Left one, right one. Progress depended on little successive bargains with myself: ten steps, and you can rest a few seconds. Okay, now ten steps more. Resting didn't help; I could not recoup any energy. But standing still required less will than moving. When I stopped I was only my body's struggle to breathe, while walking forced my mind to get involved, bullying my feet.

The succeeding ranges of naked peaks on the far side of the valley pierced clouds sunk to half their height. We were now above those clouds, but other cloud layers higher up dropped a steady, icy drizzle. I wore the hiking boots I'd bought on sale for gentler, better oxygenated climbs in the North Carolina mountains; my winter jacket;

a five-dollar plastic poncho from Walgreen's; and, over long underwear and leggings, an ankle-length cotton skirt—a gesture of cultural respect now wrapping my thighs like a sodden rope. We climbed for more than two hours, a straggling group, each person negotiating individually the bargain between body and mind, the path ascending, the rain coming down harder, the footing growing increasingly slick. Diminutive Tibetans passed us, climbing steadily with no apparent effort, rhythmically spinning prayer wheels or silently counting mantra, the 108 beads of a *mala* pressed one by one between small thumb and tapered forefinger. We stepped aside deferentially and stuck out like sore white thumbs, a head taller than the tallest of them.

The religious Tibetans I'd met in Lhasa were calm and open-hearted to an extent most "I"-oriented Americans can hardly fathom—like the line-standers in the Jokhang so pleased and honored by my interest in their Buddha's blessing they welcomed my stepping in front of them. A highlight of my entire sojourn in Tibet would happen a week later on a frigid, wind-swept lakeshore when a solitary elderly woman, circumambulating, stepped into my path, thrust her prayer wheel into my hand, and grinned at my unsuccessful attempt to smoothly spin the heavy brass cylinder mounted on a thick stick worn smooth from generations of hands. She would seize my face in genuine gap-toothed joy when I recognized and spoke along with her, not too awkwardly, the mantra she recited. But on this higher, holier, grimmer path to the sky burial ground, our uncouth presence clearly offended. The Tibetans' deeply lined faces remained unsmiling, and hard dark glances asserted they had no idea why we were there. With no common language, no way to explain to them the permission we'd been granted, embarrassed and afraid of reprisal, I kept my head down and concentrated on my feet.

Walk fast. Keep going. Up and up, into the clouds and the drizzle they're full of.

My parents are buried on a hillside in southwest Virginia about two miles from the house we lived in. Their graves lie side by side, together with a third plot awaiting Betsy. My mother's grave is in the middle. There is no monument—the regulations of this modern cemetery prohibit them, to facilitate mowing. Small, rectangular bronze markers, flush with the turf, bear their full names and their life spans. After each parent's burial, it took more than a year and many phone calls to the cemetery's management company to have their death dates added to their markers. My parents had bought a package deal, including all the interment costs and perpetual care of the sites, for one low price. I know it was a low price. My mother made this clear when she told me about the purchase, a decade or more before her death. A good deal was key, because it permitted inclusion of Betsy in the plan, and my mother knew her responsibilities for her cognitively disabled child stretched from cradle to grave—the child's grave—regardless of whether she got there first.

The cemetery is large, spanning several knobs of a low ridge at the edge of town. Thousands of graves. The effect of that much closely mowed, treeless, featureless topography is a broad expanse of barren space. The view from the grave sites, when I turn my back to town, is rolling farmland: cow pastures and corn fields and tobacco patches, dotted with old frame houses and rusty mobile homes, sectioned off with sagging barbwire. The palette leaf-green, grass-green, goldened, or sere, according to season. My mother was buried in mid-January, my father in early February. The temperature, both times, rose only into the teens. The ground was hard-frozen, the wind cutting. The graveside portion of their services had to be brief to the point of cursory.

Even when I visit them there on a humid summer day, the place feels desolate. No peace. No beauty. Plenty of emptiness. Usually a breeze.

The sky burial ground lay in a slight concavity atop the sheer ridge line at just under 17,000 feet. That we'd arrived at the destination of our strenuous, rain-soaked ascent was evident from the plumes of aromatic smoke—juniper branches smoldering on dampened fire pits. A flimsy slat fence demarcating the ceremonial site sagged beneath miles of prayer flags strung the length and square of it—the top layers crayon-bright red, blue, green, yellow and white; the successive under-layers paled first to pastel then dissolved to grey shreds from long exposure to the elements. On the uphill side of the burial field, a dozen or so vultures had lined up with the keyed patience of white-tie dinner guests awaiting a signal from their host.

In the very center of the site, at a distance of a hundred yards from the path I walked, a sky burial was underway. Men grunting with effort and commitment heaved mallets above their shoulders and hurled them down, crushing the bones in a cut-apart corpse, preparing offerings, thus, for the vultures' consumption; expiating in this way the karma of devout Buddhists who must, in a climate where no agriculture is possible, kill and eat animals to stay alive; burying, in this way, the religious dead in a terrain where no trees provide firewood for cremation and permafrost renders gravedigging impossible.

Our leader herded us nervously. "Walk fast," he said. "Keep going." Some mistake had occurred. He'd been told no burial would happen this day. Even with permission to be here, we should not witness this secret ritual, but we also could not turn back; circumambulating in the wrong direction would exponentially compound our offense. Because at this ridgetop the way was temporarily not steep, a measure of relief in my muscles and lungs melded with adrenalin, enabling me to hurry as I was told. I dreaded what I'd see if I looked. I took seriously the religious and cultural affront I'd commit by looking. But how could I not look upon something so fantastically and gruesomely holy? I glanced, then glanced away. I propelled my leaden feet forward. I heard what I will not forget: the sound of heavy force falling hard on human bodies—a tonality of *thunk* that insists the struck object was once juicy, once sentient, not stone, not dirt.

A body destined for sky burial—a heavy four-cornered bundle wrapped in old but richly colored carpet, lifted from the open bed of a dusty small truck by two men struggling with its dead weight—had arrived at the monastery courtyard simultaneous with our group the prior morning. Traipsing from the bus to our seats on cold paving stones for the ritual dances, we'd regarded the parcel amid us with no particular interest until later, when our guide explained what we had seen. Driving one foot, then the other forward through mud, risking one and then another furtive look, I wondered if the body on the field—its quartered torso and orphaned limbs, the pale strewn viscera and the ample blood, all of which my mind recognized but refused in that moment to label—was the same body, that unknown being's path into dissolution running parallel to our living paths a second time.

We circled past the burial ground on its downhill side, then ascended along the back side where the path ran lower than the field, screening from sight the ritual we could still hear. Tibetan pilgrims crowded the path, which fell away on the other side into a gorge rendered bottomless by our altitude and the low-slung rain clouds that filled it. At a spot three-quarters of the way around the burial ground, well uphill of the ritual and removed from the attention of the Tibetans, our group stopped to string up our prayer flags with the many thousand others, and to burn the incense and juniper boughs our Tibetan guide and the bus driver had carried up in bulky bundles strapped to their backs. Our smoke plume streamed up with the rest, the rain making a good smudge of it. Some members of our party, practicing Buddhists or not, joined in these ritual acts, but remembrance and mindfulness had both deserted me. Wet to the bone despite my plastic poncho, cold beyond the bone, exhausted, hungry, winded and wretched, I sat down in the mud. There was nowhere else to sit, and I had no more strength to stand.

Not a one of the many Yous I've attached to came to mind. I was as alone as I have ever been.

At the peak of my unintended pilgrimage, I burned with resentment at my circumstances and the people around me who seemed more able than I to rise above them. I had just enough awareness left to recognize the poison of that anger as an additional loss: a failure of view that seemed to negate the enormous effort of the climb.

How far I'd come, at such personal and monetary cost, and after all, it meant nothing to me.

Me. I stared back downhill at the sodden prayer flags soaking up more rain, and the vultures now feasting on what I could just make out as pieces of human flesh. I didn't think about what I saw, and I felt neither awe nor fear. Through a scrim of antipathy about all that emptiness, I just saw what I saw: what it all comes to in the end, for every ambition, and every body.

The strained first-foursome Christmas among V.T., my children, and me contains a single instance of genuine togetherness. And because life is strange, and sometimes simply offers up the storyline a writer is always seeking, this happens in a tattoo parlor.

The event begins as another four-way choke. V.T. and I drive into Tampa from the beach, feeling jittery. J and B arrive together, in her car, from their dad's. We meet up in an empty parking garage: some stiff hugs and awkward handshakes; a few words, echoing against concrete slabs. Lefty's given up his one-man shop in the strip mall for a booth in an upscale tattoo parlor in Ybor City. Less overhead and more traffic, probably—at least once the sun goes down. Eleven in the morning mid-week, though, Ybor is close to deserted. With last night's party litter already swept up, our tongue-tied stroll along vacant sidewalks feels like we missed a parade by several days.

The reception area of the parlor earns that name: a velvet loveseat and overstuffed armchairs in striped silk damask. The color palette rich, and on the tasteful side of bordello. A half-dozen tattooists operate from two rows of stations tightly lining both sides of a narrow shop space twice as deep as it is wide. There are no partitions, not the least nod to privacy, and, save for the reception area, nowhere to sit except in Lefty's black leatherette chair. Our party of four, especially V.T., who is tall, and I, who am so evidently the mom, draws baleful glances from everyone except Lefty. He's cordial in his ultra-cool way. He remembers me, man-greets V.T., nods like a homie to J (who's sent many customers his way), and is immediately professionally solicitous with B. Lefty's grown a thick bundle of bound-back dreads since I last saw him and has new and frighteningly larger black spacers hollowing his earlobes.

I ask B's back, on his way into the leatherette chair, "Does your dad know?"

"No."

The monosyllable suggests I should have known better than to ask. I take in V.T.'s take on that information—arched brows.

I process this amid the shuffle to fit five bodies into space meant for two. The receptionist's credenza forms one wall of Lefty's station; when I lean against it, she tells me sharply that I may not do so. I walk away huffy, pick up a magazine, and sink in the red velvet couch cushions. But no one joins me. Turning pages I don't want to read, I feel very left out. V.T. and J have squeezed into two corners of Lefty's square space, and I end up squatting on the floor by B's legs, more or less eye level with Lefty's rolling stool and his buzzing needle gun.

B's sitting up, shirtless, the mantra already stenciled on:

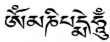

Om Mani Peme Hung, six Tibetan characters not unlike tribal tattoo in their short calligraphic curves and barbed serifs. The syllables line up on his chest beginning just below the left nipple and head round his side underneath his arm. For now, that arm lies bent atop his shaggy blond head. He is eighteen and lean, a reasonable proxy for Adonis except for the unkempt hair. I am uncomfortably aware of the cool stares and dead silence our uncool tableau elicits from the other tattooists; there are no potential customers inside or outside the shop for our weirdness to scare off but we are not what these night creatures want to see this early in their morning. In tacit solidarity, all of us, including Lefty, ignore their snubbing. We can't find anything to say to each other but we hang in, together, in discomfort.

This inking goes fast. B hardly sweats. Two years older with half a year of dorm life under his belt since his first tattoo, his skin's not so tender any more. In almost no time—ten minutes?—the stung flesh is raised up proud. The mantra, pure sound of limitless compassion, now embossed in blue-black pigment on B's fair young skin. Around each letter runs an angry red rim of needle tracks, and over the whole thing the coat of protective ointment glistens.

I get up from my squat, middle-aged knees screaming from a punishment I know better than to inflict on them. A wad of twenties passes from my hand to Lefty's. Merry Christmas, B. So long, Lefty. Within a year or two he will move to L.A. and disappear from our lives—permanently, I assume.

The four of us step out of the shop into pale, unwarm winter sun. We amble along deserted sidewalks. We all agree we are hungry, but the idea of lunch together, suggested by V.T., does not fly. In the parking garage, we repeat the strained hugs and handshakes, peppered with relieved good-byes. We get into our cars and drive our separate ways.

No part of this was not awkward. We've conducted a ritual linking, B's flesh carries its symbol, and…what happened, exactly? Has anything changed? I remember how it felt like this the first time. An anti-climax. A group letdown. Now we have one more tattoo in our family. That we did it—everybody showed up and no one acted out—it means something. The question is what.

Neither V.T. nor I have mentioned *his* ink to B or J. About that he says to me, in the car, on the way back to the rented house at the beach, "Good thing we didn't, I'd have to drop trou for them to see."

Months later, B will tell me by phone—the news arriving unsolicited—that his dad finally saw the new tattoo, the six syllables of compassion, boldface round his chest. I ask for the reaction.

B says, "He didn't say a word. Whatever that means."

The day after my father's funeral, I emptied his room at assisted living. No one pressed me to do this quickly. Despite the rocky beginning to his time there—that unauthorized tap into the television cable, and the sexual assault on my mother that brought in the police—he'd become a well-loved and respected citizen. During the halcyon days of his romance with Bonnie, he and she had been the facility's greeters for visitors and new residents; the director and the social director still chuckled fondly over memories of them as First Couple, and more than one of the good-hearted country women who dressed and fed and wiped him during his last days there sought me out to recall how, as long as he could still get around, he made the staff's jobs easier by fixing the things no repairman would come for.

The room I entered was not the cozy suite he'd shared with Bonnie. The space where he served out his last year of life, a single room in a different wing, was nearly as bare as a cell. Its only furnishings were a bed he never used and a nightstand, lamp, and dresser (of the chain-hotel sort, nice but generic, provided by the facility); the huge push-button recliner he slept in, two units of freestanding metal shelving of the kind usually found in a garage; and my mother's canes, walker, and wheelchair, aids he progressed through just as she had, only more quickly, and after longer resistance.

Emptying the meager contents of the drawers and the closet into black plastic sacks, I worked fast. Kept moving because I needed to be *done*. Clearing items from the shelves—a hammer and some screwdrivers, a few books (Kipling and electrical engineering texts), his college fraternity paddle, a framed photo of my mother as 20s flapper surrounded by gauzy clouds—I wanted to believe the objects I handled said something about what mattered to my father at the end. But I knew better. Sara helped move him in black days right after Bonnie died when he had no more will to want anything; she had put into his room the items she found significant.

Only the clock I took down from the shelf was really about him as I knew him: a cheap, round, white plastic face with easy-to-read large numerals and black, battery-operated hands, including a second hand ticking audibly, screwed firmly into an eight-inch chunk of pressure-treated 4 X 4. He'd once built handsome, plain furniture—bookcases, benches, and hope chests—from carefully fitted, luminously sanded planks of cherry and walnut, but in his very old age when his hands and eyes and brain no longer cooperated smoothly, he made dozens of these ugly, purely functional clocks—requiring only two screws and a trip to Walmart or Lowe's for clock faces and precut lumber—then gave them away to anyone he could corner into accepting one. The facility director, all his still-living friends, friendly strangers, his healthcare providers, visiting ministers, Bonnie's daughters, and of course my sisters, me, and my children, we all got one. On the bottom of the 4 X 4, they are dedicated, dated, and signed—*S.D. Hale*—in thick black marker. The clock he gave me now resides in my writing room, on a bookcase three feet from my desk. When I encountered one of these clocks in an unexpected setting, the estate attorney's office, for instance, the recipient would invariably explain its presence with wide-eyed chagrin that echoed the moment he or she could not say no to so determined a gift-giver: "He wanted me to have that."

Yes, he did.　He wanted to be remembered, as useful and good-hearted.

The two Hefty bags and one grocery box I carried from his room went next to Margaret's house where I was staying.　I spread the contents on the floor of her basement den, and sorted mercilessly.　I threw away a good bit.　I saved the photos, the books, and the fraternity paddle for Sara.　What was usable—clean underwear and socks and never-worn pajamas—I sacked up again to give away.　When I drove to the Salvation Army on my way out of town, the office was closed but two giant green bins in the parking lot had open chutes, high off the ground to discourage trash pickers.　I had to lean back, throw hard, and arc the bags in.　Because I couldn't imagine what else to do with them—I tossed in my parents' canes, and the walker.

Then I drove away.

In the aftermath of the together-tattoo redux, V.T. and I spend Christmas Eve day, the last time we'll see each other for months, alone on the cold, windy beach, wearing sweats for warmth.　The sun, the sky, the water are achingly beautiful.　But blowing sand stings our faces.　And my throat—the strep—hurts like hell.　We wrap up like mummies in our beach towels, hats and sunglasses, sit close, and take turns lifting a soap bubble wand to the wind's mouth.　Together, we watch rafts of iridescent bubbles stream over sea oats into the dunes.

The bubbles rise, very real.　They dissolve, very gone.　My teacher once said, watching a child blow bubbles that settled in long grass like dew, glistened there, persisted, and burst: *Like that, your delusions. Like that, your life.*

The path down from the sky burial ground proved more treacher-
ous than the path up. We slipped and slid in a sheep trail barely wider
than our boots and as deep as our ankles, the excrement in its crease
sometimes human because the pitch was so steep a shepherd could
have squatted nowhere else. The travail didn't end when we reached
the monastery. We sat a long stint in a cold anteroom awaiting the
conclusion of our leader's conference with the abbot. Finally, having
eaten and broken camp, we rode the bus down the valley and up a
different peak to a fabled hot spring where Padmasambhava, revered
as the founder of Buddhism in Tibet, is said to have subdued and
converted a serpent god. Despite temperatures near freezing and the
never-ceasing drizzle, the half-dozen of us most desperate for either
warmth or some relative cleanliness stripped to our underwear and
waded into the rock-walled pool, gender-segregated by a wooden wall.

I submerged to the earlobes in water a hot-tub-perfect one hundred degrees, utterly clear, and pleasantly mineral-scented. The same
group of American travelers who'd pronounced the roof-top restaurant in Lhasa safe for western diners left us a warning of tuberculosis
incubating in that spring, but whether because they'd been so wrong
about the food that felled me or because I couldn't care at the end of
that particular day what might befall me in the future, I dismissed the
warning. I'll never know if I exposed myself to TB (or the typhoid or
hepatitis-A for which I'd had myself immunized in the States) but I'd
hardly stopped grinning from my body's first flush of enervation and
delight when three small snakes—brown, wedged-headed, the length
of my forearm and the width of my index finger—launched themselves from crevices in the rocks, swimming vigorously straight toward
me and my bathing companions.

My mind stiffened but my body moved—fast, and out of their
path. Watching them slither from sight into the cracks of the opposite rock wall, my brain unjammed and generated explanation: disturbed by our arrival, the snakes swam out to check us out. My gut
unclenched: okay, okay, snakes are sentient beings, too—live and let

live.

Days after the climb to the sky burial ground, on a remote stretch of desert highway still many kilometers from the hotel in Lhasa, our bus passed a lone monk prostrating his way down the pavement, progressing body-length by body-length from whatever distant village he inhabited toward the city, the spiritual center of his religious practice, accomplishing in what might be a years-long effort this once-in-a-lifetime holy journey in the most devoted way possible—face down on the path. Wholly absorbed in his effort, thin and dusty, tire-tread pads bound to his hands, knees, abdomen, he took no notice of our gawking from the bus windows' height, but another monk, his helper, trailing him on a battered bicycle pulling a little two-wheeled cart of provisions, smiled and waved at the staring white faces pressed to the glass.

Watching that pilgrim on the pavement grow smaller as we sped on toward our destination on tires powered by diesel fuel, I felt how extremely small were my headache and body ache and hunger and weariness—in relation to all that others feel, and endure.

~

My father's guns linger in our lives long after his death. He hadn't been allowed to take them with him into assisted living, of course, so when he moved there he verbally bequeathed his firepower to the next and only male in his line, B. At age eleven, then, my son found himself owner of the pellet gun we'd all fired together, the .22 with a scope my father used on birds, and a 16-gauge shotgun.

When we emptied the house, B's uncle, Sara's husband, took the .222, maybe just to mitigate the absurdity of a city-dwelling pre-adolescent receiving *four* long guns. B's three weapons traveled to Florida, first to a closet in my house, and then, when I moved north, to his father's place. But at twenty-one, claiming his majority, B asked his

uncle for that last gun he thought belonged to him. It came to live in
V.T.'s and my house temporarily, lying beneath the guest bed in a hard
shell case we bought B for Christmas. He cleaned the rifle lovingly,
seated on the rug in our living room as we looked on, then took it
home to his place, a bachelor apartment in a college town.

He has made a deal with his sister to rectify her exclusion on the
basis of gender from her grandfather's legacy; he's given her the shotgun, just as soon as she has time to drive to Florida and bring it to
her home.

I confess it surprises me, my gentle son's affection for these weapons. He takes a gun safety course, goes hunting, and kills a six-point
buck. Meticulously he researches, via the internet, the provenance of
each gun. They are pieces of history, he says. Because of him, I now
know the .222 came into being in May of 1936, just months before
my parents married.

After the arduous ascent to the sky burial ground, after the unset-
tling dip in the holy hot springs, the group returned to the Kyichu
Hotel oasis in Lhasa. I took a long shower, lukewarm, in a bathroom
with no stall and no curtain, but also no snakes and plenty of soap. I
ate the available version of comfort food—spaghetti with yak-meat-
balls—in the restaurant downstairs, and after a night's solid sleep in
the blessed hard warm bed, I got up extra early in order to be first in
the always-long queue for a seat at one of the two internet-connected
computers in the hotel lobby. I'd told all my email correspondents
back home in the States I couldn't check my inbox from Tibet but
with urgency and some difficulty, because both the keyboard and the
desktop icons were in Chinese, and because we were all due on the
bus in ten minutes, I typed a short message to V.T., the mirror I most
needed to gaze into just then, to reassure myself I was still who I
thought myself to be, after all I'd just been through.

My sentences offered love, support, and brief touristy highlights of the trip so far. I felt smugly virtuous about what I withheld: how sick I'd been, how inconsolably lonely I was, how confused I remained about why I came here. I didn't want to trouble him with matters he could do nothing about. When I clicked Send and my inbox refreshed, a loving brief message from V.T. popped in.

Simultaneous email. The serendipity of an almost real-time connection across twelve time zones and 13,000 miles thrilled me. I climbed on the bus rejuvenated and rebalanced.

All was right with my world, inside and out; You, deeply desired, desiring me back, proved it.

Not until I was back in the States—airsick and profoundly exhausted from twenty-two days in Tibet followed by thirteen hours in the air, barely able to stand upright, but doing so to call V.T. from a standup booth in Newark airport because that was the only phone I could find and I had to find *him*—not until then did I discover what was withheld from *me* in that email I clung to: a second major surgery, barely three months after the first one.

He was alone. Just a day or two out of the hospital, unable to drive, struggling to eat a little and get some work done. But he was cheerful. Glad to hear from me. Very loving.

Standing in Newark, I was furious at him for not telling. For destroying, by telling me now, my illusion of our perfect, unobstructed connection. For revealing, instead, that its bright affirming flag, its flash of satisfying heat, was a notion I had: momentary, dissolving, launched by my desire into the silence of our separate solitudes, our simultaneous but still solo efforts to get on with the lonely business of living, or dying.

In my agitation, I completely forgot that in the arms of what I perceived to be my death in Lhasa I'd willingly turned loose of him— and all my other attachments. I'd long forgotten, too, what I vowed, silently, to my own heart, when we took up our together path, by phone, on the same day he told me he might die: to accept the uncertainty of him—the miswired body, the overgenerous heart, the freewheeling mind—as my karma. And to carry the affliction that is my anxiety about all that onto my path.

I'd promised—and forgotten—to allow You, dangerous *and* life-giving, to *be* the path on which I stretched myself until my death or yours, swallowing the bitter dust with the sweet sustenance, inching toward spiritual understanding.

I would not realize for a long time after I returned from Tibet that two companion awakenings found me in my accidental pilgrimage there: the clarity about death I cherished that night at the Kyichu Hotel, and the gritty truth about life I wished I had not seen at the sky burial ground.

I would not really know until I wrote this down, my father's no-nonsense clock ticking the seconds away nearby, that I carry both awarenesses with me still. Two opposed and simultaneous truths, the tension between them a prompt of *dren-pa*—remembrance—toward *shey-zhin*—mindfulness.

⁓

Laid out in crucifixion position and tied down to be cut open, V.T. heard a nurse and the anesthetist, both women, remark on his tattoo as they prepared to put him under.

"Isn't that *pretty*."

Their feminine voices rang like bells, he told me, as his consciousness slid away.

⁓

Early one morning some years after her death, I saw my mother in a dream. Her face, in profile, was sad. She was intensely inward—all the space in the world between her and the world, between her and me. We passed each other in the narrow space between the sink and the tub in the green-tiled bathroom of the house where I grew up. I noticed she was not as old as I thought she would be; she was much younger than when she died. She had heft to her body, and her face had flesh and strength even though it was still the skin of a mask that hid her real self.

Her hair had not yet gone white. It was thinned out, as at the time of her death, but still dark as it was when I was smaller than she. When we passed in the bathroom I saw her hair combed straight behind her ears and a white towel draped on her shoulders. I understood she was about to wash her hair, a task that near the end of her days in that house became a preoccupation of hers because of its difficulty, and the likelihood she'd lose her balance when she leaned over. She knelt, as I watched her, in front of the toilet, which was filthy and shit-stained, as it never was in my youth, as it always was in the last years of my parents' shaky residence in that house they built together. I understood, because of the towel and the submission in her knees that she was going to wash her hair in the toilet, and my immediate utter revulsion was checked only by my sudden comprehension that this was all she could do. Here was the only basin she could reach in her crippled, compromised, circumscribed condition.

Compassion rose through me—a stinging tenderness that dissolved my will—but still I could not stop myself from voicing the disgust that gagged me. *"Don't do that,"* I told my mother sharply. In my dream I turned away. I knew she'd do it anyway. I knew she had no choice, and I knew I had no choice but to know that.

I remembered while still inside this dream that I had dreamed already she would do exactly this in exactly this way. I marveled at my prescience, at what that might mean. In my memory of the earlier dream I saw the swipe of her dark hair against the fouled slope of the white bowl; I saw the black stream of her wet hair on the white towel when she was done. Bacteria and the residue of excrement from the toilet would be transferred to her hair, but wouldn't the effort at washing have removed *something*, some oil or loose dirt that is the reason we want to wash our hair?

Inside this lucid dream I will myself to turn around, undo my cowardice and resentment, see the other side of You.

You are not me and yet we are forever entangled, our bonds both accidental and self-inflicted.

Not the form nor the terms of intimacy I'd prefer.

But You, mirroring back to me my notions about You, show me what I otherwise would never see clearly: me.

Twenty years have passed since I first stumbled into my teacher's path. She has grown very old. Her health is in decline. It's been several years since I've seen her, and months pass between the times we speak by phone. She calls or I call and often we miss each other. When we connect, we mostly say certain quick prayers in a call-and-response ritual that has become a comforting mode of communication between us, after many years' repetition. Sometimes she also says, *I never forget you.* Sometimes I say that to her. Each of us always says, Thank you. And every time there is the same firm instruction, too: *It your duty to realize.* She means: *The only thing in your way is you.*

When V.T. arrives to live with me the summer after B's Christmas inking, he's closed the gap in his own tattoo circle, once again without a word to me. In the cramped and noisy apartment where we start our life together, I trace with my forefinger on his outer thigh the eight-spoke wheel, dark blue shadowed in red, linking last year's two undulating ribbons of blue wave, and offsetting the whirling disk of fire scarred into his tender inner thigh.

In Buddhist iconography, the Dharma wheel stands for the joy and the sorrow of *samsara*, perpetually turning one into the other.

At the end of this same summer, J enters medical school. In high school she dressed like a skater, black and baggy, metal-studded. Now she attires herself conservatively although her politics, expressed in health care access terms, become more visibly and actively radical. She cloaks her tattoos carefully when she dresses for the classroom or the hospital. Still, a .jpeg of her ankle barb turns up for a while as her profile picture on Facebook.

I'll accept that I cannot know her but know that she loves me, whoever she is, and I'll be mostly okay with that conundrum. That none of us know anyone, including ourselves, as well as our minds insist we do: this will be, by then, a little bit clearer to me—sometimes. When I ask J during her second year of med school—at the turning point in the anguish, when we both sense she's going to stick it out and succeed—whether she intuited at nineteen, long before her decision to become a doctor, that the tattoo she had intaglioed on her back from cervical vertebra to coccyx was her personal version of the universal emblem of her future profession, the caduceus, she said, "No."

Then, after one beat of silence: "Yes."

After one more beat, she lands in the middle. "Sorta."

There comes a dangerous moment, almost an everything-lost moment, in a season not Christmas, not quite, although V.T.'s arrival in my life was supposed to be like Christmas forever: everything I'd ever wanted, right there, in reach, mine, finally. He and I have bought a house. The plans for our late autumn wedding are almost complete.

We are together.

Side by side on our new couch, we watch cable news. On the screen, the endless back-and-forth, surge-and-flow of charged emotions, prognostication, worst-case-best-case extrapolations—a historic presidential campaign conducted amid a historic tanking of the economy and the near collapse of the banking system. When I return from the kitchen with a cookie for me and a glass of ice water for V.T., something has happened to us.

Just as my gaze travels to the television screen, I sense a sharp look from him. As if I have changed. My brows tense with the sharp questions I ask: What is it, what's up? He responds with a grin that irritates because of some weirdness in its import or its timing.

"I love you," You say. I sit down. You lean closer. Warm, sincere, flushed with joy. Your skin is flushed, too, something I almost don't notice.

Two, three times I verbalize my question. What's up? Two, three times You duck, repeating your profession of love. Then You tilt the world. You ask mildly, "You went somewhere? You left the room?"

You have left this world and come back. For a span of some few seconds, only your body sat on our couch. Long enough for me to peel the cellophane from a package of shortbread cookies and fill a glass with water from the dispenser on the fridge door.

You are the man who blew up your whole life to join mine, telling me: *I am the next opportunity for freedom in your life.*

You are a man with nine lives, or maybe ninety-nine. I have no way to know. You keep dodging bullets doctors label fatal. Those surgeries. The tumors that riddled your lungs only a year ago through two sets of X-rays, then, in the next sets of films, gone. The irregular brain circuitry you were born with, and the resultant ever-morphing electrical problems that create insomnia, arrhythmias, migraines, and lightning headaches—power surges like the one that just jolted your mind blank.

There is nothing I can do about any of this. Except sit with it, beside you, not-knowing what's up next.

People who love us tell V.T. and me they are happy for our mid-life marriage but sometimes they also signal concern about something less friendly associates simply blast us for: we have married in haste. I want to ask them, I am beginning to tell some of them, "How long do you think we have? How long do you think any of us has?"

The clarity I don't want but cannot not-know is as heart-pounding as the thin air at 17,000 feet: not one single one of us knows when death will arrive, or well-being end.

Like that, your life.

On the third Christmas subsequent to the stilted first foursome in Florida, B and J come home for that holiday for the first time, "home" being now V.T.'s and my house on a wooded ridge in North Carolina, above a bend of the Swannanoa River. This Christmas happens as two threesomes; because of their exam schedules, B joins us for a few days before he heads to his dad's in Florida, then J does the same. The visits go well. V.T.'s not their dad and never will be but they like him and we have fun.

But here's the thing: there's tattoo talk, again.

The first and only serious subject B broaches, within hours of his arrival, is his intention to get a new—third—tattoo. He asks not our permission, of course, but our reaction. Our acquiescence. To an infinity sign.

"Where?" I ask.

"Here," he says, left hand slapping the right side of his chest. Opposite, and balancing, the compassion mantra.

"Hmm," I say. "How big?"

Same size.

Color?

Black.

V.T. is reading the newspaper on the couch. B and I sit side by side at the breakfast bar. The room is real quiet and stays that way for some seconds.

"Won't that look like a number 8?" I ask.

"It's an 8 on its side. People will know what it means," he says.

I picture my son's slender chest looking more and more like a billboard or a webpage, cluttered with logos. I don't say that. B pushes for a response. I hedge, and finally verbalize that it's his decision. Then I ask why that symbol, particularly. What I get from what he answers is that it has to do with limits, and no limits. His limits, and stretching them.

As much as I can understand about the irritation I feel has to do with not getting what I want. What I need my often silent son to proffer, reveal, discuss, is something about all that baffles me in his choices, his sufferings, the way he spends his time, and—okay, I admit it—how he feels about me, my choices, and the way I spend my time.

B's offering us intimacy, in neither the form nor the terms I desire. Will I always want something other than what he—they, my children, the people I love and need—can give me?

Closing out the topic that night, B says we must know that if he's thought about it this much it means something to him. We are ready to respect that. We acquiesce, by saying nothing more.

The next morning V.T. leaves on the breakfast bar for B drawings and a printout from the internet of the *ensō*, the single-brushstroke open circle representing in Zen meditative painting the felt-but-not-cognized knowing: that incompletion is an essential and inherent aspect of existence.

We leave it—the tattoo thing—at that.

Except that, when B has gone on to Tampa and J arrives to take his place in our house, and I mention his tattoo talk, she tells me she's got her next one picked out.

We're on the couch, sunk deep into its cozy softness.

"Okay," I say, "what'll it be, and where?"

"The Celtic symbol for healing," she says. "On my wrist."

She shows me a picture, on the screen of her cell phone, of a triskelion, three small wheels of tight, concentric spiral, flush on one side but open on the other, spinning out energy. Constraining *and* emanating momentum.

I gaze at her fine-boned wrist, the translucent skin, and beneath it, the tracery of blue, beating veins.

"That's going to hurt," I say.

"Yes."

When she graduates from medical school, seated beside me on the shuttle from stadium parking lot to the convocation hall—the bus packed like a rush-hour subway, the atmosphere sweaty—she shows me her wrist. A babble of agitated voices cocoons the two of us. J's gesture is unprefaced. Silent. It simply is. Peeking from the margin of her doctoral gown, the triskelion, a fresh wound, ink blue-black and flesh proud.

About the Author

Christine Hale is the author of a novel, *Basil's Dream* (Livingston Press, 2009), which received honorable mention in the 2010 Library of Virginia Literary Awards. National Book Award finalist Joan Silber says "*Basil's Dream*...seems to prove fiction can go where other forms can't." (see www.christinehalebooks.com)

Ms. Hale's creative nonfiction and short fiction have appeared in *Arts & Letters, Hippocampus, The Sun, Shadowgraph,* and *Prime Number,* among other journals. A fellow of MacDowell, Ucross, Hedgebrook, Hambidge and the Virginia Center for the Creative Arts, Ms. Hale has been a finalist for the Autumn House Non-Fiction Contest, the Sonora Review Essay Contest, the Glimmer Train Short Story Award for New Writers, the Dana Award in Creative Nonfiction, and the Rona Jaffe Foundation Writers' Award.

A native of the southern Appalachians, as were her parents, Ms. Hale grew up in Bristol, Virginia. She received an MBA from University of North Carolina at Chapel Hill and an MFA from Warren Wilson College. She worked in investment banking in New York City in the early 80s, began teaching writing in 1996 at the University of Tampa, and in the intervening years worked as a freelance writer and editor in business communications in New York and Tampa. From 1989 to 1992, she lived in Bermuda. A former Beebe Teaching Fellow at Warren Wilson College, she now teaches in the Antioch University – Los Angeles Low-Residency MFA Program as well as the Great Smokies Writing Program in Asheville, North Carolina.

Apprentice House is the country's only campus-based, student-staffed book publishing company. Directed by professors and industry professionals, it is a nonprofit activity of the Communication Department at Loyola University Maryland.

Using state-of-the-art technology and an experiential learning model of education, Apprentice House publishes books in untraditional ways. This dual responsibility as publishers and educators creates an unprecedented collaborative environment among faculty and students, while teaching tomorrow's editors, designers, and marketers.

Outside of class, progress on book projects is carried forth by the AH Book Publishing Club, a co-curricular campus organization supported by Loyola University Maryland's Office of Student Activities.

Eclectic and provocative, Apprentice House titles intend to entertain as well as spark dialogue on a variety of topics. Financial contributions to sustain the press's work are welcomed. Contributions are tax deductible to the fullest extent allowed by the IRS.

To learn more about Apprentice House books or to obtain submission guidelines, please visit www.apprenticehouse.com.

Apprentice House
Communication Department
Loyola University Maryland
4501 N. Charles Street
Baltimore, MD 21210
Ph: 410-617-5265 • Fax: 410-617-2198
info@apprenticehouse.com • www.apprenticehouse.com

CPSIA information can be obtained at www.ICGtesting.com
Printed in the USA
LVOW11s0139210916

505507LV00002B/10/P